More Praise for *Beyond E-Learning*

"Marc Rosenberg offers a bold vision for the future of corporate learning that clearly shows how our intellectual technologies can most effectively integrate with hardware and software technology. Rosenberg illustrates his vision with case studies of effective working examples that are already in use. A must-read for all who want to stay on the leading edge of corporate learning."

—Saul Carliner, assistant professor, Graduate Program in Educational Technology, Concordia University, Montreal

"Once again, Marc Rosenberg is ahead of the crowd. *Beyond E-Learning* is a powerful business book masquerading as a training book. If you read only one book on getting results this year, make it *Beyond E-Learning*."

—Jay Cross, CEO, Internet Time Group

"Marc Rosenberg's work is the greatest concentration of contemporary wisdom and experience around e-learning to date— including his own and that of the most seasoned professionals who truly make performance happen. *Beyond E-Learning* will therefore make better decision makers of leaders such as CEOs, CFOs, and CTOs and, equally, will make better managers and practitioners of those charged with ensuring organizational performance through human performance."

—Gary J. Dickelman, president and CEO, EPSScentral LLC

"Once again, Marc Rosenberg has written a 'must-read' book for those involved not only in e-learning in their organization but anyone who must understand how to improve workforce productivity. *Beyond E-Learning* is a road map that will help you find your way through the ever-changing, ever-expanding, everevolving phases of learning and performance improvement."

—Heidi Fisk, executive director, The eLearning Guild

"Context is everything, and in *Beyond E-Learning* Marc Rosenberg sets the context to put technologies, techniques, and deliverables into perspective. The perspective should drive rich strategy development that extends beyond simplistic uses of electronic resources. It also stimulates the creative thinking necessary for true change in how we create and support performance and learning."

—Gloria Gery, Gery Associates, consultant and strategist in EPSS and performance-centered design

"Another winner from Marc Rosenberg! *Beyond E-Learning* shows you the best ways to combine technology, learning, and collaboration to deliver improved workforce performance within your organization."

—Victoria Macdonald, e-learning strategist, BMW Group

"Learning technology is rapidly becoming viewed as 'mission-critical' in progressive organizations, and is one of the few technologies that touches not only every employee in an organization but often several audiences in the extended enterprise of partners, distributors, suppliers, and customers. In *Beyond E-Learning*, Marc Rosenberg provides readers—whether you are a business leader, training professional, or a student of the field—with the processes and concepts you need in order to be prepared for this new era of using learning as a strategic advantage."

—Kevin Oakes, president, SumTotal Systems, Inc.

"If you are interested in improving organizational effectiveness and business results, *Beyond E-Learning* is a must! Marc Rosenberg offers a wealth of practical suggestions on such topics as workplace learning, change management, and leadership, all of which add up to a road map for successful performance improvement efforts."

—Robert Reiser, Distinguished Teaching Professor and program leader, Instructional Systems Program, Florida State University

About this Book

Why is this topic important?

Beyond E-Learning comes at a time of great transformation in how individuals and organizations learn and how they transfer learning into performance and value. Training—in the classroom and online—remains as important as ever, but it can't do it all. E-learning is much more than "e-training." The accelerating pace of knowledge growth and change, as well as the increasing pressures of the marketplace, require that we look for innovative approaches to complement training. Our responsibility for learning should not stop at the end of class. The technology-rich workplace requires new technology-enabled tools and strategies for workplace learning—anytime and anywhere, including knowledge management collaboration and communities, and performance support. These approaches and others are demonstrating important benefits in improving access to information and the ability to share it with others.

What can you achieve with this book?

Moving beyond e-learning requires that we reinvent the way we talk about and practice it. We must look beyond a singular training mindset. After reading this book, I hope you will come away with an expanded focus on new learning possibilities, focused on the workplace as much as the classroom, and freed from the myths and assumptions that have constrained us:

- Business leaders, from senior executives to front-line supervisors, will see how learning, and e-learning, will become more integrated into the work—and the life—of their organizations.

- If you are a training professional, from an instructional designer to a chief learning officer, you will be challenged to reconsider your role and see the expanded opportunities you have for influence.

- If you focus primarily on technology, from the business side or the information technology side, this book will provide you with the business and learning perspective that will give your technology value.

- Consultants in the learning and performance arenas will gain some new insights into how they can help their clients learn faster and better and how to position workplace learning as a driver of business results.

- If you are a student in the learning and performance fields, this book will stimulate your thinking about the profession and its emerging new directions and, I hope, provide many opportunities for discussion and debate.

How is this book organized?

Beyond E-Learning takes you on a journey from where we are right now to where we need to be. Although we begin with considerations of e-learning and learning technology, we end focused much more on performance. The first of three parts, "Beyond E-Training," begins with a realistic assessment of the current state of e-learning. Part Two, "Beyond the Classroom," showcases many new non-training approaches that expand the notion of e-learning, learning in general, and performance improvement. In Part Three, "Beyond Learning," the book describes several cultural issues you must take into consideration if you want your efforts to be successful *and sustainable.*

Throughout the book are woven stories of how organizations are using new technologies and new approaches to learning to extend their reach and impact beyond the classroom. In addition, essays by leaders and practitioners punctuate my presentation with their own unique thoughts about the field and the opportunities before us. A series of appendixes provide additional information on e-learning topics, an assessment, and a resource list.

About Pfeiffer

Pfeiffer serves the professional development and hands-on resource needs of training and human resource practitioners and gives them products to do their jobs better. We deliver proven ideas and solutions from experts in HR development and HR management, and we offer effective and customizable tools to improve workplace performance. From novice to seasoned professional, Pfeiffer is the source you can trust to make yourself and your organization more successful.

Essential Knowledge   Pfeiffer produces insightful, practical, and comprehensive materials on topics that matter the most to training and HR professionals. Our Essential Knowledge resources translate the expertise of seasoned professionals into practical, how-to guidance on critical workplace issues and problems. These resources are supported by case studies, worksheets, and job aids and are frequently supplemented with CD-ROMs, Web sites, and other means of making the content easier to read, understand, and use.

Essential Tools   Pfeiffer's Essential Tools resources save time and expense by offering proven, ready-to-use materials—including exercises, activities, games, instruments, and assessments—for use during a training or team-learning event. These resources are frequently offered in looseleaf or CD-ROM format to facilitate copying and customization of the material.

Pfeiffer also recognizes the remarkable power of new technologies in expanding the reach and effectiveness of training. While e-hype has often created whizbang solutions in search of a problem, we are dedicated to bringing convenience and enhancements to proven training solutions. All our e-tools comply with rigorous functionality standards. The most appropriate technology wrapped around essential content yields the perfect solution for today's on-the-go trainers and human resource professionals.

Pfeiffer   *Essential resources for training and HR professionals*
www.pfeiffer.com

To Ben, Sherry, Marvin, Phillip, and Miriam

Beyond
E-Learning

Approaches and Technologies to Enhance Organizational Knowledge, Learning, and Performance

Marc J. Rosenberg

Foreword by David Holcombe

Afterword by John Larson

Pfeiffer
A Wiley Imprint
www.pfeiffer.com

Published by Pfeiffer
An Imprint of Wiley
989 Market Street, San Francisco, CA 94103-1741
www.pfeiffer.com

For additional copies/bulk purchases of this book in the U.S. please contact 800-274-4434.

Pfeiffer books and products are available through most bookstores. To contact Pfeiffer directly call our Customer Care Department within the U.S. at 800-274-4434, outside the U.S. at 317-572-3985, fax 317-572-4002, or visit www.pfeiffer.com.

Pfeiffer also publishes its books in a variety of electronic formats. Some content that appears in print may not be available in electronic books.

Library of Congress Cataloging-in-Publication Data

Rosenberg, Marc Jeffrey.
 Beyond e-learning : approaches and technologies to enhance organizational knowledge, learning, and performance / by Marc J. Rosenberg ; foreword by David Holcombe.
   p. cm.
 Includes bibliographical references and index.
 ISBN-13: 978-0-7879-7757-3 (alk. paper)
 ISBN-10: 0-7879-7757-8 (alk. paper)
 1. Web-based instruction. 2. Organizational learning. 3. Computer-assisted instruction. 4. Internet in education. I. Title: Approaches and technologies to enhance organizational knowledge, learning, and performance. II. Title.
  LB1044.87.R678   2006
  371.33'44678—dc22

                                        2005024331

Acquiring Editor: Matthew Davis   Editor: Beverly Miller
Director of Development: Kathleen Dolan Davies   Manufacturing Supervisor: Becky Carreño
Production Editor: Mary Garrett

Printed in the United States of America

Printing   10   9   8   7   6   5   4   3   2

Contents

Part Three: Beyond Learning

List of Illustrations

Figures

Tables

Foreword

So here you are, standing in a bookstore holding a copy of this book and contemplating whether to purchase it. Or perhaps you've already purchased the book and have finally found time to sit down to dig into it. Either way, it is important that you understand that you are holding a vision of the future of e-learning in your hands. I mean this in all seriousness. This book is genuinely prophetic.

I have watched the evolution of learning technologies for almost twenty years. I've seen firsthand how e-learning practitioners have struggled to put these ever more sophisticated technologies to work in a variety of innovative ways and met with widely varying levels of success.

The problem is that most of these efforts are focused on the technology itself, rather than how to apply it, in concert with other strategies, to solve a greater challenge: what the purpose of e-learning really is, what e-learning's role is within the larger context of performance improvement, and, perhaps most important, what our changing roles are as e-learning—and learning—professionals.

Marc Rosenberg has taken a much wider, comprehensive view of e-learning by focusing on the ultimate goal of building the smart enterprise: an organization where the ability to capture and disseminate knowledge to those who need it is at the core of its operational excellence. He has seen the light and put it on paper, and that is no small feat.

In this book, Rosenberg puts forward a cogent and broad-based definition of e-learning, defines a viable learning and performance architecture (a framework for illustrating the interrelationships between various technologies and strategies for learning and performance improvement), outlines the role of e-learning within that architecture, and explains how the architecture works in support of the smart enterprise. Along the way he has also managed to redefine the role of e-learning professionals, and learning professionals in general.

By reading this book now, you will be making an investment in your future and in the future of your organization's performance improvement efforts. You will come away with a clearer picture not only of what you need to do but why you need to do it. You'll develop a keen understanding of how to manage your role to ensure that you are armed with the skills you need to make your efforts congruent with the core of your organization's business.

This book is full of insight. Consider, for example, Rosenberg's position on blended learning. He challenges the commonly accepted definition that *blended learning* means simply blending classroom training with synchronous or asynchronous e-learning. He argues that the real blended learning we should all strive for is the convergence of training, information repositories, communities and networks, experts and expertise, and performance support. This is the blended learning that can truly enable the smart enterprise. But he doesn't just stop there. He then gives powerful examples of how organizations have put this into practice.

How does this new view of blended learning affect you? Profoundly, because if your view is that e-learning is just training, then your view of what can be done is limited. If you adopt Rosenberg's broader view of e-learning, you'll become much more effective and involved in all these elements. Learning technologies can be leveraged and integrated with information repositories. They can enable communities and networks, connect experts and expertise with those in need, and, ideally, work in concert with performance support technology to nullify the divide between learning and performance. Learning professionals must be armed with both this broader vision of the role of e-learning and the skills necessary to enable them to make it a reality.

As another example, briefly consider knowledge management (KM). Rosenberg argues that knowledge can't really be "managed" from a top-down perspective. Rather, it is something that is to be exchanged and shared, and to be really useful, it must be kept fresh, accurate, relevant, and accessible by all those who use it. But isn't this also the goal of all forms of learning? To make critical, accurate, relevant knowledge accessible whenever and wherever it's needed? As he points out, this clearly lies at the crux of learning and performance.

How does this vision of e-learning and KM affect you? Again, profoundly! The narrow view of e-learning is that technology is used to put relatively static educational content in front of an employee or customer. The broader view is that e-learning leverages dynamic information repositories to put critical content within easy reach of workers. It is critical to understand that this is where e-learning is going and then cultivate the skills necessary to make this happen becomes essential.

Let's look at the example of e-learning and performance support (EPSS). Many hold the view that these two are diametrically opposed ways to enhance performance, and the common view is that they are unrelated. This holds true to the extent that in most organizations that actually do have a vision for EPSS, responsibility for its development and maintenance is assigned to departments other than those where more traditional online training is being produced and managed. But Rosenberg argues here that learning and performance support are fundamentally connected because they are part of the same framework. Once you accept this and begin to explore their interrelationships, it becomes clear that for each to be successful, they must be managed and woven into a seamless resource where the line between learning and the actual support of workplace performance is blurred.

How does this vision of the relationship between e-learning and performance support affect you? Once again, profoundly! If you accept the premise that e-learning and EPSS are connected, then it becomes your responsibility to begin cultivating the skills necessary to make these interrelationships work. This means expanding your own vision for what you need to learn beyond traditional training skills to include performance support development strategies and technologies. This shift in your focus will enable you to serve as a catalyst to bring this vision to your organization, and it will put you at the crux of your organization's business, which is exactly where you want to be.

I offer these examples of Rosenberg's vision here to give you a taste of the broad vision this book provides. To really understand how this vision works and how you can put it into practice, you need to read this book now, and read it carefully. It will shake up your view of your role and will energize you with a new understanding of what you can accomplish.

It's true that to a certain extent, your having the vision and the ability to put the vision into practice is limited by the resources, capabilities, willingness, and culture of your organization. But I guarantee that if you cultivate Rosenberg's vision and set your sights on working toward achieving it, you will find yourself a leader in this important and valued transformation of the way you and your organization learn, and sooner rather than later.

Santa Rosa, California   David Holcombe
September 2005

◆ ◆ ◆

David Holcombe is president and CEO of the eLearning Guild (www.elearningguild.com), a global community of practice for e-learning professionals. He can be reached at dh@elearning guild.com.

Acknowledgments

If I have seen farther, it is only because I have stood
on the shoulders of giants.

—Sir Isaac Newton

There is no way I could have written this book without the contributions, help, and advice of so many professional colleagues—my giants—who are also among the smartest people in the business. This was not just a writing exercise but a true learning experience, and I have all of them to thank for it.

I long ago recognized that no single individual knows everything, especially me. I am gratified to include the viewpoints of some wonderful essayists who have added their insight and perspective to mine, making the total far greater than the sum of its parts: Jay Cross, Lance Dublin, Steve Foreman, Diane Hessan, William Horton, Nancy Lewis, Elliott Masie, Kevin Oakes, and Allison Rossett. Thanks also to David Holcombe for writing a wonderful Foreword and John Larson for an excellent Afterword. There is no better way to frame this book.

I also extend my deep gratitude to the individuals and companies that allowed me to share their stories in this book: J. R. Clark and Debra Ross (H-E-B Grocery), Elliot Rosenberg and Rob Lauber (Cingular Wireless), Ghenno Senbetta (Powered Performance), Jennifer Smith (Molex), Melinda Bickerstaff (Bristol-Myers Squibb), Linda McKula (DiamondCluster International), Eren Rosenfeld (Accenture), David Coleman and Andrew Waller (Unilever), Joanna Miller (Tufts University), Tony O'Driscoll (IBM), and Ed Arnold.

In the six months or so it took to write this book, I appreciated the many reality checks and countless suggestions from my two primary readers, Steve Foreman and John Larson. Steve brought a savvy e-learning and knowledge management business sense to the table, and John kept me true to the principles of instructional design, learning, and performance improvement. Their advice was invaluable. In addition, I thank Saul Carliner, David Erekson, Jeff Leeson, and Victoria McDonald for their invaluable input and advice.

I thank my editor at Pfeiffer, Matt Davis, and his colleagues, Kathleen Dolan Davies, Laura Reizman, Susan Rachmeler, Mary Garrett, and Beverly Miller for their professionalism and support throughout this project. Thanks also to Marcia Conner and Cambridge University Press and Robert Reiser and Prentice Hall Publishers for their kind permission to reuse some of my material previously published in their books.

I am also grateful to all my colleagues at AT&T, OmniTech Consulting, and DiamondCluster International for all that I have learned from them over the years.

Finally, some special acknowledgments: to Harold Stolovitch, who gave me some sage advice at a critical point in this project; to Jay Cross, for his professional generosity; to Allison Rossett and Gloria Gery, who have helped me crystallize my thinking over the years; and to my friend Joe Wions, who always kept after me about work-life balance and doing what I want to do. I'm still working on that one, Joe.

When I completed my first book, I promised my wife, Harlene, and my son, Brian, that I wouldn't put them through the craziness of writing another one. I guess I did, but I could never have done it without their continuing love and support, for which I am truly blessed. And now, to their glee, I can clean up my office.

Hillsborough, New Jersey   Marc J. Rosenberg
September 2005

INTRODUCTION

Getting the Most from This Book

E-Learning! We need to talk about "e-forgetting,"
because to be successful at e-learning, you have to
forget the ways of your past.

—Tom Peters[1]

Human knowledge is growing exponentially. A great paradox of our time is that the more we must learn, the less time we have to learn. So we are faced with a seemingly insurmountable challenge: How do we keep up to speed on everything we must know, precisely when we must know it?

Mass education became popular at the point in history when apprenticeships became impractical because there were too many knowledge seekers and not enough knowledge providers. Since then, we have relied on schooling, where one subject matter expert, or master, teaches dozens or hundreds of people at one time. But the world of learning is rapidly changing. With knowledge becoming so expansive (and often fleeting), demand for learning growing, and an increasing diversity in what individuals must know, even the best master teachers cannot reach all who have to learn with any semblance of timeliness and effectiveness. Our strategy now must be to capture knowledge so that it can be instantaneously accessed and shared. The only way to do this at anything close to the speed of change is to apply new thinking about learning technology and, more important, new thinking about learning itself. The technological revolution that spawned our fast-paced, information-centric world can also help us master it.

A colleague suggests that with respect to e-learning, organizations go through three phases. The first is to get lots of content out there ("we need to get into e-learning"). The focus is on the quantity of courses (classroom conversions and off-the-shelf purchases) and an investment in the technology to deliver them. Success is measured by how much you do, how quickly you do it, and how many courses you offer. The second phase comes when quantity is no longer a viable measure of success without quality and impact ("we need to get better at e-learning"). The focus here is to identify which e-learning programs have the greatest payoff, even if it means cutting back on others. Experimentation increases in new forms of design and delivery, including blending classroom and online programs and implementing virtual classrooms. Success is centered on innovative instructional applications and higher cost-benefit ratios. Finally, the third phase represents a shift in e-learning's emphasis from training performance to business performance ("we need to support workplace learning and performance across the organization"). Here the goal is to cross over from formal learning to both formal and informal learning, and to design more comprehensive solutions that span training, knowledge sharing, collaboration, and performance improvement, all in the context of work. Business measures like productivity, customer and employee satisfaction, organizational agility, and marketplace performance are the metrics that matter here.

Wherever you see yourself and your organization with regard to e-learning, the purpose of this book is to help you successfully move to phase three and beyond. To do this, we must expand the parameters of what e-learning is and how it can be strategically applied in the workplace. The rise of e-learning has provided a great opportunity to demonstrate value, but only if we go beyond traditional notions. Now is the time to step forward and redefine what it means to learn and perform in a true business context and to transcend the classroom to consider seriously how we integrate learning much more into the context of work. We must change the conversation about e-learning from when and if we're going to do it, to how it is changing, what it is becoming, and what it will look like when we get there.

Audience

Beyond E-Learning doesn't begin with the basics. To keep this book on the right trajectory, a more advanced and strategic treatment of learning and e-learning, it assumes you have a good working knowledge of the field. And while I absolutely recognize the importance of quality training, I assume that you are already familiar with and even experienced in training best practices (or are working with training professionals who are).

Although this book was written mainly for an experienced audience, it can provide useful information to a wide variety of readers. Business leaders, training professionals, technology professionals, consultants, and students will all benefit from the perspectives and information presented in this book.

If you are expecting this book to address only the future of learning technology, you may be surprised. As I wrote this book, I discovered that the more I got into how e-learning will expand and evolve, the less relevant e-learning, on its own, became. And the more I got into the impact of all of this on organizational learning and performance, the less I saw training, on its own, as the center of the learning universe. So for me, going beyond e-learning is, in a sense, putting e-learning and training aside (but without ignoring them) and moving on to bigger issues, opportunities, and challenges. Thus, this book is focused not on the training side of e-learning but on the more advanced workplace learning and performance side.

Learning and Training Are Not the Same

Many organizations approach most learning challenges as training problems, and most efforts to create a learning culture tend to end up primarily with a training culture. But these two are not the same. Learning is a basic human activity that takes place everywhere and every day. Every role or function within an organization has some form of learning attribute, and the people who do the work are constantly learning.

The use of technology to support learning is commonly referred to as e-learning. From training delivered at a specified time and place, we have moved to a model that transcends place and space, where instruction is continuously available. In the late 1990s, when the Internet made e-learning more practical on a massive scale, investment and interest in the field soared. Since then, the e-learning industry has also gone through some tough times. Many firms have come and gone. Growth and optimism were replaced with cost cutting and disillusionment, investment slowed, and jobs were cut. But the industry that emerged from this era is more focused and more reliable.

> Is a profession that doesn't know what to call itself having an identity crisis, or morphing into something new and better?
>
> —Pat Galagan, ASTD[2]

E-learning is here to stay, but that doesn't mean it should stay the way it is. From a learning perspective, we should see the Internet as much as a library as a classroom, and embrace information sharing as much as instruction. Technology is essential, but it alone will not get us where we have to go; we must be ever vigilant about quality and also make sure the culture of the organization supports e-learning—and learning in general—rather than hinders it.

The Changing Nature of Learning and Learning Technology

> Courses, by definition, capture yesterday's knowledge.
>
> —Diane Hessan and Eric Vogt, Communispace[3]

Now that the giddiness over learning technology has subsided, corporations (and not just training departments) are asking, "What's next?" What will expedite learning, performance, and knowledge sharing? How are future learning innovations made possible by new technologies? How do we best take advantage of what learning technology has to offer, without overdoing it, and what else should we consider when we think about new approaches to learning and performance? Nobody assumes that learning is inconsequential or that technology doesn't have a role to play. But a redefinition of its characteristics, role, and value is needed.

In considering these questions, five realities are fundamentally changing how we think about the learning landscape:

- **Technology-based learning is here to stay.** It enables organizations to conquer both time and location in the development and support of employee skill and knowledge. It enables real-time content updating and facilitates the interconnectivity of people separated by time zones and organizational walls. Interoperability and security issues are being addressed and are no longer considered major barriers. Quality online training—what we have traditionally referred to as *e-learning*—continues to grow, as it should.
- **Believing that face-to-face classroom training is going away is both misguided and wrong.** The classroom will continue to serve a critical function in any learning strategy. It provides a place where people can interact, experiment, collaborate, and create. And while this is possible online, the classroom's (or laboratory's) unique nature provides a great environment for these activities (making high-quality classroom programs more important than ever before). In addition, there will certainly be times when the presence of a live, expert instructor or facilitator is essential: to explain, observe, guide, and give feedback. Thus, both traditional and online training have significant roles to play in the future of learning. The key will be in determining when each should be used and what new instructional, informational, and support configurations will be made possible by these delivery strategies, both individually and blended.
- **Justifying the expense of learning is no longer a cakewalk.** Even the argument that an up-front investment in learning technology can save money in the long run may not be enough if the performance results are not there. More than ever before, investment in any type of learning strategy requires an expectation, if not hard

evidence, of business value. This will clearly drive changes in the articulation of what should be measured, including the expansion of success criteria beyond educational results ("Did they learn?") to performance results ("What can they do?"), as well as a much closer tie to business results ("What is the value to the business?").

• **Organizational learning and performance are facilitated through strategies and techniques that go far beyond training alone.** This expanded view transcends the classroom, bringing learning and learning technology to the workplace, the home, the hotel room, and many other locales. Although e-learning began as a new way to deliver training, it cannot remain that way because it is no longer able to adequately support all the learning needs of individuals and organizations by itself—if it ever was. It has moved in a new, somewhat unanticipated direction: a direction not always reminiscent of an instructional framework.

• **The workplace has fundamentally changed.** For better or worse, we are fully engulfed in what the Gartner Group, a business and technology research service, calls the "e-workplace," a 24/7 virtual world were work activities transcend the office and the traditional notion of the nine-to-five job.[4] Living and prospering on "Internet time" requires a complete rethinking of what it means to learn, where learning takes place, and what learning looks like. E-learning is part of the journey to this new reality of business, and of work.

Hindsight enables missteps of the past to be seen clearly, and these five realities provide new insights into the future. Like the rest of the Internet and the knowledge economy, the e-learning phenomenon is finding (and creating) its own path and moving in new directions, as am I.

Lessons Learned

The future ain't what it used to be.

—*Yogi Berra, baseball legend*

Having worked in university, business, and consulting settings for more than a quarter of a century, I have seen and participated in some great work, as well as some misfires. I have noted the accomplishments of many learning professionals but have also seen far too many layoffs. I have watched as new technologies were adopted with great fanfare, and then seen them junked when "the next big thing" came along. Through it all, I have always viewed the glass as half-full, not half-empty. Along the way, here are some lessons I have learned:

- **We have overrelied on technology.** Although technology is important, we have often been too quick to embrace it, especially to solve current problems—a cure-all mentality—without considering what future challenges and consequences might be. We should think of technology as an enabler, not as a strategy. It's the highway, not the destination; the means rather than the ends. The success of any learning initiative is much more likely to depend on management policies, leadership, and organizational culture than on new or better technologies.
- **We have spent too much time in the training center.** Compared to how other business operations use technology, we have typically come to the table with too little, too late, often running our own show without the cross-functional collaboration that is necessary for long-term success. We may be overprotecting our turf just a little. We should truly integrate ourselves more with other key business operations.
- **We have often spoken a foreign language.** We have at times marginalized training's contribution by emphasizing our own internal metrics, such as student days, tuition revenue, the size of our course catalogue, and other similar measures without adequate consideration of the business or performance problems we are trying to address. We should tone down our own jargon and speak the language of our clients.
- **We tend to think this is easy.** We often look for simplistic solutions to learning, which fly in the face of its true complexity and importance. This is tough stuff; what we do is in part "rocket science."

We must avoid trivializing human learning and performance and recognize that this is hard, professional work.

- **We want immediate results.** Innovation always lags the innovator. New ideas need a gestation period, a time for experimentation and thought. Changing the way people learn will take deliberate steps, but it will also take time. A strategy that encompasses a long-term view with interim milestones is an essential first step.

These observations and experiences—these lessons learned—have shaped the writing of this book. But despite our missteps, we have an undeniable drive to be successful. We are constantly experimenting, and our concern for making a difference keeps us going. We are on the cusp of a major revolution in learning, learning technology, and performance improvement, not just at work but across our society. Continuous lifelong learning—anytime and anywhere—is not just an ideal; it is an essential part of modern life. Because of this, the world *will* beat a path to our door. Whether you are using learning to transform your entire business or simply want to transform your training department, my hope is that this book contributes to getting you ready.

Notes

1. Peters, T. (2001, October 29). Presentation at the annual Tech-Learn conference, Orlando, FL.
2. Galagan, P. (2003, December). The future of the profession formerly known as training. *T&D Magazine, 57*(12), 26.
3. Hessan, D., & Vogt, E. (1999, November). Presentation at TechLearn conference, Orlando, FL.
4. Gartner Group. (2003, October 3). *Client issues for the knowledge workplace*. Stamford, CT: Gartner Group.

Part One

BEYOND E-TRAINING

"E-learning" is *not* "e-training." It is too important to be limited solely to instructional solutions.

1

Myths and Warning Signs

> Learning is a much more complicated phenomenon
> than can ever be limited to a classroom. In
> organizational learning efforts, the confusion of
> learning and training is fatal.
>
> —*Peter Senge*[1]

Training has a significant role to play in any successful business. Organizations need highly skilled employees and great skill-building programs. Faced with the ongoing challenges of constant change and an insatiable need for knowledge, organizations have embraced technology-enabled learning as a way to keep up. But sometimes the implementation of learning technology becomes the objective rather than the means to a valued end. There is no question that learning technology is getting better and that it can support successful, sustainable learning. But the perfect use of technology to deliver bad or unnecessary training, or training that's offered to the wrong people at the wrong time, is worthless for the most part. E-learning is indeed a revolution in the way people learn and improve their performance. But like most other things, overindulgence (or, more often, misapplication) seems like the right thing at the time, but afterward, you wonder what the point was, or whether you should do it again.

This chapter is about where e-learning is and where it is going. Once the hype of the e-learning craze has gone, what's left? What's myth and what's real? How can another binge be avoided? What's worth keeping, and what needs to change? It is a wakeup call for e-learning zealots and Luddites alike as the field embarks on new paths.

Overpromised and Underdelivered

The future of learning technology is full of promise, but charting its trajectory is not easy, as can be seen from its shaky past. Although computer-based training (CBT) has been around in various forms for more than thirty years, until recently, most business and training leaders considered it marginal or were not quite sure how to best take advantage of it.

In the past, training organizations dabbled with CBT, putting out an occasional course that promised to revolutionize organizational learning, only to find that poor design and a lack of workstation standards and network connectivity hampered the program's effectiveness. Furthermore, course content required continuous updating, and development cycles were long. It's no wonder that classroom training continued to dominate the learning landscape. Then the Internet was born, and the common Web browser platform began to mitigate technology challenges. Because programs could be updated instantly, online training could keep up with the pace of change, or so it seemed.

The Hype

With the advent of the Internet and the "e-enablement" of many business operations, such as customer care, sales support, e-commerce, supply chain management, and customer relationship management, investment and enthusiasm in e-learning exploded. Like every other industry in the Internet economy, e-learning company valuations went through the roof. The hype was on, fueled by industry experts whose books, speeches, and company Web sites proclaimed the revolution to be in full swing. There was nothing e-learning could not do. Consider this single well-meaning comment by Cisco Systems' CEO, John Chambers. Of all the pronouncements about the e-learning revolution, Chambers's remark was one of the most quoted and perhaps the most famous: "The biggest growth in the Internet, and the area that will prove to be one of the biggest agents of change, will be in e-learning."

The same organizations that once touted their classroom offerings now wanted to put much of it online. Training organizations were eager to do with online training what they had done with classroom training: become a one-stop shop for all training needs throughout the enterprise. Content was purchased by the bucketful, loaded onto servers, and made available to all. Some companies put all or part of their training operations in the hands of third-party service providers. Many organizations operated on the assumption that more training was always better than less. But many training organizations that "went online" continued to measure themselves the same way, advertise courses the same way, and use the same processes, skill sets, and organizational structures as they had for classroom training. They applied their old business model to the new "e" business. This was a mistake. In their study of the use of e-learning in higher education, Robert Zemsky and William Massy note, "The hard fact is that e-learning took off before people really knew how to use it."[2] At the end of the 1990s, this was also true within many corporations. And just as the irrational exuberance over e-learning was peaking, the Internet bubble collapsed.

The Fallout

> In the rush to turn online education into a business, the roof caved in.
> —New York Times, May 2, 2002

What a difference a few years make. The e-learning industry was hit as hard as any other by the Internet crash. Investment slowed significantly and in many cases came to a screeching halt. Most critical, executives looked at their e-learning investments and wondered where the value was.

E-learning became marginalized in some organizations; the bills for the large investments that were made in the previous years were now coming due, and e-learning was seen as an expense that could no longer be afforded at anywhere near the current pace. When business value proved to be more elusive, it was harder to build the case for e-learning. Although a solid business case is certainly appropriate, getting a hearing and a favorable response became much more difficult, and many training organizations were ill prepared for the type of scrutiny they were now getting to their requests for funds, personnel, and even permission to move forward. Organizations were questioning not only the value of technology-based learning but also the value of training in general. Training looked increasing like an unnecessary cost. Layoffs increased, and whole training functions were outsourced.

In many cases, business managers at all levels either had differing views from each other or didn't completely understand what technology could do for learning. For example, a study of senior human resource (HR) managers noted that while most managers had ideas for learning solutions, they were not sure if their approach was correct; they had a weak or nonexistent strategy. As far as technology was concerned, most solutions addressed only part of their needs, and they didn't quite fit the most pressing issues. Complementing this lack of clear direction for learning technology was the fact that implementation was often in silos, different areas of the organization were doing different things, and budgetary constraints were significant and long-term.[3]

Of course, lots of companies have maintained their commitment to training in all forms. But in many organizations, there is no doubt that the overselling of learning technology, sometimes without a comprehensive strategy or clear vision, combined with new economic realities, has caused a lot of rethinking about learning.

From customer to analyst to investor, the consensus is that e-learning still has a few things of its own to learn.

—Information Week, May 13, 2002

Is the Glass Half-Empty or Half-Full?

For all the efforts of two generations of research and practice, the most recent data suggest that e-learning is still a small piece of the overall training pie. A 2004 *Training Magazine* survey reported that only about 17 percent of all training is delivered by computer (another 8 percent is delivered by an instructor via a "virtual" classroom), and as much as 70 percent of all training is delivered in the classroom (another 5 percent was allocated to "other").[4]

In many cases when e-learning does get off the ground, it fails to deliver on expectations. Martin Sloman and Mark Van Buren reported that as much as 62 percent of all learning technologies fail to meet expectations. These researchers also cited a study by DDI (Development Dimensions International) that, after studying 139 companies in fifteen countries, found that 75 percent of the respondents rated the effectiveness of e-learning as less than five on a ten-point scale.[5]

Do these findings suggest failure or greatly diminished expectations, or is e-learning advancing out of the wisdom gained from past experience? Can training organizations alter their mission to more effectively employ e-learning even as e-learning continues to evolve? Is the glass half-empty or half-full?

Those suggesting the glass is half-empty argue that e-learning can never live up to its promise and that those associated with it are not to be taken seriously (or as seriously). They say that advocates of e-learning have squandered opportunities to demonstrate real value and have lost credibility. The half-empty contingent suggests that training organizations are failing to get outside the classroom model in a serious way. They note that with lots of money already spent, it will be hard to get more and that a critical mass of funds and personnel will be almost impossible to bring together. Naysayers point out that the emphasis of technology over instructional design has so diminished the professional skill sets of practitioners within many organizations that those skills are no longer identifiable, and that too much time and effort is still being spent on "Webifying" classroom courses rather than redesigning learning to leverage the true interactive nature of the Web. Those who forecast the end of e-learning, as it is practiced today, say that layoffs, downsizing, outsourcing, and offshoring are not just a short-term reality but represent a significant and permanent shift in how organizations will run training. Their perspective is that e-learning has not demonstrated that it is consistently better than classroom instruction from a learning perspective, so why bother?[6] This points to a not-so-promising future, where past disappointment about e-learning will make it harder for people to accept the next iteration.

> Everything looks like a failure in the middle.
>
> —Rosabeth Moss Kanter [7]

For their part, proponents of a glass half-full suggest that e-learning is embarking on a new phase or journey that will be both different and more valuable. They suggest that there are real success stories that need to be found and used to reeducate key constituencies about the power of e-learning. Furthermore, they note some positive trends. The increasingly competitive and information-rich marketplace has finally gotten the attention of executives around the power of the knowledge-centric workplace, new technologies promise greater abilities to do it right, with better integration and lower redundancy, and customer e-learning, as an adjunct of successful e-commerce initiatives already in place, presents a huge opportunity for all forms of e-learning. They argue that a poor economy (global, national, or industry specific) is not a time to cut back; rather, it is an opportunity to retool, relearn, and start fresh. They point to a revitalized training and e-learning industry that is trying to respond with new ideas and better, easier-to-use products, a hopeful sign. Although learning effectiveness from e-learning is often only as good as classroom training, this is not a reason to abandon it, say e-learning proponents. E-learning is significantly more efficient, accessible, and updatable, which provides a positive business rationale. And in some situations, e-learning techniques can do better, especially when live training is too risky, complex, time-consuming, or expensive to be done with the necessary authenticity to be effective. Finally, those in e-learning's corner say that the e-learning hype, and subsequent disappointment, has caused everyone to take it all more seriously, carefully, and thoughtfully. The field has sobered up.

> Now that we've cleared out the riff-raff, we can get down to building the future.
> —John Perry Barlow, originator of the term cyberspace and former lyricist for the Grateful Dead[8]

While the downside indicators are all too real, the upside potential of e-learning is tremendous. Business research firm IDC sees corporate training, including business skills and information technology training, rebounding from the downturn, with a robust expansion going forward. And e-learning will be a significant part of the recovery, IDC notes, with "increased use of the Internet as a training creation, delivery, and management tool; increased familiarity by U.S. workers with collaborative technologies, which will drive demand for synchronous content and shared learning technologies; and new technologies and services that foster e-learning implementation, richness of content, and other improvements."[9]

The glass is indeed half full, but it's a different glass than the industry drank from in the past.

The Myths of E-Learning

myth (n): a notion based more on tradition or convenience than on fact.

—American Heritage Dictionary

The overhyped promise of e-learning was in part fueled by nine myths:[10]

1. Everyone understands what e-learning is.
2. E-learning is easy.
3. E-learning technology equals e-learning strategy.
4. Success is getting e-learning to work.
5. E-learning will eliminate the classroom.
6. Only certain content can be taught online.
7. E-learning's value proposition is based on lowering the cost of training delivery.
8. If you build it, they will come.
9. The learners are the ones who really count.

Buying into these myths has led individuals, organizations, and entire industries to make decisions based on beliefs about the ease and acceptance of e-learning that are, at times, naive. But the myths are not historical in nature; they continue to influence e-learning strategy and decision making. Understanding and getting past them is the first step toward moving forward to a more sanguine, successful, and durable strategy.

Everyone Understands What E-Learning Is

There continues to be significant confusion about the term *e-learning*, as with a host of other terms, like *online training*, *Web-based training*, and even older terms such as *computer-based training*. This is complicated by differentiations between *asynchronous*, or completely self-contained e-learning, and *synchronous*, or virtual, leader-led e-learning (sometimes referred to as a "virtual classroom"). Adding in new fields and technologies makes defining *e-learning* more complex. Even the word *learning* attached to the expression is a source of confusion. Without agreed-on definitions and a common framework for thinking and talking about e-learning, confusion reigns.

Sometimes a change of name is significant—and sometimes it's not. To many practitioners, e-learning equals e-training. To them, e-learning is simply courseware online or e-training. The paradigm that e-learning equals e-training keeps the field moving down a path that's much narrower than it should be. Even the continued confusion between training (the means) and learning (the ends) lingers in the professional collective psyche.

E-Learning Is Easy

Wish it were so, but in fact, it is hard work. Better tools do not equate to better skills. Building and deploying great e-learning that is both effective and efficient takes real effort, discipline, and experience in fields such as instructional design, information design, communications, psychology, project management, and psychometrics, not to mention a healthy consideration of needs assessment and evaluation. Think about word processing; the tools are getting easier all the time, but that doesn't mean everyone can write the next Pulitzer Prize–winning novel.

The general assumption is that technology is the hard part and that most of the work and investment goes into getting the technology right. This is partially true. New technologies are often fraught with bugs, cost overruns, and a more significant learning curve than expected. And if you're not careful, technology issues can be all-consuming. But getting the technology right is nothing compared with getting the learning right. As the saying goes, "The delivery truck may be important, but it's what's in the truck that really matters."

E-Learning Technology Equals E-Learning Strategy

One of the biggest mistakes organizations make is leading with technology before a strategy is established. Too much money is spent too soon, resulting in disappointment and resistance to investing more when the proper time for the investment arrives. This isn't just an e-learning myth; organizations have often invested too much in new technology before they really knew what they were going to do with it or what its value really was. This is not to say that learning technology is unimportant—far from it. But you can't select the right learning management system, authoring tool, or any other part of your e-learning infrastructure before you have a comprehensive learning strategy (not just an e-learning strategy) that positions the technology appropriately.

Success Is Getting E-Learning to Work

In this context, what does "getting *it* to work" mean? For too many, it means getting the technology to work. This leads to a false sense of security that once e-learning is "out there," you've accomplished your mission. But from a value standpoint, deploying e-learning is meaningless. It's what's done with e-learning that matters. True success for e-learning is in how well it strengthens performance and the business. And that takes careful measurement and a long-term view—a learning and performance strategy.

If you agree that just getting it to work is not an adequate success criterion, you might believe that having a large online catalogue of courseware is. Having fifty, one hundred, or even five hundred courses online, or having 10 percent, 50 percent, or as much as 90 percent of all training online certainly defines quantity, but it doesn't define value. A library of courses, large or small, is of little use by itself. Real success is what impact these courses have on the organization. How targeted are they toward business needs? What performance outcomes are you expecting? These are the types of questions you must answer when defining success.

E-Learning Will Eliminate the Classroom

In order to get approval for the money and resources to see e-learning deployed, many organizations promised dramatic reductions in classroom-based offerings, even to the point of agreeing to get rid of the classroom option altogether. But it hasn't turned out this way, and promising to eliminate the classroom is a promise that cannot and should not be kept. Classroom-based face-to-face training continues to have an important role, albeit a somewhat changed one. One way the classroom may change, for example, is by moving from a heavy emphasis on disseminating facts to providing an environment where collaborative teams can discover, invent, or otherwise solve complex problems. Those who believe e-learning will kill the classroom are as misguided as those who believe e-learning is a passing fad.

Only Certain Content Can Be Taught Online

This argument, often raised by sponsors as a reason not to support e-learning, is untrue. With the right instructional design approach, almost any type of knowledge or skill can be developed and delivered online, including so-called soft skills like leadership or critical thinking. Of course, some skills development may require reinforcement through other formats, such as classroom training, opportunities for practice, online tools and resources, or access to coaches and experts. If you think broadly enough about the possibilities e-learning affords, you will find a way to employ it successfully in almost any discipline.

E-Learning's Value Proposition Is Based on Lowering the Cost of Training Delivery

E-learning does lower the cost of training delivery. And while executives may appreciate any cost savings they can get, they will really appreciate the substantial benefits e-learning can generate in worker productivity, speed of learning deployment, and shortened times to competence. E-learning's real economic value is in the money it saves its clients by shortening the time it takes to improve worker skills and knowledge so they can be productive sooner.

If You Build It, They Will Come

In the movie *Field of Dreams,* Kevin Costner's character built a baseball diamond in the middle of an Iowa cornfield because he heard a voice telling him, "If you build it, he [his father] will come." Getting employees, or partners, or customers to rush toward e-learning just because it's there is wishful thinking. More likely, getting people to use and accept e-learning, especially over the long haul, will take work—in change management, communications, and leadership—and time.

Although it's true that users need help in getting comfortable with e-learning, if you communicate well and provide the help and encouragement they need, they will likely give it a try. The biggest roadblocks often come from executive sponsors and other senior stakeholders. Some are quick to provide support in words only, but when it comes time to pay for it, they're nowhere to be found. Others create nearly impossible hoops for you to jump through before they will support e-learning, and sometimes, even when you meet all the requirements, support really isn't there. Although it can be difficult, finding executive sponsors who will truly commit resources, including people and money, and invest their personal time in your cause is a beautiful thing and an important criterion for successful e-learning.

The Learners Are the Ones Who Really Count

Sure they count, but a focus on learners to the exclusion of other constituencies reflects traditional training organization thinking at a time when the training function must be much more integrated into the business mainstream. If all you think about is whether learners learn, you are likely missing where the real value is: in the job performance and business impact. This means satisfying executive sponsors, frontline managers, partners, suppliers, customers, and others who may certainly appreciate that people learned, but really want to know what it all means for the organization, and for *them*.

Don't Call Them Learners!

Another myth to consider is that the people who take training or e-learning are "learners." Of course, they are engaged in learning, and perhaps during that time, the term fits. And while everyone, by their very nature, is a learner and is constantly learning, referring to people who participate in training only as learners rather than who they really are—workers or employees (salespeople, engineers, accountants, technicians), managers or executives, customers or suppliers, or any other role that is a more accurate description of what these people really do—can be too simplistic and tends to encourage a perspective that often fails to get beyond traditional training thinking. This myth is more semantic in nature, and some might find it too picky. But thinking about e-learning in new ways has to start with existing paradigms that might be holding you back. Calling people what they really are is a good beginning, but if you must use a generic term, a better one might be *performer*. Although learning is both essential and at the core of what this book is about, this book will not refer to those in a learning mode as learners.

The problem with myths is that they are often assumed to be truths. The old adage, "garbage in, garbage out," is more likely "garbage in, gospel out." In other words, people act on what they believe to be correct and are sometimes slow to recognize that the direction they are heading in may be the wrong one. When your actions are based on false assumptions or inappropriate practices, the negative impact of the decisions you make can be significant.

> There is one thing that should be said loudly and clearly: trainers need to realize that things are going on that don't fit their assumptions, their own training backgrounds, and the way they typically have been doing their jobs.
>
> —Peter Drucker[11]

Warning Signs

Most organizations have e-learning strengths and weaknesses. E-learning strengths open doors of opportunity, innovation, and value. Weaknesses, if left unattended, can lead to waste and disillusionment. Knowing where you stand, and what to do about it, makes all the difference. If you're inside a business or a government agency, how do you know if your learning (and e-learning) initiatives are in jeopardy? From the perspective of an outside consultant or service provider, how do you know that your client is moving in the right direction? Look for these nine warning signs:

1. **Technology without strategy.** Are you focusing on technology first and above all else? Are you implementing technology without close collaboration with your IT department? The tendency of many organizations is to overstate the role of technology as a component of a successful and sustainable e-learning strategy. Technology is important, but it is a terrible place to start and insufficient, by itself, to sustain a successful e-learning program over the long-term. And if you pursue a technological course of action that is incom-

patible with the capabilities of your organization's IT infrastructure, you may be headed for disaster if critical business operations are adversely affected.

2. Weak focus on business and performance requirements. Are you in the training catalogue business? Trying to be all things to all people? The inability to directly link e-learning programs, or any other training program, to specific business and performance needs dramatically reduces your value in the eyes of your constituents and sponsors.

3. Minimal e-learning expertise. Is your e-learning program getting ahead of your e-learning capabilities? Insufficient skills in e-learning management, design, development, and deployment and an inability to leverage talent from other sources (such as other parts of your business, external partners and suppliers, academic institutions) can significantly slow your progress.

4. No attention to the unique attributes of e-learning design. Do you see e-learning as simply an online manual, lecture, or slide presentation? Failure to apply specific techniques in instructional, informational, and software design to truly take advantage of the unique interactive capabilities of e-learning diminishes the quality and innovativeness of your efforts.

5. Weak assessment. Do you know whether people are actually learning? Do you know what they are learning? Can you determine if their on-the-job performance has changed? Too often, learning and performance assessment and other measures of quality are put on the back burner as everyone's energy is focused on other aspects of e-learning, such as technology issues and content presentation. This can leave you guessing about the real impact of your work.

6. No focus on informal, workplace learning. Are you limiting the role of e-learning to formal, online courses? Failure to extend the power of learning technology directly to the workplace and provide knowledge sharing, collaboration, and support to workers in the context of their jobs constrains your role to a much smaller sphere of influence than is necessary or desirable.

7. No governance. Are you unable to make collective decisions about e-learning strategy and operations? Failure to control redundancy and infighting across multiple training organizations, and no vehicle to represent the potential of e-learning to senior management, are two major contributions to inefficiency and waste.

8. Weak sponsorship. Do you get lots of positive words from the top but little action? Misidentification of leaders most likely to support e-learning over the long term or pursuing an e-learning strategy without solid executive support can leave you much more vulnerable when budgets are cut or priorities change.

9. Failure to manage change. Are you launching e-learning programs without getting people ready for this major change in how they'll learn? Embracing a new way to learn is not so easy for many people. Winning the support of employees so that they will willingly accept and ultimately prefer e-learning is a major challenge. Without a change management and communications plan, your e-learning initiative might just be a flash in the pan.

Additional details on these nine warning signs are provided in Appendix A.

Rethinking E-Learning at H-E-B Grocery

Organizations can defy the myths of e-learning and mitigate the warning signs. They can think creatively about how to use technology to enhance learning and performance. When they do, the rewards are there. But the result may not look like the e-learning they were familiar with. So companies, even those with little experience in e-learning, can succeed just by thinking a little differently. That's what H-E-B Grocery did.

San Antonio–based grocery company H-E-B operates hundreds of stores in Texas and Mexico. The privately held firm prides itself on the way its thousands of partners (its term for employees) serve customers, a point of differentiation for the business. This is especially important for frontline workers like checkers, who spend the most time with customers and in many cases are the only ones who speak directly to them.

H-E-B management noticed that the productivity of checkers fell if they couldn't identify produce items or took too long to look up the price of specific fruits and vegetables. When checkers have difficulty telling the difference between casabas and cantaloupes, for example, they have to take additional time to verify the right product in order to ring up the right price. In a business with razor-thin margins, even small delays or misidentifications can add up to significant monetary loss, not to mention slower checkout lines and frustrated customers. For checkers, produce is a moving target, as the assortment comes in and out of season all year long. For many years, H-E-B's solution to produce identification was traditional classroom training (for new checkers), manual produce identification tests (for existing checkers), and job aids.

Traditional E-Learning Is Not an Ideal Solution

Converting a classroom training event into an online course would seem a reasonable and flexible solution, but it was not. First, the specific performance problem—reducing produce identification errors—required the checker to differentiate among hundreds of products and then quickly look up the correct code. Any traditional online course would require lengthy recognition tests and undoubtedly many retests until mastery (accomplished through lots of memorization) was achieved. Then retraining would be needed as new products were added. There would likely be lots of training activity but little performance change.

At the time, H-E-B's infrastructure was not at the level it needed to be for complex e-learning solutions. The slow network speed would require too much wait time for lessons to download, and the information technology (IT) organization justifiably wasn't going to spend millions of dollars to upgrade the bandwidth just for checker training. So the company was faced with a dilemma: it needed to solve the performance problem (accurate produce identification and pricing), but traditional training—classroom or online—was not going to work. An innovative solution was required.

A cross-functional team was assembled to create the solution. The result was the "Produce Challenge," a program and a strategy to maintain knowledge and improve performance by creating a weekly online produce test with built-in content remediation and a little bit of business logic. The team recognized that the performance problem could be addressed only through an ongoing conversation with checkers about produce. In addition, the company could put some focus on new and current produce items in the stores, target individual weaknesses, and include a little bit fun and competition, all in a very short time.

Bringing Learning Directly to the Workplace

The Produce Challenge is essentially a weekly two-minute drill consisting of ten questions from a pool of hundreds of items. It is designed to work within the existing infrastructure and bandwidth. Checkers might be presented with two images and be asked to select the correct one. For example, in Figure 1.1, the checker is being asked to identify a bell pepper. First, checkers select the right produce and then get a small nugget of instruction about it.

The clock is always running, and when time runs out, the checker gets a score that is compiled with his or her previous results in a database. Missed items are captured in the database and re-presented to individual checkers in subsequent weeks until they get them right. The program includes remediation for missed items, and the content is customized based on the store product mix.

There were more obstacles to overcome. Checkers didn't have access to computers, and there was little room for e-learning workstations in the stores. The team compelled store leaders to use the computers on their desks for the Challenge. Levels of computer literacy were all over the place. Many checkers had little computer experience, so the design featured very simple mouse movements.

Figure 1.1   H-E-B Grocery's Produce Challenge

Source: H-E-B Grocery Company.

Results

From the partner perspective, the Produce Challenge was well received. More than 90 percent of H-E-B's checkers take the challenge every week. The amount of shrinkage (product loss) saved and productivity gained in the first year alone has more than paid for the program. J. R. Clark, a member of H-E-B's training organization, Partner Learning and Development, thinks this is partly because it was quick, easy to use, and a bit of fun (as with arcade games, everyone wants to make the top 10 list). The company also put a lot of promotion and measurement around it, not just when it launched but as a continuing element of the strategy, certainly a contributing factor.

Executive support has grown and deepened. The marketing vice president commented that he felt more comfortable increasing the product mix because he knew checkers would be more likely to ring produce correctly (thus generating better data and less shrinkage). Now, training supports a wider selection of products for consumers, which is consistent with H-E-B's customer-centric strategy. More "Challenge" programs are under way.

> One challenge on the content design side was to let go of that conventional binders and classrooms approach. Designing training in two-minute repetitions instead of four-hour events required a mental shift. We never expected participation rates to be so high and sustainable. The culture has visibly shifted, and it sets us up to deliver more e-learning going forward.
>
> —J. R. Clark, H-E-B Grocery

The lessons learned from H-E-B's Produce Challenge are several. An e-learning program does not always have to look or act like a course to succeed. The format of the Produce Challenge is part game and part test. Repeated, short-interval programs can be very effective, with limited lost productivity. Each checker would have to take the Challenge every week for more than two years to equal the time off the job of the original four-hour classroom course. When there's a business problem to solve, predispositions about e-learning fade; what counts is whether it will work. Finally, the power of e-learning grows when it can be integrated with business intelligence—when the real world of business is fused into the way people do and learn their jobs.

Putting E-Learning in the Context of an Overall Training Strategy

As the H-E-B story clearly shows, not all e-learning initiatives succumb to the myths and warning signs. E-learning can build confidence not just in e-learning but in training (and the training department as well). E-learning that solves business problems provides an opportunity for connections with upper management and fosters further innovation. But too often this is the exception rather than the rule.

> Unfortunately, things here are not good. Our mistake was getting our corporate university recognized in the press as world class. Our executive management has felt for some time that they could not afford such a group.
>
> —*Training professional who was subsequently laid off*

Companies often try to do too much with training, including e-learning, to solve problems the function is ill equipped to cope with, such as using training as the primary or only tool to change a culture. But does learning something new translate into a change in attitude or belief? Does diversity training *alone* create a more diverse company? Is sales training *alone* enough to improve the productivity of the sales force? Can customer care training *by itself* improve a call center representative's demeanor on the telephone?

Will simply adding e-learning to these questions fundamentally change the answers? Although training is often a part of achieving these and other business goals, it usually cannot accomplish them alone. Poor supervision, interpersonal rivalries and competition, a bad working environment, outdated tools and processes, unsatisfactory incentives and rewards, and unusable documentation are just some of the many other factors that block successful performance, achievement, and productivity. Training, whether in the classroom or online, is likely to be wasted, and ultimately lose its support, when it is delivered in an atmosphere where these issues are not considered, addressed, and incorporated into the solution.

DILBERT: © Scott Adams/Dist. by United Feature Syndicate, Inc.

How can the value and impact of e-learning be improved? Does e-learning represent a true revolution in training, or is it just one important step on a larger journey that will revolutionize how organizations think about and approach learning and performance improvement overall? The answer that is emerging, from past experience and from a more realistic view of the future, is that it is the latter: part of a fundamental transformation that is much bigger than training.

Notes

1. Senge, P. (2004, May). Interview: The future of workplace learning and performance. *T&D Magazine*, p. SS45.

2. Zemsky, R., & Massy, W. (2004). *Thwarted innovation: What happened to e-learning and why*. Report of the Learning Alliance, University of Pennsylvania, p. iii.

3. Karrer, T. (2004, February 9). The perfect (performance) storm. *eLearning Developers' Journal*. http://www.elearningguild.com/pdf/2/020904mgt.pdf.

4. Dolezalek, H. (2004, October). Twenty-third annual industry report. *Training Magazine*, pp. 20–36

5. Sloman, M., & Van Buren, M. (2003, May 18). *E-learning's learning curve: Will they come, will they learn?* Paper presented at the ASTD Conference, San Diego.

6. Refer to www.nosignificantdifference.org for a review of the many studies that have tried but failed to show a difference.

7. Kanter, R. (2001, November 13). *Evolve! Life and learning in the digital culture of tomorrow*. Presentation at the Chief Learning Officer Summit, Boston.

8. Barlow, J. (2001). Business meeting presentation, St. Petersburg, FL.

9. IDC Research. (2003, September). *U.S. corporate and government e-learning forecast, 2002–2007*. Framingham, MA: IDC.

10. Thanks to Lance Dublin (www.lancedublinconsulting.com) for contributing several of these myths.

11. Drucker, P. (2000, December). Interview. *T&D Magazine*, p. 27.

In the Land of E-Learning Myths

A Knight's Tale

Lance Dublin

Myths began as invented stories that the ancient Greeks used to explain why things are, where things came from, who did something, and how human beings should be (that is, what human ideals and values are). Think of them as entertaining stories with a serious purpose. Although the word *myth* means "untrue" to some people, to others the word embodies a different kind of truth—one that expresses their deepest and truest values, fears and concerns, hopes, and beliefs.

Myths have been powerful forces for centuries. From ancient times right up to the present, they have been used as the basis for the most critical decisions, ranging from war to exploration to invention. They are powerful forces because they are larger than life—almost mystical, in fact. They hold the promise of wondrous accomplishments, great feats, and superpowers beyond imagination. People want to believe in myths: fire-breathing dragons to slay, wizards and sorcerers casting spells, superheroes leaping the tallest buildings in a single leap.

I am constantly amazed at the role myths play in the learning business today. Based on myths, I've seen careers made, strategies developed, vendors engaged, technologies installed, and monies spent. All too often these myths formed the basis for justifications and served to obfuscate the real issues at hand. Since myths by their very nature are not fact based, it becomes easy to fit the myth to the "truth" we want to believe, such as "all learners want e-learning." It is hard to debunk a myth, be it that thunder comes from Thor's hammer or e-learning is "always better-faster-cheaper." Myths seem to take on a life of their own, seeming to be true because they represent plausible explanations.

If we let our worldview and our decisions be governed by myths, we can be sure that we will be living more in the land of fantasy than that of reality. We will continue to find ourselves spending more time justifying and explaining than making things happen. We will continue to find ourselves with a false sense of certainty as we become ever more convinced that the myth is in fact true or even *the* truth. This is a slippery slope, and we will soon find ourselves unable to change our perceptions and see clearly, unable to distinguish fact from fiction and myth from reality. And we will never reach the pot of gold at the end of the e-learning rainbow. (Or is that just a myth as well?)

I am frustrated by the power and long life that so many of the e-learning myths seem to have. No matter what the data show, the myths continue. It's as if we are afraid to challenge a myth because it would cast doubt on our very purpose and the very existence of a whole industry. So we end up making excuses and creating explanations to prove that the myth is true.

I have been in situations where people have held on to a position based on their belief in the myth even when confronted with hard data. "If you build it, they will come . . . and be happy" is a great example. The data show that learners don't flock to e-learning courses because they are online. Nor are they always happy with whatever they can find. Nor do they even always want a course, "e" or instructor led.

In fact, the data show that people in business settings want just-enough, just-in-time answers to questions and solutions to problems rather than abstract concepts and knowledge checks, no matter how good the Flash animation. They register for online courses, search the table of contents to find just what they want, work through that module, and then log off to go apply what they've just learned. The learning management system records this as a failure, a dropout, when in fact they got just what they wanted just when they needed it.

But this myth about e-learning prevails, and hours are spent trying to figure out the cause of this "failure." Was it the wrong content, bad instructional design, or not enough interactivity? Was there not enough simulation, or too much entertainment and not enough application? Seldom do I find anyone challenging the myth itself.

Maybe businesspeople just want to use a search engine to find the right content! Maybe they value speed over entertainment. Maybe they value simplicity over animation for animation's sake. The reality may well be that in today's world, e-learning should really be learning to the power of "e."

Ah, but were not all e-learning myths actually true and the world really full of fire-breathing dragons and damsels in distress. That would seemingly make my life much easier because debunking myths and finding truths are indeed the work of knights. And I could then engage the knights of the e-learning roundtable in this quest. But, alas, these knights do not exist, and I do not believe in these myths.

So I continue on my own quest to challenge e-learning myths whenever I hear of them and wherever I find them. For although I am not a knight, I know we'd all be better off replacing the wishful thinking of myths with some hard doses of reality.

◆　◆　◆

Lance Dublin is a management consultant, speaker, and author specializing in corporate learning and organizational change. He can be reached at ldublin@pacbell.net and www.lancedublin.com.

2

Learning, E-Learning, and the Smart Enterprise

The problems that exist in the world today cannot
be solved by the level of thinking that created them.
—*Albert Einstein*

Managers and trainers alike have long hoped that technology can
be a panacea for any number of organizational and business problems. Just the availability of new learning technology is often seen
as a reason for using it. But as comfort and experience with technology grow, there is an increasing understanding that it's a tool for
organizational learning, not its solution. Simply going from classroom training to online training does not guarantee more or better
learning or improved business performance. In fact, when used
inappropriately, technology can be a hindrance—and a costly one.

Yet there are a myriad of appropriate and highly beneficial roles
for learning technology, if applied correctly. To understand how
technology can be used to facilitate learning, it's important to look
beyond traditional training perspectives.

This chapter introduces the smart enterprise, an organization
where learning adds value to the business, and the four components
that support it: (1) a learning and performance architecture, (2)
change management and communications, (3) learning and performance leadership, and (4) a proper environment for learning and
performance improvement to succeed. All four components are
necessary to build and maintain a smart enterprise; to ignore even
one is to impair individual and organizational performance. And
technology, used appropriately, supports them all, imparting integrity
to the entire structure, like rebar in concrete.

The Smart Enterprise

Enterprises must accomplish more in a shorter time frame. The speed of knowledge transfer is becoming a determinant of how fast an enterprise can perform.

—*Gartner Group*[1]

Organizations are full of smart people: scientists, executives, salespeople, engineers, administrators, factory workers, technologists, and hundreds more titles and roles that make up a business or government enterprise. For the most part, these are well-educated and wholly competent individuals, the products of years of education, training, and experience. Whether they are located in one building, one city, across a country, or around the world, they are selected for their role because they have the knowledge and skills to enable them to do their job successfully. Although some particularly bright people might end up in one company or another, most businesses have their share of the best and the brightest.

So if all organizations have smart people, why don't they all perform equally well? This is a complex question, and it goes to the heart of how organizations succeed. Certainly there are many factors. Economic conditions may dictate the health and success of a business. The telecommunications industry, believed to be essential to the new economy, was decimated by the 2000–2002 recession. Being a market leader may mean the difference between staying in a line of business or abandoning it. Jack Welch, former CEO of General Electric, liked to say that in any industry, you'd better be either number one or number two in the marketplace. Otherwise you should get out. Lean and cost-effective operations can also tip the scales between success and failure. Japanese car manufacturers gained an initial toehold in the United States not on quality issues but because they could build, and therefore sell, automobiles at a much lower cost. Today the Koreans are trumping the Japanese in this area. Such is the natural flow of business.

An equally important factor of organizational success is the ability of the organization, and its people, to perform in a coordinated and systematic way. How well, and how fast, a business or government agency can adjust to changing market conditions, transform a new discovery or idea into new products and services, or respond to changing customer needs is critical. And the enterprise's capacity to adjust, transform, and respond is a direct reflection not simply of the ability of its smart and capable people, but the ability of those people to work together and adapt as a smart enterprise.

What Is the Smart Enterprise?

Smart enterprises are places where a learning culture thrives.

> A **smart enterprise** is a high-performing organization that allows knowledge and capabilities, enabled by technology, to grow and flow freely across departmental, geographical, or hierarchical boundaries, where it is shared and made actionable for the use and benefit of all.

A smart enterprise begins with a high-performing workforce, supported by a performance-enhancing workplace environment. It is an organization where this knowledge is collectively, systematically, and efficiently applied for valued purposes, such as business growth, operational improvement, product development, new market acquisition, defense against competitors, customer satisfaction, and the enhancement of employee performance—as individuals and as teams. For some organizations, it is a reality: they have implemented smart enterprise strategies in a department or business unit or addressed a specific challenge or opportunity. But it is also a vision: an ideal state that gives organizations something to shoot for as they seek to strengthen the role of learning and performance improvement solutions. Looking at the characteristics of a smart enterprise more deeply, there are five key points to emphasize:

- **A focus on knowledge and application.** The smart enterprise is sustained not by capital expenditures or bricks and mortar, but by what the collective employee body knows and is able to do as a result, especially when the "doing" is creative, insightful, or innovative, even if it involves trial and error. It therefore follows that learning is an essential element in facilitating the growth and sharing of knowledge. It also implies that knowledge is accessible and available to those who need it, when they need it, wherever they need it.

• **The effective use of technology.** Whether they are small or large, twenty-first-century organizations are more dynamic, mobile, flexible, and virtual than ever before. Pervasive connectivity and mobile computing will contribute to increasingly decentralized work where, from 2007 going forward, beginning in the United States, knowledge workers may spend most of their time working outside the traditional office.[2] Whether this prediction is optimistic or not, the fact remains that technology will increasingly be a critical force in maintaining and increasing productivity through business process automation, self-service, and disintermediation. Further increases in productivity must come from applying technology to support new models and environments for learning and performance. The smart enterprise employs technology to provide access to the vast array of new learning resources across the organization. This goes far beyond courseware to a variety of information repositories, expertise, tools, and other knowledge and performance assets.

• **A systematic and a dynamic approach.** The smart enterprise is the antithesis of a haphazard organization. It exists only through the systematic coordination and collaboration of the smart individuals who comprise it and the knowledge each carries. This is not to say that lockstep rules and procedures are required. On the contrary, what is required is a balance between processes (and the flexibility and capacity to allow them to change and evolve) that encourage and support collective efforts and the flexibility and openness that encourages innovation. The smart enterprise should be in a continuously formative state, collecting feedback and data and iteratively analyzing and improving itself. Maintaining this delicate balance is one of the main challenges of smart enterprise leadership.

• **An emphasis on both individuals and teams.** The smart enterprise is centered on the performance of teams, organizations, and business units, and this is a reflection of the knowledge and capabilities of individuals who make up these groups. Most activities around training, coaching, and other human resource functions have typically focused on the development of individual employees. But in the smart enterprise, these activities must also be focused on how individuals learn, work, and perform *together* over the long haul across functional areas and business units. This requires a whole new way of looking at how these services are provided.

- **A performance foundation.** Despite the focus on knowledge and learning, it is the performance of the enterprise that counts. From a business perspective, simply knowing something is insufficient. Without using knowledge to create value, the effort put into creating and disseminating that knowledge is often wasted. And the metrics that matter to the organization are its readiness measures, including productivity, individual performance metrics, team or small-group performance metrics, and business metrics, as dictated by its strategy, and operational goals and objectives. Increased sales, more efficient operations, enhanced shareholder value, and higher customer satisfaction are examples of appropriate business performance measures. Even in nonprofits and governmental agencies, delivery of service and measuring the performance of that effort will continue to grow in importance.

> The transition of the workforce from brawn-power to brain-power rivets attention on what the people in an organization know, and how to collect, stir, store and refresh it.
>
> —*Allison Rossett and Kendra Sheldon*[3]

Origins of the Smart Enterprise

The work of Peter Senge[4] and Chris Argyris and Donald Schön[5] has resulted in the definition and popularization of the learning organization, one characterized by continuous collaboration and knowledge sharing, invention, and innovation. It is an organization that not only learns from its experiences but reflects and adapts its behavior going forward.

A learning organization is not a training organization; training, including online training, is not adequate alone to foster a learning organization. For all the courses that are available, they are predominantly one way, episodic, and event driven rather than part of how people actually work, collaborate, and learn.

Many of the attributes of a learning organization are more human than technological. Issues of trust, reflection, dialogue, and feedback are all essential and often best conveyed in a personal way. Yet technology offers many opportunities to capture and increase knowledge and then make it available to more people. It supplements (but does not replace) the personal interactions that may be more difficult in today's decentralized, virtual world. The value of the smart enterprise lies in the strategic convergence of organizational learning principles with the tools and technologies that can support them.

Here is just one possible approach. The Gartner Group has suggested a new type of technology integration, called the smart enterprise suite, that emphasizes collaborative processes and knowledge work, more akin to organizational learning requirements.[6] At a minimum, vendors may offer separate tools and technologies under a single marketing bundle. Others may offer increasing levels of technical integration of existing applications and services, and a few might even develop suites from scratch.

Thus, in a smart enterprise, the principles of organizational learning are supported and enhanced by new approaches and technologies that bridge the gap between formal classroom learning and informal workplace learning and support.

Breaking the Bonds of the Course

"We need a course" is probably the most overused statement ever delivered by, or to, a training organization. As prominent as this statement is and as important as the training function is, when organizations follow it blindly, it presupposes that the best solution to an identified performance problem is always and only training. Maybe it is, and maybe it isn't. Unfortunately, for far too long, many training departments have been quite happy defining their function only as providers of courses. In the worst of cases, they are seen just as order takers. "Want a course? Sure, no problem. How many would you like?"

To be more influential in the smart enterprise, e-learning must be reinvented. While continuing to provide a viable instructional option in a formal learning setting, it must also move toward informational solutions that focus more prominently on the specific jobs people do. It must move beyond courseware and classrooms and into work. To reinvent e-learning is, in many ways, to reinvent learning itself.

Building the Culture

One of the major failures that contributed to 9/11 was the inability or unwillingness of various agencies to share and coordinate information. With bits of information all over the place, no one knew what was actually going on.

—Former Illinois governor James Thompson, 9/11 Commission member[7]

Achieving a smart enterprise culture is not easy. The silo nature of many organizations, where communication and collaboration across departments is practically nil, creates huge barriers to collaboration, knowledge sharing, and learning. In the fight for resources, business units are often loath to cooperate with one another. Employees, fearful of their job security and eager to be noticed, may seek an advantage by hoarding information rather than sharing it.

DILBERT: © Scott Adams/Dist. by United Feature Syndicate, Inc.

In the smart enterprise, interrelationships and interdependencies abound. There are fewer silos, and those that exist are much weaker. Team-based work and collaboration are the rule rather than the exception. Knowledge sharing is rewarded, and true organizational learning is a defining characteristic rather than just a lot of training. The whole is greater than the sum of its parts.

Training's Role and Limitations

Before alternatives to training can be introduced, it is important to understand training's continuing and often important role in organizations, as well as its continuing and often significant limitations.

Classroom Training

Classroom training is by far the most recognizable approach to facilitate learning. The benefits of classroom training have been well documented. It is relatively quick to develop and deliver, especially for small numbers of people, but it becomes more costly and time-consuming as those numbers go up. It allows an expert instructor to lead the learning process, which is especially important if the content is new, unstable, or complex. Classrooms themselves provide great opportunities for teamwork, group problem solving, and bonding among participants. Finally, qualified instructors can observe and provide expert feedback and serve as coaches and advisers in real time. They can facilitate in-depth discussions, set the stage for experimentation, and help participants deal with failures and risk. Nevertheless, there are significant limitations to the classroom model:

- **The classroom cannot scale.** Its ability to meet demand is limited by available instructor staff, the number of people to train, and desired class size. The greater the demand and the sense of urgency, the more tenuous is the organization's ability to meet the need through quality classroom training.

- **The classroom cannot handle the speed at which knowledge is changing.** Internal and external information is constantly changing, requiring expensive, productivity-inhibiting retraining. This problem is exacerbated as the number of people who need the information grows.

- **Classroom costs are rising.** Costs for instructors, travel, and facilities raise the costs for classroom training significantly. More important, there is tremendous cost if those who need new knowledge right away have to wait for a seat in a training class to open.

- **It can be difficult to assemble a homogeneous roster for a class.** As work diversifies and the knowledge and skill requirements of employees diversify as well, it becomes increasingly difficult to offer a classroom course that can precisely meet the needs of everyone who attends. The result is that some are bored, others can't keep up, and many may see all or part of the course as irrelevant.

- **Classrooms don't allow flexible scheduling.** As companies become more virtual, more decentralized, and more flexible in how they run their businesses, waiting for a specific class start date or traveling to a specific course location is often seen as unnecessary and wasteful.

- **There is a lack of qualified instructors.** Instructors should be subject matter experts and have the experience necessary to teach and advise employees while they are in class. (If they are not experts, valued learning may suffer; if they are not schooled in teaching methods, learning transfer may suffer.) But their supply is limited, as is the time they can devote to actual teaching.

- **Message consistency may be an issue.** Multiple instructors, spread out across time and distance, cannot always be counted on to deliver a consistent message. Their expertise and experiences, not to mention their teaching skills, may be divergent enough to create situations where different groups of people hear different things and receive dissimilar instruction. In some cases, this is not a problem; in fact, the diversity may be welcomed. But increasingly, requirements for consistency—for safety, security, legal, compliance, performance, and competitive reasons—are becoming much more critical.

- **Classroom training is time-consuming and interruptive.** Employees (or partners, suppliers, and customers) are looking for efficient learning alternatives. Every day they are under pressure to make the best use of their time. Going to class may not always make it to the top of their list of priorities.

Despite these limitations, classroom training remains a powerful tool when used for appropriate purposes. There is no evidence that the classroom's days are numbered or that organizations should close training centers in favor of all things technological. Companies that abandon the best attributes of classroom training or rush to unrealistic goals of putting nearly everything on the Web may find their actions very shortsighted.

Online Training

Although the classroom continues to have an important role to play, it can no longer be the sole or even the default approach. Like classroom training, the purpose of online training is to deliver instruction: a structured set of activities designed to achieve specific learning outcomes. While online training programs try to adapt to the learning needs of the user, there is a limit to how much variability can be programmed into them. In the end, control over what content is taught, and in what sequence it is taught, is in the hands of the program. This is to be expected, as the goal of any training program is to build specific skills and develop specific competencies, and to do this, the sequence of instructional events, including the choices people are given as they move through the program, must be predictable.

Beyond the classroom, online training can reach people who are dispersed geographically, and it allows large numbers of people to participate in a course. This can markedly improve the efficiency of training, enabling more instruction to be delivered to more people at a lower cost. Courseware can be divided into smaller instructional chunks that give people more flexibility in selected training components that precisely meet their requirements. Furthermore, being able to reach more people quickly can be a significant strategic advantage. Many companies have not been able to train their sales force, customer service representatives, product developers, and others quickly enough to meet ever changing competitive threats or consumer needs or to take advantage of innovation. When the workforce has more immediate access to instruction using technology, competitive advantage, in the form of a shorter time to workforce competency, is self-evident. And the ability to update online training the moment the content changes increases the organization's ability to meet the needs of dispersed people who rely on accurate content to do their jobs. Using technology to deliver a consistent instructional program to all who need it can ensure that no critical content falls through the cracks.

Here's a great example. When the U.S. government had to train tens of thousands of airport security personnel for the Transportation Security Administration, it required broad reach, nearly impossible speed, the ability to update the learning as new procedures were developed, and a highly consistent instructional program. Online training was a major part of the strategy.

Even more interesting, learning technology provides an opportunity to depict more authentic scenarios with far less risk. From the days when film and video were introduced into the classroom, it has been possible to bring the outside world into the training environment. Now, new learning technologies can increase this benefit manyfold. Through the power and creativity of simulations and the ubiquitous nature of the Internet, scenarios can be created that rival the real world, making training more relevant, more effective, more challenging, and, where appropriate, more fun. Indeed, technology-based games and simulations represent one of the fastest growing segments of the e-learning industry,[8] and the U.S. government is now fully engaged in simulations and games, even for highly sensitive areas like the military and homeland security.[9] Finally, technology is being used to monitor training results and electronically provide the kind of high-quality feedback and coaching that often seem more valuable than the course content itself. When one hotel chain chose to train its front desk personnel in the critical area of customer service, it didn't use a lecture or even an online course. It chose a creative game-based simulation where individual scenarios were presented to the employee, who earns "applause" when the right solution is selected. And if the system detected inappropriate selections, an online coach appears with additional, reinforcing content.

Of course, technology is not always applied well in training. Building technology-based training is hard and complex. It takes time and costs more to develop than traditional classroom training (although it is generally much less expensive to deliver, which is where the savings are). If the message isn't clear, there's no instructor to clear up the confusion. A greater variety of questions and reactions from participants must be anticipated and built into the product, and more effort must be made to focus on their specific interests and needs.

And technology is not always applied to the right training need. When learning technology is applied incorrectly or inappropriately, it can inhibit rather than accentuate learning and may in fact be responsible for the perception that technology doesn't work. But there are no hard-and-fast rules; almost every situation is unique to the organizational context. Think about employee orientation, for example. One argument suggests that orientation programs are ideal for online training. The content is fairly stable and relatively simple. And since most new employees need some form of orientation, the audience may be large enough to justify it. A brewing company, for example, put a lot of its new employee orientation online, enabling people to get up to speed faster than if they had to wait for an orientation class. In fact, some orientation materials were made available to prospective employees before they started work so that they could get a sense of a life of making beer. This resulted in some marginal prospects' dropping out early, before the company had invested too much money or time in them.

But a counterargument is just as powerful: leave orientation programs in the classroom (the brewery might argue, "How can they understand the business if they can't smell the beer?"). There is validity in the need for employees to bond with their peers and begin working together as a team. Here's a story from the consulting industry. A professional services firm that recruited dozens of M.B.A.s from around the country used classroom-based orientation training so that the new employees could build relationships that would help them survive the somewhat nomadic life of a consultant. Years later, many employees still rely on the people they met in orientation for advice and counsel even though they may see each other infrequently.

When applied well and to the right learning and performance need, classroom and online training does work. Training, and the instructional strategies that make it work, continues to be an essential component of the smart enterprise but no longer the only one.

Building the Smart Enterprise: Much More Than Training

Considering everything people have to know, it is no longer possible (if it ever was) for training alone to provide all the learning people need. Ask anyone how they learned to do their job or how they learned to do it better than anyone else, and they'll likely tell you that they learned in many ways. Certainly they had some training, but they also learned on the job, through watching others, asking questions of peers, trial and error, their own experimentation, and, if they were lucky, the help and support of a mentor or coach. They will also tell you that learning, especially to the point of mastery, took time, creativity, and thoughtfulness.

The assumption that taking a class or a set of classes builds quick competency is almost always wishful thinking. In fact, it's a bumpy road. You take a course, learn some new things, then go back to the job and try them out. Perhaps you learned a new skill, but applying what you've learned is often not so easy. You have to practice, ask for help, reread the student materials, and so on. Even then, with the pressures of work and the passage of time, some forgetting is bound to set in. So you wait for the next class to reinforce what you've learned, and then learn more.

By providing tools and resources that support learning and performance directly in the workplace, you are in a sense building a bridge from the classroom to the job. One way to do this is to provide workplace-accessible online training. But is this enough? Are people, in the context of performing their jobs, always able to stop working to take a course every time they have a question? Probably not. What workers are looking for is straightforward and reliable access to information and expertise that answers their questions, demonstrates a task or process, provides advice, and in general makes their work easier and better. With technology as an enabler, these recourses are available from the desktop—fixed or mobile— and provide a wealth of opportunities to learn quickly only what is needed, at the precise moment of need.

The Need for a Strong Technological Foundation

Technology does more than just support a more comprehensive set of learning and performance tools. It also has altered the nature of work. It enables more virtual work arrangements and the ability to organize globally. Teams of employees can contribute to projects from different parts of the country or the world. Partner and supplier networks can function faster and more efficiently. Work structures and process can be more dynamic, forming and re-forming as the business situation demands. The universality of desktop computing and the Internet has radically changed business and is doing the same for learning.

Technology models are changing. Older views of technology— to automate training delivery and manage the training transaction (for example, course registration)—while still necessary, no longer represent cutting-edge thinking about technology's purpose and value. Neither does a linear view, where technology-enabled learning is seen as a series of screens of content, presented in a predetermined order. New views of technology see it more likely to change or adapt to the environment and needs of the user and to provide more of a nonlinear, weblike framework for moving through content. Ultimately technology will be seen less as a way to manage content than as a way to help people grow and share knowledge organically.

Technology is a key enabler of the smart enterprise—a true bridge between individual and organizational learning. It is essential to building and sustaining learning in today's large and complex organizations. It improves the quality and expands the reach of learning products and approaches of all kinds. Equally important, it enables these resources to work in harmony, creating a far more valuable solution. It can provide a single, personalized gateway to a wide array of instructional and informational resources for each individual while maintaining a singular organizational perspective.

How Smart Enterprise Thinking Changes the Nature of E-Learning

> Think different.
>
> —*Apple Computer slogan*

The most important aspect of the smart enterprise as it affects e-learning is the direct integration of e-learning into business processes and activities rather than as a separate activity. This means that consideration of learning and performance issues takes place much earlier in the development of new systems, tools, or work processes. It also means that training organizations have to rethink how they are positioning themselves going forward. Table 2.1 illustrates some of the major paradigm changes that result when smart enterprise thinking drives e-learning strategy.

Table 2.1 E-Learning in the Smart Enterprise

Traditional E-Learning	*Smart Enterprise E-Learning*
Stand-alone operation of the training department, offering a service to the rest of the company. The training department "owns" e-learning.	Integrated into business processes, requiring specific and deep partnerships with other operational units (for example, IT, customer care, HR). E-learning is a cross-functional business resource.
Focuses on delivering courses online; instructional design is the default and dominant approach, and instructional designers, working with subject-matter experts, do much of the work.	Focuses on delivering instruction and information and enabling collaboration. Instructional design is one of many key approaches, and instructional designers are part of much broader interdisciplinary teams.
Supports new business tools, processes, and products that are about to be launched.	Involved at the start in the design of new tools, processes, and products from a learning and performance perspective.
Operates its own technology platform and infrastructure; training Web sites and tools are separate from other business resources.	Fully integrated with business platforms and infrastructure; training information is seamlessly linked with HR, IT, and other business resources.
Value driven by "customer" satisfaction and learning gain as measured by pre- and posttests.	Value driven by improved job performance and other business metrics and by lower overall cost, increased speed, and responsiveness of deployment and adaptability to changing business requirements.
Robust catalogue of products (something for everyone).	Targeted and integrated solutions, embedded in the business and reflecting key business priorities.
Permanent staff with most work done in-house.	Flexible staff, featuring large numbers of rotational experts and the strategic use of key outsourced partners.
Deliver the course, and we're done until it is updated one or two years from now.	Deliver the solution and continuously improve it through ongoing iterations.

Table 2.1 E-Learning in the Smart Enterprise, Cont'd

Traditional E-Learning	Smart Enterprise E-Learning
Philosophy: We have the knowledge, and we need to deliver it to the field.	Philosophy: The knowledge resides here, in other staff organizations, and in the field. We need to collect it, broker it, organize it, and package it from the employee's viewpoint.

Learning to Learn in the Smart Enterprise

Peter Drucker, ever on target, says that "knowledge worker productivity is the biggest of the 21st century management challenges."[10] By immersing people in a knowledge culture rather than just a training culture, they learn to be better information seekers, better researchers, and ultimately better performers. People can learn from instruction, and they can learn from information, but they don't learn the same way. Learning through instruction is a structured and managed experience; learning through information is much the opposite.

Those who know how to learn on their own and are motivated to do so are less likely to rely only on instructional solutions. They are more likely to demand direct access to well-designed content so that they can figure things out for themselves, and they are more likely to become frustrated when they can't. They learn to discern important and valid content from drivel. They begin to stop asking, "What do I need to know?" and begin asking, "Where can I find what I need to know?" As they become self-directed, they hone a critical skill: the ability to identify, access, evaluate, and effectively use information. This is a primary skill for people working in a smart enterprise.

> Knowledge is a force stronger than gravity.
>
> —Boeing Corporation commercial

Waiting a day, a week, or a month for a training course, in the classroom or online, is no longer acceptable. When you need to win a sale, solve a technical problem, design a product, or manage any other process, the ability to learn, and learn fast, is the premier asset of the competitive, smart enterprise.

DILBERT: © Scott Adams/Dist. by United Feature Syndicate, Inc.

Building a smart enterprise is not just finding better ways to do what you have always done; it is about thinking differently not just about what you do but about what learning itself is all about. To get there, as Lance Dublin suggests, you must move yourself, your people, and your organization as a whole through three cumulative stages.[11] First, you must be *efficient*; you must be able to improve what you are currently doing. Reducing costs, delivering less expensive training, and being able to deliver learning where and when people need it are all examples of greater efficiencies. Second, you must be *effective*; you must do things better, and do better things. Improving business results through formal and informal learning and employing workplace learning and support enable you to be more effective as well as more innovative. Third, to deliver value in a smart enterprise, you must deliver *competitive advantage*; you must be able to do what you have not been able to do before. Focusing on business benefits rather than learning benefits and getting more involved upfront in business processes and operations is a great start. Each of these stages is required; you cannot skip the first two to get to the third. These were the challenges Molex Corporation faced.

Molex Learns to Use Technology to Learn

Molex, the second largest manufacturer of interconnect products, knows that product and competitor knowledge is essential for marketplace success. To sell more, its general employee body must be able to talk about Molex products and articulate its value proposition in any number of industry and customer contact situations.

Generally there were significant gaps between the importance of using technology to accomplish key business tasks as well as in the proficiency level of Molex's employees. Molex recognized that continuous improvement was not something to attempt just by installing more technology; it requires helping people embrace technology as a preferred way to get their work done.

Using tools provided by Powered Performance, the company uncovered opportunities in the way people use technology to find, organize, and share product and competitive information. It also identified several areas where productivity in using Web browser resources and tools (search, favorites, task bars) could be improved.

Molex wanted to do more than improve product and competitive knowledge; it also wanted to improve the ability of employees to use software productivity tools and the Web to make this happen. It could have launched a lot of more traditional product and competitor-focused training courses, in the classroom or online, as well as classes in personal information management and productivity. It did some of this, but for the most part, it went down a different path.

In specially designed work sessions, employees received brief instruction on productive searching and other Web-based information management skills. During these sessions, each participant applied the various tools and techniques to address his or her own specific needs. At the end, they not only built the beginnings of their own personal knowledge library but developed advanced skills in information research as well.

Molex found that with these new skills in hand, employees were able to find online information faster, which resulted in work productivity increases. They were able to better differentiate quality content from mediocre content. They were able to organize increasing amounts of knowledge for future reference, and they were more likely to share what they found with others. Their comfort level in using Web-based knowledge resources increased significantly. Six weeks after participating in the program, of the participants who completed the follow-up survey, 100 percent reported improvement in their technology skills with 55 percent reporting significant or very significant improvement; 89 percent of the participants indicated good or excellent retention of information research concepts, tools, and techniques.

> In the business world as well as our personal lives, today so much of our time is spent working with some type of software and the Internet. This program is very helpful in improving the skills of our people, giving them the capability and motivation to find information themselves.
>
> —*Jennifer M. Smith, senior corporate product trainer*

Learning in this fast-paced, electronic information age is increasingly self-directed learning. People need research skills and tools and the confidence that they can find what they need, when they need it, with increasingly less assistance. With this confidence comes more openness to knowledge sharing and collaboration, the hallmarks of a smart enterprise. The old adage, "Give a person a fish and they won't be hungry for a day; teach a person to fish and they won't be hungry for a lifetime," certainly applies.

The Smart Enterprise Framework

What should be apparent by now is that even the most effective training cannot support a smart enterprise alone. New thinking and new ideas are necessary. A smart enterprise framework has been developed to provide a much more comprehensive perspective as to how to enhance learning and performance in an organization. There are four major components to the smart enterprise framework (Figure 2.1):

- Learning and performance architecture, which constitutes the bulk of this book, and is covered in Chapters Three through Seven
- Change management and communications, covered in Chapter Eight
- Learning leadership, covered in Chapter Nine
- Performance environment, covered in Chapter Ten

Figure 2.1 Components of the Smart Enterprise Framework

Change Management and Communications

Learning and Performance Architecture

The Smart Enterprise

Employees   Partners   Suppliers   Customers

Performance Environment
(Tools, Resources, Motivation, Incentives, Processes, Talent Management)

Learning and Performance Leadership

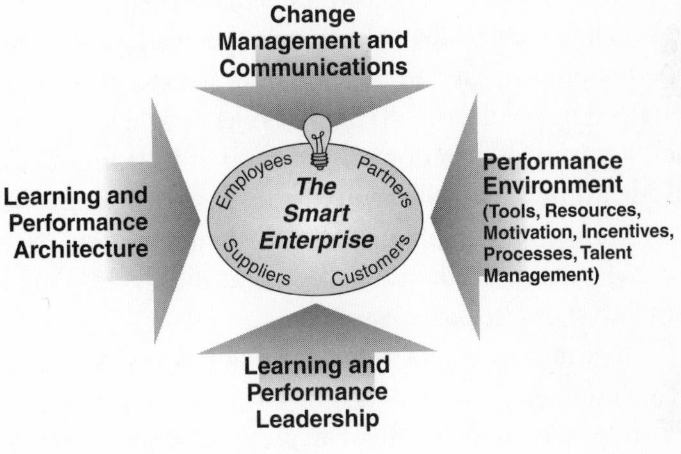

Introduction to the Learning and Performance Architecture

Smart enterprise thinking requires a redefinition of e-learning, from new and innovative ways to use Internet technology to deliver courseware, to new and innovative way to directly enhance learning and performance in both training and work environments. This requires the development of an entirely new architecture for learning and performance solutions, one that significantly expands the set of tools, approaches, and strategies for learning in a modern and complex organization.

The learning and performance architecture includes formal training solutions but doesn't stop there. A single solution is often suboptimal. Instead, a greater variety of solutions—instructional, informational, and collaborative—must be devised so that they work in harmony, much like the way a script, scenery, special effects, and music come together to create a film that is greater than the sum of its parts.

Introduction to Change Management and Communications

It would be nice to think that all you have to do is build great learning programs and everyone will immediately buy in to them. The fact is, training, especially online, and other workplace learning and support approaches represent such new ways to learn that people often need help adjusting to them. Some people love change, but others are wary of it or downright afraid of it. It is not enough to "sell e-learning"; that will result in only short-term gains. You have to create an environment and culture where new ways to learn are encouraged, embraced, and accepted at all levels. This effort is referred to as *change management*.

Change management ensures the alignment of people with business direction, important for any new venture, and new approaches to learning clearly fit in this category. All change management efforts seek to accomplish three things:

1. Establish an environment for change, making sure people, systems, and processes are ready to support new learning approaches.

2. Foster high performance, ensuring that people can benefit from new approaches to learn in the way that counts most: with higher performance.

3. Sustain workforce commitment, keeping the change management effort ongoing so that employees don't inadvertently revert to their old ways.

Communications is a particularly important tool of change management. A solid communications strategy makes sure that people are not just aware of new ways to learn but prefer them. This is critical for a smart enterprise.

Introduction to Learning and Performance Leadership

No major change in the way people learn is possible without strong leadership. Good leaders—leaders who are also good sponsors—from executives to department managers do more than approve budgets; they support the initiative. They act as role models and active participants. Instead of allowing new learning strategies to linger at the periphery of the organization, they help integrate them directly into their business operations. It is vital that you have solid leadership support for your initiative. Without it, it will likely not succeed.

In addition to having good leadership support, you must be able to lead your own organization to high performance. You will have many decisions to make about the balance between classroom and online training and about how you approach nontraining alternatives that are becoming increasingly important. And finally, you will have to work within some form of governance structure so that the learning and e-learning resources of the organization are used wisely.

Introduction to the Performance Environment

You can't learn your way out of a bad process without fixing the process as well. You can't always train everyone for more complex work; sometimes you have to replace them with more capable people. You can't train employees to work harder when the incentives and working environment encourage just the opposite. And you can't train people to be more innovative if your culture punishes risk taking and innovative thinking. These are just some examples where learning solutions don't work, at least not alone.

Organizations that fail to consider the total support environment, such as instituting appropriate rewards and incentives, fixing broken work processes, and making sure people have the resources to be successful, run the risk of developing less efficient and less effective solutions, including learning solutions. In a smart enterprise, this should never happen. By focusing first on performance rather than training (or even learning), you avoid jumping to a solution, such as a course, before you know what the problem is and whether there is value in solving it.

Smart enterprise thinking always begins with questions like, "What are we trying to accomplish?" rather than questions like, "How can we use training?" This requires much more initial analysis and decision making. And most important, it requires an open mind to solutions that have nothing to do with learning (or at least only partly concerned with learning) and more to do with the culture, constraints, incentives, resources, tools, and support people have for doing their job. Fix the environment, and learning can flourish.

With this smart enterprise framework in mind, it is time to dig into its components, beginning with the learning and performance architecture.

Notes

1. Gartner Group. (2003, December 1). *Predicts 2004: Knowledge support*. Stamford, CT: Gartner Group.
2. Meta Group. (2004, January 22). *On the road to knowledge management*. Stamford, CT: Meta Group.
3. Rossett, A., & Sheldon, K. (2001). *Beyond the podium: Delivering training and performance to a digital world*. San Francisco: Pfeiffer, p. 245.
4. Senge, P. (1990). *The fifth discipline: The art and practice of the learning organization*. New York: Doubleday.

5. Argyris, C., & Schön, D. (1996). *Organizational learning II: Theory, method and practice*. Reading, MA: Addison-Wesley.

6. Gartner Group. (2002, May 10). *The smart enterprise suite is coming: Do we need it?* Stamford, CT: Gartner Group.

7. Comments made at a hearing on July 22, 2004, following release of the report of the commission investigating the terrorist attacks of September 11, 2001.

8. Brennan, M., & Kao, G. (2004, May). The promise and reality of technology-based simulations. *CLO Magazine*, 3(5), 52–55.

9. Zeller, S. (2005, January). Training games. *Government Executive*, 36(22), 45.

10. Drucker, P. (1999). *Management challenges for the twenty-first century*. New York: HarperCollins, p. 157.

11. Dublin, L. (2004, October 19). *Critical steps for developing an effective learning strategy*. Presentation at the E-Learning Producer Conference, Orlando, FL.

Learning Decisions and Disruptions!

Elliott Masie

Learning and training professionals should not sleep too soundly. There is disruption in the air! Ever-changing technology, evolving worker characteristics, faster-moving business requirements, and a maturing perspective about the learning organization will disrupt many of our well-designed strategies and approaches. And that will require crisp thinking and brave leaders to make a new wave of learning decisions.

For example, think about mobile technologies and instant messaging (IM) in the workplace. Your cell phone and your child's use of IM to collaborate on homework with seven other classmates are technologies that did not start as corporate tools. In fact, most organizations don't have a clue how to really use these devices. Yet employees, both young and older, are using their cell phone and IM as informal, and often unapproved, tools for learning, collaboration, and knowledge access. Executives use their BlackBerry to send text messages to each other in boring meetings, and sales reps IM their friends who are working in competitive organizations, asking for context and background on a pending sale. Both of these actions are disruptive; they happen as covert, or even illegal, actions, yet they are powerful tools for knowledge and learning, introduced and even funded by workers themselves.

Your organization must make a few key learning decisions about how technologies like mobile phones and instant messaging will be harvested as learning and performance tools:

- **Technology learning decisions.** Will organizations issue mobile technology that will weave the workforce into a 24/7 social network?

- **Methodology learning decisions.** How will mobile technology and IM capabilities be woven into learning events? For example, what if we issued a device to each new employee to support them through an orientation process, even providing a visual map of seasoned colleagues near them for "welcome to the company" conversations?

• **Compliance learning decisions.** How do we keep companies in compliance with legal and ethical requirements as these new capacities are developed? Do knowledge-sharing conversations with friends in other companies expose your organization to legal liabilities?

• **Integration learning decisions.** How do we weave these new technologies into existing learning and knowledge delivery models? Can we offer people access to instant coaching from peers around the enterprise as a blended learning extension of a classroom offering? And how do we integrate the use of emerging technologies into existing learning management systems and models?

• **Financial learning decisions.** These disruptive technologies also can challenge budgeting and financial assumptions. I am a trustee at a college that is experiencing a $500,000 a year reduction in revenues from dorm room phones because students are using cell phones instead of land lines. And every time the college calls the student's cell phone, it's a long-distance call for it. Imagine shifting that model by issuing a free phone, with a local number, to each first-year student arriving at the college.

There are other looming disruptive technologies and phenomena that will have deep impacts on learning and training professionals. Here are a few that we are tracking:

• **Trophy expectations of the millennials.** The label for students in college now is the *millennial generation*. They have had a different style of upbringing that can disrupt learning and training assumptions. One example is trophies. They have been told by their parents and teachers that "every person gets a trophy, not just the winner!" This may translate to a very different reaction to performance review and supervision. One of my friends, a vice president of human resources, had a new experience recently when he received a telephone call from the parents of a new employee to complain that their daughter should have received a higher "grade" on her performance review.

• **Find it.** Watch for search engines to disrupt many of our assumptions about course design and even training catalogues. I already want to use search engines to find my way to the key learning objects, or at least the most important modules, rather than browse a catalogue or training portal pages. As search engines become more personalized, more integrated with social networks, and more corporately tuned, this will force some interesting learning decisions.

• **Simulate it.** Simulations and gaming technology will be deployed in ways that we can't even imagine yet. The ability of a worker to do an instant simulation of a task, prior to doing it in reality, is potent. For example, prior to making a repair to an automobile, a technician will have the ability to do an instant simulation. He or she can practice the best approach and even see what would be the most productive or profitable technique. Simulations will be expected and comfortable to our newer generations of learners and yield significant results to our organizations.

Ah, disruption! Some of us hate it. Many of us thrive on it, as I do. I believe that true learning organizations welcome these disruptions. But it requires the learning and training function to make key and often new learning decisions. Have courage!

◆　◆　◆

Elliott Maisie is president of the Masie Center (www.masie.com) and founder of the e-Learning Consortium. He can be reached at emasie@masie.com.

Part Two

BEYOND THE CLASSROOM

Training works, but if training were the only way to learn, everyone would be in class all day, every day.

3

Building a Learning and Performance Architecture

You cannot create value from any one
investment—you have to bundle them.
—*David Norton*[1]

In the beginning, there was classroom-based, instructor-led training. And the training director looked around at the full classrooms and the crowded training center and declared it to be good. Indeed, corporate training had come far, from small training rooms to fabulous corporate universities. If enrollments were any indicator, training was more popular than ever.

Tucked away in one corner of the training center was the CBT (computer-based training) group. Since PLATO's time (not the ancient philosopher but one of the original CBT systems pioneered by the University of Illinois in the 1960s and 1970s), training organizations have dabbled in learning technology. A few folks with far different skills (and sometimes far different attitudes) experimented and occasionally produced a course. Most courses were of marginal value, primarily due to the significant limitations of the technology and people's discomfort or confusion with it. Nevertheless, these intrepid pioneers tried mightily to demonstrate the power of these early incarnations of e-learning. And the training director looked at these efforts, often with amusement or bewilderment (or both), and declared it wonderful that the organization was so committed to the future.

As long as they weren't *too* committed. After all, it was classroom training that people wanted. It was classroom training that paid the bills. It was classroom training that sustained the staff.

And, of course, it was classroom training that everyone was comfortable with. The cash cow of instructor-led training and the facilities used to deliver it were safe and secure.

In the *Star Wars* saga, the Empire dismissed the small rebellion as insignificant until the rebels were able to muster "The Force." Then their challenge to Darth Vader and company became real. In the e-learning saga, the Internet was the force to reckon with. Mastering it meant that learning technology had power, legitimacy, and reach. The battle was joined. On one side were the long-entrenched forces of classroom-based, instructor-led training. On the other were the emerging rebellious e-learning faithful, backed up by an ever growing and increasingly sophisticated technology, industry, and profession.

> You must unlearn what you have learned.
>
> —*Yoda*

Once the Web became commonplace and e-learning took off, the established training functions had a choice to make. Some embraced the new ways of e-learning, while others initially fought or ignored it. Training directors were under increasing pressure to "get into" e-learning if for no other reason than to lower delivery costs. They were also challenged with redefining their metrics, funding models, processes, staff skill sets, customer expectations, and physical assets. Those who didn't adapt had difficulty fitting e-learning into their old business models. Those who did found it difficult to change existing mind-sets and culture not only within the training organization but in the broader company as well. Now in the limelight, e-learning advocates were under increasing pressure to demonstrate value, a task more challenging than they had imagined. It was not the panacea they had said it would be.

This chapter focuses on a new post-Internet definition of *e-learning*, one that encompasses all of the new opportunities to bring instruction, information, and support to the workplace. It defines a new architecture for e-learning—and learning in general—that is essential for the smart enterprise.

Blended Learning: The Good and the Bad

Many companies have jumped on and off the e-learning bandwagon several times. Organizations that rushed to put all training on the Web risked weakening their overall training program in the name of cost savings (which may be elusive if job performance— what a worker does to accomplish something of value—or business results, such as profit, market share, productivity, or innovation, suffer). Organizations that moved too slowly missed out on the efficiency and benefits offered by technology.

Here's a typical story. During the Internet bubble, when Lucent Technologies was soaring, it could easily afford classroom training and the costs that came with it. So online training was only 10 percent of the company's total training activity, and training centers bulged with activity. When the crash came and training budgets shriveled, Lucent completely reversed itself and tried to provide over 90 percent of its training online. But it found that an overreliance on one delivery strategy was neither as economical nor as effective as the company assumed. A balance of about 65 percent classroom and 35 percent online training ultimately became its more reasonable—and realistic—goal.[2]

Like Lucent, what most companies are looking for is a way for e-learning and classroom training to coexist and even benefit each other. One approach has been to adopt blended learning.

The popular, albeit limited, definition of *blended learning* is the integration of group and self-paced instruction, usually manifested through classroom and online delivery. This view correctly recognizes that there are situations where classroom training, with a qualified instructor, is most appropriate; there are situations where online training works better; and there are times when a prudent combination of both approaches is best. Decisions on how to blend are based to some degree on instructional design considerations, that is, how best to present training materials to facilitate effective learning (and ultimately improve performance), and on business considerations, including cost and productivity issues, such as speed of deployment, scalability, time in training, and updatability. To many organizations, blended learning seems so logical that they have embraced it as a fundamental tenet of how they will work going forward. But this view of blending is often too limiting. It assumes only an instructional approach, when other approaches may be more appropriate and more cost-effective. When the solution (online or classroom training) is preordained, other opportunities are too often ignored. Sometimes this is a result of an organization's limited viewpoint, and other times, the concept has not had sufficient time to mature. Either way, the concept of blended learning is changing and expanding.

The Learning and Performance Architecture

ar-chi-tec-ture (n): a unifying or coherent form or structure.
—Merriam-Webster's Collegiate Dictionary, 11th edition

A **learning and performance architecture** is a systematic integration of approaches (electronic and nonelectronic) that facilitates both formal and informal workplace learning and support and, ultimately, improved human performance.

The architecture describes a model of how these approaches relate to each other and is based on five important truths about where learning and learning technology must go to fulfill the promise of the smart enterprise:

• **Most learning takes place on the job.** Employees learn from the peers, the corporate intranet, trade publications, and trial and error. To assume training is the only place where learning occurs is to so severely limit your options and perspective that you will be hard-pressed to demonstrate any real and lasting value to the organization.

- **Learning is not training.** It transcends the classroom and is critical to the successful accomplishment of work. Think of it this way: training is one of many approaches to facilitate learning, and learning is one of many essential activities that support individual and organizational performance. Learning is a much broader concept than training.

- **Training, even online training, is incapable on its own of supporting all the learning needs of employees, partners, suppliers, or customers.** The need for new skills and knowledge and the need to build sustainable competence require a broader set of solutions than just instructional ones.

- **Technology has demonstrated a powerful capability to enable workforce productivity, and it can do the same for learning.** From personal computing to global networks and the Web, technology has contributed mightily to a productivity boom. But technology does not drive or create the smart enterprise or a learning and performance architecture; it supports them.

- **Learning effectiveness (what people learn) is extremely important in the smart enterprise, but it does not, in and of itself, constitute the ultimate value proposition.** That comes from the improved level of workforce performance (what people actually do), which contributes directly to business success. While determining if the user "liked" or "valued" a particular training program, or if pre- and posttest scores indicate that learning occurred during the training is useful information, such measures do not provide the evidence of business value that is required. What really matters is whether you improved performance and whether that performance benefited the effectiveness and efficiency of the organization (including metrics such as sales, revenue, profit, waste reduction, customer satisfaction, productivity improvements, employee retention, responsiveness and flexibility, and innovation). This is why identifying appropriate performance measures at the start is so important in setting the direction for any learning initiative; the right metrics are the best guideposts to ensure you reach your performance goals.

Redefining E-Learning

Within the learning and performance architecture is e-learning—not e-learning as it is traditionally practiced but a broader, more inclusive definition of *e-learning:*

> **E-learning** is the use of Internet technologies to create and deliver a rich learning environment that includes a broad array of instruction and information resources and solutions, the goal of which is to enhance individual and organizational performance.

In this definition, both instructional and information solutions are employed. Not all learning requires an instructional solution. Certainly doctors need lots of formal training. But they also learn in other ways, such as reading journals, talking with peers, and accessing new medical research data. Salespeople are trained to sell, but then rely on up-to-date competitive and product information to be sure they know the market well enough to be successful. Emergency first responders are highly trained, but on a daily basis, they also need access to databases of emergency procedures, high levels of communication with experts and commanders, and the ability to quickly form teams to solve real-time problems. In all of these nontraining environments, doctors, salespeople, and first responders are still learning.

Instructional design purists say, "Information is not instruction." So what? If information helps me become a better performer, just tell me. Don't insist that I take an entire course. If I can add more value with a better connection to the 'Net, a subscription to a reference service or a direct line to the local expert, then give it to me. Give me a way to do my job better—I don't care whether or not you call it instruction.

—*Jay Cross, Internet Time Group*[3]

Building the Architecture

Figure 3.1 depicts the e-learning components of the learning and performance architecture. Note that only online training is included at this point; classroom training will be integrated later. Also included are several new and expanded ways of approaching e-learning: information repositories, communities and networks, and experts and expertise, all bundled as knowledge management, and performance support, which stands on its own. These new approaches are introduced next.

**Figure 3.1   The E-Learning Components
of the Learning and Performance Architecture**

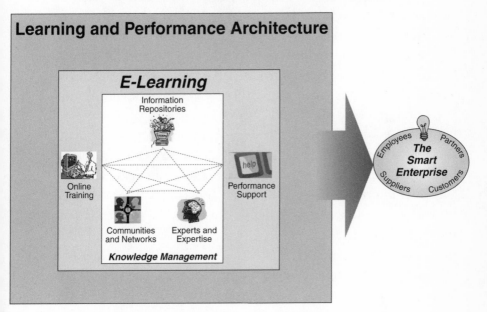

Knowledge Management

Although knowledge management is explored in depth in Chapters Four and Five, it is important to introduce and define it here in order to understand how it fits into the overall learning and performance architecture model:

> **Knowledge management** is the creation, archiving, and sharing of valued information, expertise, and insight within and across communities

of people and organizations with similar interests and needs, the goal of which is to build competitive advantage.

Knowledge management (KM) is about sharing knowledge; simply gathering it and storing it is not enough. KM's goal is to get knowledge from those who have it to those who need it. It enables organizations to create, acquire, organize, and make available their intellectual capital, which Mark Van Buren suggests includes more than just information about human capital (what people know and can do). It also includes information about innovation capital (the capability of the organization to innovate and create new products and services), process capital (the organization's processes, techniques, systems, and tools), and customer capital (the value of the organization's relationship with its customers, such as market share, revenues, and growth).[4] In addition, knowledge management focuses on creating opportunities for collaboration between individuals and teams so that intellectual capital can be shared. This helps organizations get a better handle on the critical questions: "Who is doing what?" and "Who knows what?"

Most people engage in some sort of personal knowledge management—the tools and practices individuals use to keep their own information in order. Some of these approaches are quite familiar: a diary of information kept over a year, a list of favorites in a Web browser, content in a personal digital assistant (PDA), even important e-mails sorted by topic, client, or project. In fact, the hard drive of a personal computer, especially the "my documents" folder in a Windows-based machine, represents in many ways an individual's own, unique KM strategy. Now the challenge is to take KM to the next level: the organizational or enterprise level.

Knowledge management can also be defined by its objectives, such as these developed by professional services firm Ernst & Young:[5]

- Connecting people with other knowledgeable people
- Connecting people with information
- Enabling the conversion of information to knowledge
- Encapsulating knowledge, to make it easier to transfer
- Disseminating knowledge around the firm

Why is knowledge management important? Consider these findings from IDC.[6] Knowledge workers spend from 15 to 35 percent of their time searching for information but are successful in finding what they seek only 50 percent of the time or less. Forty percent of corporate users cannot find the information they need to do their jobs on their intranets, and this inability to find or share information has tremendous organizational costs for typical businesses. In its research, IDC estimated that "the cost of intellectual rework, substandard performance and inability to find knowledge resources was $5,000 per worker per year." Think about it: if you spend as much time searching for information, with the same success rate noted in these studies, even a 10 percent improvement in your knowledge management productivity would be significant. Now multiply your gain by the total number of knowledge workers in your business, and the benefits become substantial.

> Our scientists spend at least 20 to 25 percent of their time looking for stuff.
>
> —*Melinda J. Bickerstaff, vice president for knowledge management, Bristol-Myers Squibb Company*[7]

Equally important is the need to prevent what David DeLong calls "lost knowledge," manifested in an organization's inability to retain intellectual capital and know-how over a long period of time, so that it survives the tenure of those who created it. DeLong cites NASA's brain drain, following the end of the *Apollo* moon program, and "a general loss of capacity to replicate one of the greatest achievements in the history of mankind," as a classic example.[8]

A study by consulting firm Accenture found that nearly half of the employees questioned said their firms had no plans to capture their knowledge when they retire, and only 20 percent said they anticipate going through a rigorous knowledge transfer process. Think of the risk that may be incurred when knowledge "walks out the door," and imagine the benefits an organization gains by reducing its need to reinvent or rediscover that knowledge![9]

Knowledge Management Components

Knowledge management is composed of three interconnected and interdependent components: information repositories, communities and networks, and experts and expertise.

Information Repositories. For anyone who has worked with huge binders of outdated documentation and has tried to keep up with color-coded page updates, new approaches to managing documents and other physical knowledge assets have been nothing short of a revolution in information management and distribution, as well as a revolution in learning, because of the enhanced ability to update a broadly distributed workforce and keep content up-to-date in real time. When information is easier to find and is more accurate, more people will use and learn from it. The massive adoption of the Internet as a primary information source bears this out. People learn from a host of Web sites when they shop for a car, seek medical advice, and make investment decisions, for example. And although they don't think about it, they tend to favor the sites where technologies and practices help them gather information more easily and with greater confidence.

> I never bother to remember anything I know I can look up.
>
> —*Albert Einstein*

Information repositories are created by codifying the collective knowledge of the organization—documents, Web sites, training courses, user manuals, procedures and processes, business data, employee information, and a host of other types of information—and making it readily available through increasingly easy and powerful technologies that are embedded within organizational systems. They are organized and managed in ways that make finding, using, and contributing knowledge easy. Libraries have been doing this work for years; in fact, the Dewey Decimal System may represent one of the best-known knowledge management strategies; it is so well known that it is generally taken for granted. Imagine the chaos if every library in the country had a different scheme to organize, store, and access resources. Organizing a content domain into logical knowledge categories; creating easy ways to find, create, and update information; and presenting knowledge in a readable and understandable fashion are just some of the requirements of good knowledge management. Very popular Web sites like Dell (technical support), WebMD (medical information), Edmunds (automobile shopping), and Britannica (online encyclopedia) have information repositories that facilitate access to large amounts of content.

But to use information repositories well, you have to know not just how to use the online tools but also to understand what content to look for and how to conduct searches. So in many cases, training programs are increasingly emphasizing technology-based information resources and the skills to use them (for example, effective search techniques).

Communities and Networks.   People learn from more than courses and information repositories; they also learn with and through others as they build relationships with coworkers, partners, suppliers, customers, and other constituencies. When this happens, the effect is to democratize knowledge in the organization, creating a culture that supports more collaborative work and collaborative learning.

There has been a lot of success at making training more interactive and collaborative. But what happens outside the classroom? In conference rooms, at lunch, over the telephone, and in many other ways, people share knowledge. This is nothing new; working together is not only good business, it is human nature. When people get together to solve a problem, accomplish a task, evaluate a situation, or formulate a plan, they learn from each other. They take these experiences to their next meeting or project and learn even more as they go along. The challenge now is to get more value out of collaboration: to preserve, share, and build on the work that people do together.

Sometimes one group of people does not know what other groups are doing. Another team—across the hall or around the world—might be doing the same work, perhaps better or perhaps worse. The work that one group sets out to do may have already been done, even been implemented, and nobody else knows. This redundancy of effort slows innovation, adds cost, and puts the organization at a business disadvantage. Online collaboration and community tools help organizations eliminate redundancy by overcoming time and distance. They make the benefits of watercooler or lunch table conversations available more quickly to more people, improving everyone's awareness of what is going on.

> The more enterprises come to rely on people working together without actually working together—that is, on people using the new technologies of information—the more important it will become to make sure that they are fully informed.
>
> —*Peter Drucker*[10]

Experts and Expertise. Essential to the success of any collaboration effort is the availability of experts and expertise. But even if you know who the experts are, they may not have the time to help. And some people who are indeed experts either don't know that they are or shy away from identifying themselves because they fear they will be inundated with requests for help. Anyone who has ever tried to develop a course or write a technical document knows how hard it is to find and hold on to a true subject matter expert.

Technology is offering some solutions to increasing access to expertise. Online directories containing more than just contact information help people identify the right person to talk to. The ability to use knowledge networks and communities of practice to disseminate expertise makes it easier to support larger numbers of people who need help or can help you.

The idea of experts and expertise does not stop with simply providing specific, codified business or technical knowledge. Expertise is also manifested in coaching and mentoring. In these roles, experts are more than a source of knowledge; they are also advisers who are charged with providing guidance, corrective feedback, and performance assessment.

Performance Support

Many people need the help of an accountant or other expert to prepare and file their tax returns. But millions of people are now filing their returns without hiring a professional. How do they do it? Turbo-Tax, Tax Cut, and other similar tools guide users through the complex tax return process and make it easier in many ways. They hide unnecessary information unless or until it becomes necessary. They do the math behind the scenes. They ask questions and try to anticipate users' problems. They provide more logical ways to navigate the process and translate tax jargon into language that's easier to understand. Automatic links to specific Web sites ensure that the software is updated if the tax code changes (without requiring the user to read the tax code). Finally, users can work on their returns in one sitting or sporadically over a few months and at any time of the day, making the process not just easier but also more convenient.

That's an example of performance support, another part of the learning and performance architecture:

> **Performance support** (or electronic performance support) is a tool or system, often computer based, that provides electronic task guidance and support to the user at the moment of need.[11]

The idea is that with the right tools, people can perform at a higher level than they would have been capable of on their own.

Performance support has been around for a while, in the form of job aids and troubleshooting guides, for instance. But the advent of technology has enabled more complex tasks to be handled through electronic performance-support systems (EPSS). These systems run the gamut from end-user PC software, which can simplify difficult computational processes, to complex manufacturing systems (enabling one skilled operator to run an elaborate process), customer care, and project management systems that can change the very nature of how a job is done or how an organization works.

The logical extension of performance support is the embedding of smart enterprise learning tools and approaches directly in the actual work. This has two major implications. First, it makes what you do to support work processes an integral part of those processes. Learning and performance solutions are integrated into work design itself. Second, work design actually replaces learning design. Learning and performance improvement solutions that help people master complex work activities and processes start to give way to efforts to improve, even reinvent, them. (Performance support is discussed in depth in Chapter Six.)

Adding Classroom Training and Coaching to the Architecture

Additional nontechnical approaches—classroom training, and mentoring and coaching—can assume their appropriate place in the model (Figure 3.2).

Positioning Training in the Architecture. In the learning and performance architecture, training is not the thousand-pound gorilla. Instead, it is just one of a broad array of tools to facilitate learning, which facilitates performance. Although the goals and methodology of classroom and online training are similar and both require the most work disruption (although online training is usually less disruptive than classroom training), they differ in how the programs are controlled. Classroom training, including synchronous or virtual classroom training, is under the control of the instructor, and

**Figure 3.2 Expanding the Learning
and Performance Architecture Beyond E-Learning**

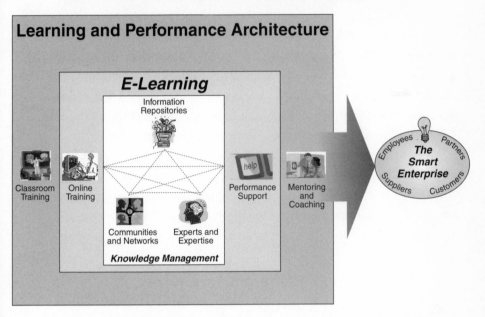

asynchronous, stand-alone online training is under the control of the program's logic. On the classroom side, the instructor's skill and the effectiveness of the course design are major contributors to the overall quality of the program. On the stand-alone side, the design of the course is even more important because no instructor is present to make real-time changes.

Positioning Mentoring and Coaching in the Architecture. Like classroom training, mentoring and coaching rely on human rather than technological intervention (although technology can facilitate the process), so many people see this as an offshoot of the training model. But a closer look at its attributes shows that it is more like performance support; its purpose is to guide performance directly, using methodologies such as personal communication, role modeling, and especially feedback, which, when provided at the right level of detail and at the right moment (when the performer is most receptive to hearing it), is one of the most effective ways of improving and sustaining learning and performance. It's an interesting component of the model, because in many cases, good teachers make good coaches. But most good coaching and mentoring (even emerging online coaching and mentoring) takes place in the workplace (often by a peer or the immediate supervisor) and, as much as possible, within the context of actual job performance. Although mentoring and coaching are often overlooked as a viable learning strategy, organizations with a strong mentoring and coaching culture tend to show more smart enterprise characteristics.

Most people think of mentoring and coaching as the same, and in the learning and performance architecture, they are depicted together. There is a difference, however: coaching is usually focused on specific, real-time performance improvement, while mentoring is usually focused on long-term advice, counsel, and career support.

True Blended Learning

In the right hands, every detail comes together to create a performance that's greater than the sum of its parts.
—*Oppenheimer Funds commercial*

In most organizations, employees typically get about three to ten days of formal training a year (the mean is slightly over four days).[12] This roughly averages out to between 2 and 5 percent of someone's work time in a year (based on about 220 to 240 total workdays). Formal training includes all classroom courses, but it also includes all technology-delivered training, asynchronous and synchronous. The rest of the year is spent on the job—about 95–98 percent of the time. Yet learning never stops; it just changes from formal instruction to informal learning—for example, accessing information (from print materials, video, the Web, and others), asking questions, watching others, mentoring, and trial and error. In Figure 3.3, the learning and performance architecture is divided between formal learning and informal workplace settings.

Figure 3.3 Formal and Informal Learning Within the Learning and Performance Architecture

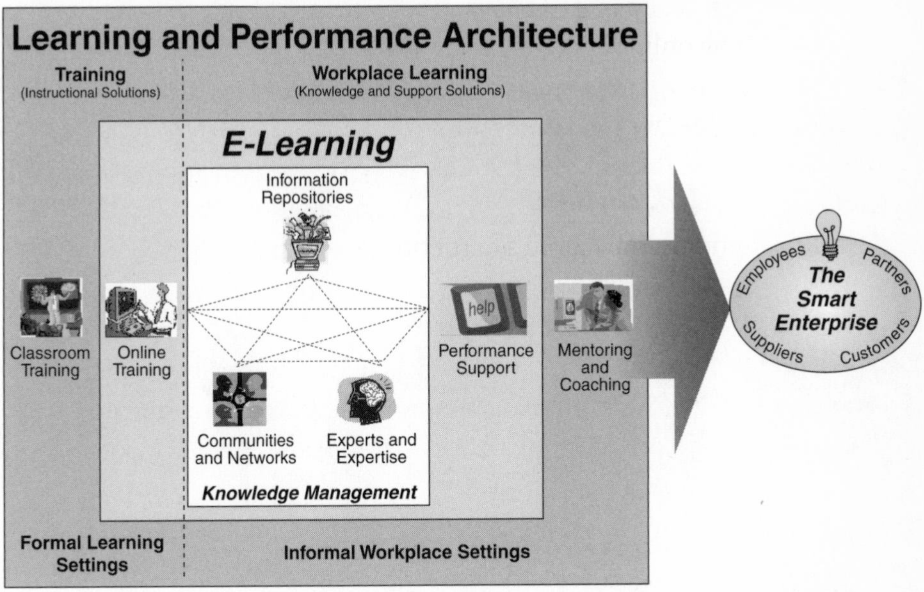

Unfortunately, discussions about training and e-learning usually end with the formal learning side; for most organizations, that is where the role of blended learning ends as well. But what about the rest of the time, when people are on the job? How should the broader view of e-learning be used in call centers, on the factory floor, at the customer's location, in the executive suite, or at home?

If learning takes place all the time and in all roles, functions, and locations where work is performed, then you must look beyond training for approaches that fit these situations. If learning extends beyond the training function, then e-learning must as well. E-learning is more than online training, or e-training. And blended learning is more than blended training.

In the emerging view of blended learning, shown in Figure 3.4, the course is no longer the default or only container of the solution. An expanded view of blended learning includes the combination of training (formal) and nontraining (informal) approaches that support the smart enterprise (such as knowledge management, performance

Figure 3.4   Learning and Performance Architecture as True Blended Learning

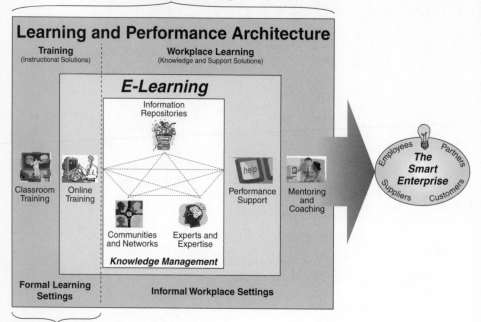

support, and coaching) in ways that improve the effectiveness and efficiency of learning. More limiting definitions, which simply focus on integrating online and classroom training, may improve the quality and efficiency of the instructional solution, but they do little to move learning—and e-learning—where it needs to go: to the workplace.

Push Learning Versus Pull Learning

Traditional learning—classroom and online—generally involves "pushing" content, in a fairly structured format, to employees, customers, or partners and suppliers. From an economic perspective, this represents a supply-side view: training organizations determine in advance what individuals have to know, and then produce specific course products that teach only what has been predetermined as being needed. Individuals can select what they want, but only from a finite list or catalogue of program offerings. Consumers of learning resources often see the training department as a mass manufacturer or "retailer" of course products from which they can "shop." This view has dominated the training business for a long time, and it limits the options available for enhancing learning in the workplace. A working learning and performance architecture cannot function on push learning alone.

By adding the informal, workplace side of the architecture to the overall learning equation, you begin to get into demand-side learning, where people "pull" content that meets their particular needs from a wide array of high-value but less structured resources like information repositories, communities, and experts. The pull perspective recognizes that it is often impossible to determine in advance what any one person, let alone an entire organization, really must know, when he or she should know it, and at what level he or she needs to know it. In this view, consumers of learning resources tend to look beyond the training department to any resource that satisfies their learning need. Each user's approach to learning can be unique. If they are smart enough and the resources are well designed, they can often construct a personal knowledge library on their own. They are much more in control, deciding for themselves how much to read, how deep to go, and how long to stay with the resource. A smart enterprise is full of people who do this every day.

The overall goal of a sound learning and performance architecture is to appropriately blend push and pull learning across formal and informal settings. There are many situations where it is extremely important that people learn a skill in a precise and predictable way. This requires, for example, very well-designed training that is pushed to the right audience at the right time. But there are other times when it is impossible to cover everything someone needs to know through push alone, especially when different people need to know different things at different times and at different levels of complexity. By creating an environment where they can pull what they need from well-designed and highly accessible resources, you create much more of a flexible, real-time learning culture.

Advanced Blended Learning: Early Examples

In the early and mid-1990s, examples of a more expansive view of blended learning were already emerging. Some incorporated performance support tools, while others implemented knowledge management. Here are two successful examples that received a great deal of attention using technologies that were available before the mass adoption of the Internet.

Apple Computer's Reference Performance and Learning Expert. Early on, Apple Computer recognized that in order to compete successfully, it needed its distributed sales and technical field force to be up-to-date all the time on products, competitors, promotions, pricing, and strategy. It was clearly impossible to fly everyone back to Cupertino, California, every time there was a change in the product line or in the marketplace. And it determined that simply sending out reams of paper and hoping that everyone would update their sales and technical binders was wishful thinking at best. Of course, Apple's sales and technical employees were first trained in selling skills, product knowledge, computer technology, and other topics, but once they were in the field, Apple knew that keeping them there would enhance their productivity profitability. So the company created ARPLE, the Apple Reference Performance and Learning Expert. ARPLE was distributed on CD, as quickly as every two weeks, to be sure that the field force was always up-to-date. Apple integrated the use of ARPLE into its training programs and developed a knowledge management process to ensure that information was always accurate and distributed in a timely fashion. Over the years, ARPLE moved from a CD-based system to a client-server system and ultimately to the Web.

Lexus Labs. Los Angeles–based Internal/External Communications (IEC) debuted a product it had built for the Lexus Automobile Company, to be deployed in Lexus dealerships across the United States.[13] The program, Lexus Labs, focused on providing salespeople at dealerships with timely product and competitive knowledge. The program included simulations, traditional training, a variety of sales tools, and a complete product and competitive database, enabling salespeople to get comparative information about other brands. It did not replace basic selling skills training; it augmented the training.

Lexus Labs dramatically improved salespeople's knowledge and their ability to address customer questions and concerns quickly. The response from the training industry to this product was amazing. Although initially CD based, the program grabbed the attention and imagination of both training professionals and business executives. At trade shows, hundreds of training professionals would crowd the IEC booth to look at the innovative program, which merged simulation, true multimedia, robust information databases, and Hollywood production values. While this and other early projects were expensive, costing several hundred thousand dollars or more to produce, companies like IEC (there were many others as well) demonstrated that it was possible to develop and deliver captivating and effective technology-based learning that incorporates a much broader array of resources than was common practice.

Going Beyond Sales Training at Cingular Wireless

Today companies are experimenting with new models of blended learning, and enhancing their traditional training with some new learning approaches. Here's one such story from Cingular Wireless. Cingular Wireless, one of the largest cellular providers in the United States, needs to maintain its edge in the extremely competitive cellular telephone industry. This means more than great products and great service; it needs highly trained, proactive people to execute its business strategy. The true test of the effectiveness of training in a business is not when a company is doing well and there are plenty of resources to build and run a robust training program, but when the business is underperforming and needs to realign its direction in order to improve its performance. The following are strong indicators that a company's business sales channel is primed for new approaches to learning and performance development:

- New customer acquisition costs are higher than in any other channel, but the net gain in customers is among the lowest.
- Account executives (AEs) do not know or do not follow the company's sales process and do not understand the company's objectives or their role in the channel and in the business as a whole.
- AEs tend to "farm" existing clients rather than "prospect" for new ones, performing more like order takers who are waiting for the phone to ring than business developers who are proactively finding new customers and developing the business.
- AEs get inconsistent support in the field, which varies from sales manager to sales manager and across the company in general.

Frequently companies in this situation also suffer from inadequate selection processes. People are hired into sales positions without regard for the capabilities they bring with them. Turnover is higher than desired as new employees discover that much of their job revolves around making sales calls and following up on leads—activities they are not prepared for and don't want to do.

Sometimes sales training courses purchased in the marketplace may be too generic and may produce little benefit. When training content is not tied to the company's business strategy or sales process, no level of participation will ensure that employees will have the knowledge and skill required to do their jobs.

Cingular executives were well aware of these challenges and knew that changes had to be made. But they didn't just want them to be cosmetic. They wanted a systemic solution that touched every performance lever in the business. For training, this created an outstanding opportunity. Management was open to more training, but what type of training should be proposed and what else would be needed to make the training stick over the long term?

The Cingular training team attacked the problem not just from a training perspective but from a learning and performance perspective. Their use of blended learning was not merely a mixture of classroom and online content but a more holistic architecture of a learning and performance solution.

Training Gets Real

The training program was completely revamped. Eighty percent of it became self-paced, focusing almost exclusively on moving through the Cingular sales process. This did not mean that the self-paced part of the program was traditional paper or online courseware. The training team quickly recognized that the training had to not just mimic the job; it had to *be* the job: making real sales calls and writing real business contracts. To get these tasks completed, the participants needed to learn to use a variety of online work tools and incorporate them into their work routines.

Prerequisite learning was strictly enforced. If participants didn't complete prerequisite modules on orientation, navigating the Cingular intranet, and understanding Cingular products and services, courses primarily delivered online, they would not be allowed to participate in the rest of the program.

As authentic and effective as the training program was, Cingular understood that learning and performance could not be maintained through excellent training alone. To be successful, the business had to blend in a much broader array of solutions and focus more directly on workplace learning.

Preparing Supervisors

In any company, individual and team performance can be enhanced or diminished depending on the coaching capabilities of the supervisor. Unfortunately, too many training initiatives are so focused on job incumbents that there is little time or money left to get managers ready to support their people. This can be a fatal mistake: local managers wield tremendous power, and if they are not prepared, uninformed, or just don't care, they can quickly derail any positive impact from even the best training.

The Cingular team developed five days of training to help managers understand what employees were learning and the expectations the company had for them. Managers also developed skills in all the work tools their account executives would be using. Most important, they received training in how to coach their staff throughout the process, backed up by new metrics designed to recognize and reward managers for their support and involvement.

Business Tools and Support

In the past, training and workplace tools were addressed separately. The training department was responsible for courseware, and other parts of the business, such as the sales organization or the IT organization, were responsible for tools. The result was the hardening of organizational smokestacks and the creation of other collaboration barriers between the two functions.

Cingular recognized that to support the sales force, it had to provide tools for continuous learning and performance directly in the context of work. Moving forward, the interdependency between training and electronic performance support tools was built into the overall sales support process. The new training program positioned mastery of these tools as one of its primary objectives. Because of this, the tools were seen as an extension of the learning and performance process beyond the classroom.

In addition to a sales force automation suite, a variety of online tools were deployed to 1) transmit knowledge to the field, 2) speed learning, and improve performance in a number of areas, including competitive, industry, and product information, account planning, presentation, and contract support, and 3) promote success stories.

Managing the Knowledge

With new business processes deployed, a new training program implemented, and new electronic work-based learning and performance support tools in the hands of every salesperson, Cingular had to ensure that no one would be buried under too much information. Content management specialists were put into each region, serving a critical role as editors and publishers of information within the region. They collect competitive and business intelligence from the field sales force on a regular basis and republish it back to the entire team. They also serve as liaisons to corporate headquarters to facilitate the sharing of best practices and other high-value knowledge across the enterprise.

> The most important lesson we got out of this experience is that while good training is a place to start, you can't improve performance through courses alone. You have to build learning opportunities into every aspect of the job.
>
> —*Rob Lauber, executive director of learning services,*
> *Cingular Wireless*

Results

Traditional measures of training effectiveness clearly showed that the revised training program was doing what it needed to do in the classroom. But Cingular also understood that training effectiveness was just one of many benchmarks for evaluating the company's ability to use a broad learning and performance architecture. For the turnaround to be successful, both sales and retention results had to improve dramatically. Indeed, during the first three months of the program, the performance of AEs enrolled in the new program was up 297 percent, and overall retention rate was up 231 percent.

Why was this program so successful? Cingular points to four reasons:

1. It didn't view the challenge (reviving the channel) as merely a formal training problem and the solution as merely training redesign. Training was a factor, but so was thinking about how learning and performance could be maintained in the workplace, long after the training was concluded. So training focused on teaching AEs how to use technology and tools so they could learn on their own.

2. The company leveraged several nontraining functions to support the new direction. It tweaked recruiting so that more qualified people, who were more likely to achieve success in the sales job, were hired. It placed supervisors at the center of the process, with training and support geared directly to them and with new incentives that encouraged them to help their people succeed.

3. Cingular also knew that salespeople, like other professionals (even the most capable ones), are ineffective without the right tools. So it used technology to improve and expand the tool kit of knowledge management and performance support resources that are available to AEs, wherever they are and whenever they need it.

4. Perhaps most important, Cingular understood that success must be measured in business terms. Satisfaction with and learning gained from training was good, but it was not enough. Only when Cingular demonstrated that the total learning and performance architecture, when deployed, did improve business performance was the project deemed a success.

The convergence of sound training design, a host of work-based support strategies, and a sound enterprise technology platform helped Cingular achieve remarkable performance gains in the sales channel. This model is currently being replicated across other channels and business units in the company. And as a side benefit, the training organization has garnered new respect by Cingular's leaders and more opportunities to participate directly in the growth of the business.

How Mastery Levels Have an Impact on Learning and E-Learning Strategies

What many companies like Cingular are discovering is that the way people learn often varies by their level of mastery in a job. This can have a significant impact on the learning approaches you employ.

In Figure 3.5, the role of learning and learning technology changes as workers move through four levels of mastery: novice, competent, experienced, and master/expert. People new to a job generally require more formal, structured learning solutions around more common learning needs and common program-driven (that is, push-driven) curricula. As they progress and become more skillful, their primary learning requirements begin to shift to more informal, on-the-job learning that is more personalized, performer-driven (that is, pull-driven) and based on their unique learning needs. The more masterful the performer becomes, the more important knowledge management, collaboration, and performance support components of the learning and performance architecture become in their learning.

This model is a solid starting point and applicable in many situations, but it is not always applied linearly. It's always important to consider the complexity of work and the context in which the work is done, as well as the needs of the workers who are doing it. For example, an expert software developer may take more advanced courses to gain additional insights, and a novice customer service representative may use a performance support tool to move to competency more quickly.

Most people operate at multiple levels of mastery. They can be novices in one area of their job and experts in another. An outstanding, experienced salesperson who is promoted to manager may be a beginner in developing leadership skills, for example. Or an auto mechanic who is an expert at diagnosing and repairing gasoline engines may have a different learning curve for new hybrid technologies.

Figure 3.5 Impact of Performance Mastery on Learning Strategies

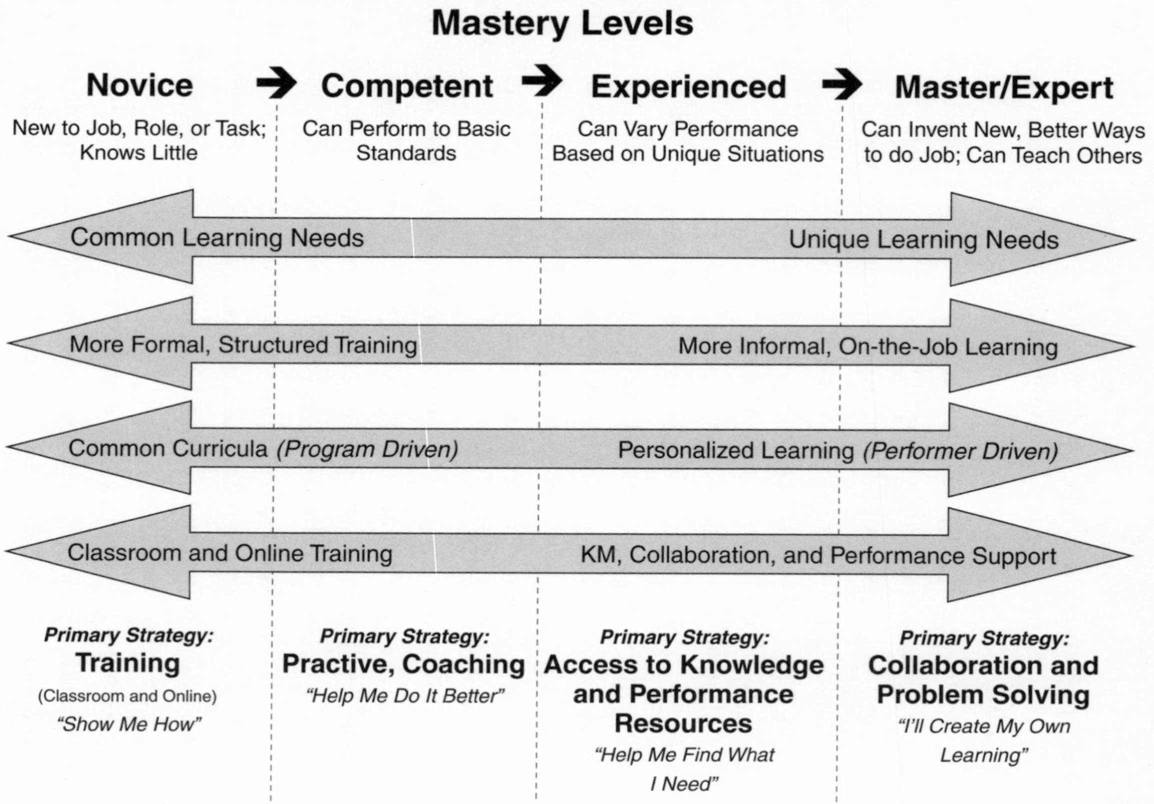

Mastery Levels

Novice	➤	Competent	➤	Experienced	➤	Master/Expert
New to Job, Role, or Task; Knows Little		Can Perform to Basic Standards		Can Vary Performance Based on Unique Situations		Can Invent New, Better Ways to do Job; Can Teach Others

Common Learning Needs ←————————————————→ Unique Learning Needs

More Formal, Structured Training ←————————————→ More Informal, On-the-Job Learning

Common Curricula *(Program Driven)* ←————————→ Personalized Learning *(Performer Driven)*

Classroom and Online Training ←————————————→ KM, Collaboration, and Performance Support

| *Primary Strategy:* **Training** (Classroom and Online) *"Show Me How"* | *Primary Strategy:* **Pracitve, Coaching** *"Help Me Do It Better"* | *Primary Strategy:* **Access to Knowledge and Performance Resources** *"Help Me Find What I Need"* | *Primary Strategy:* **Collaboration and Problem Solving** *"I'll Create My Own Learning"* |

To be sure you are considering all appropriate learning approaches and technologies across all mastery levels, ask yourself three fundamental questions:

- What approach is best to get someone *ready* to perform a task or job? Training might be a good choice here.
- What approach is best to *support* someone in the actual performance of a task or job? Coaching or performance support might be appropriate.
- What approach is best to *sustain* performance over time? Here knowledge management, communities of practice, and access to experts can keep workers continuously up-to-speed.

Answering all three questions will reveal options that might otherwise be hidden if you assume that everyone's learning needs and preferences are constant across all levels of mastery and that training is the only tool at your disposal.

Be an Architect, Not a Bricklayer

If you've ever done any brickwork, you know that it's not easy to do it right. There is artisanship to the work that combines skill, knowledge, and creativity. Just as master bricklayers are necessary in constructing a sound, beautiful building, master trainers and instructional designers are necessary in constructing sound, effective courseware. Yet bricklaying is usually just one part of an overall construction project that can also include plumbing, carpentry, and electric. Bricklayers usually don't determine the nature of the building project either; that goes to the architect. Like bricklaying, training is an essential professional craft, but it is more and more becoming just one piece of a more complex project that also includes information, collaboration, and support components. When you design solutions that take this broader scheme into account, you are acting more like the architect than the bricklayer.

The Cingular Wireless experience illustrates the challenges and the opportunities of moving from bricklaying to architecture. It underscores the benefits of changing direction and removing the isolation of training in a smart enterprise. Implementing a learning and performance architecture will require a fundamental redefinition of the role of training. Training organizations, whether they are run as large corporate universities, small training departments, or outsourced services, will have to focus far more on the workplace than just the classroom and extend the learning and performance architecture to support people directly on the job. This means that instructional solutions will not be adequate to do this alone. The components of the learning and performance architecture are sophisticated in their own right; integrating them is a major challenge, requiring not just a smart enterprise philosophy but well-developed processes and powerful technology.

To blend this wider array of solutions, training organizations will have to become much more interdisciplinary. They will have to come into what Allison Rossett calls the "big tent" of e-learning.[14] They will have to recognize that blended learning is a lot more than blended training and that true blending is a fusion of many technologies and approaches that cut across formal and informal learning solutions. And finally, training organizations will have to become much more involved in directly supporting work and the processes and tasks that comprise work. It will become increasingly important to suggest how the processes and tools of work can be made easier from the start rather than developing training to compensate for poor work design. Doing these things is the only way to build a sustainable smart enterprise.

Increasingly, enterprises will look to boost employee productivity through effective knowledge management, content management, e-learning and collaboration.

—*Gartner Group*[15]

In this regard, you should be well versed in instructional solutions, including needs assessment and evaluation. The growth areas with most promise and most challenge are those on the informal, work-based side: knowledge management (including information repositories, communities and networks, experts and expertise) and performance support. Like the architect of buildings, architects of learning and performance should be well versed in this expanded tool kit. The next three chapters delve more deeply into these new opportunities.

Notes

1. Norton, D. (2002, December). Keynote remarks. HR Masters Conference, Palm Desert, CA.
2. Johnson, H. (2004, July). Field of sales. *Training Magazine, 41*(7), 36–37.
3. Cross, J. (2004, October 5). Workflow Institute blog. http://www.internettime.com/wfblog/archives/001514.html#001514.
4. Van Buren, M. E. (1999, May). A yardstick for knowledge management. *Training and Development, 53*(5), 71–73S.
5. *Case study—Monsanto.* White paper originally published on the Web site of Ernst & Young, www.ey.com, but no longer available.
6. Feldman, S. (2004, March). The high cost of not finding information. *KM World, 13*(3).
7. Leavitt, P. (2002, November 17). *The role of knowledge management in new drug development.* American Productivity and Quality Center. www.aqpc.com.
8. DeLong, D. (2004). *Lost knowledge: Confronting the threat of an aging workforce.* New York: Oxford University Press, p. 12.
9. Accenture. (2005, May 10). *As U.S. workforce ages, employee knowledge and experience at risk, Accenture study finds.* http://press.arrivenet.com/bus/article.php/634978.html.
10. Drucker, P. (1999). *Management challenges for the twenty-first century.* New York: HarperBusiness, p. 91.

11. Gery, G. (1991). *Electronic performance support systems*. Boston: Weingarten, p. 34.

12. Sugrue, B., & Kim, K. (2004). *The state of the industry: ASTD's annual review of trends in workplace learning and performance*. Washington, DC: ASTD.

13. Like many other Internet boom companies, IEC was acquired and subsequently ceased to exist as a separate company.

14. Rossett, A. (2002). Walking in the night and thinking about e-learning. In A. Rossett (Ed.), *The ASTD e-learning handbook*. New York: McGraw-Hill, p. 7.

15. Gartner Group. (2003, February 14). *Process and technology will fuel workplace productivity*. Stamford, CT: Gartner Group.

Technology for E-Learning—and Beyond

William Horton

So you want to buy some learning technology. Stop right there. Step away from the "Add to shopping cart" button and take a few deep breaths. Before you start buying hardware and software, take a few minutes to think this through. You will save a lot of money, much of your sanity, and possibly your career. I hope this briefing will help. It is about common sense, not technical gobbledygook.

Let's start with some realistic expectations. Despite what you may have heard, technology does not educate people and organizations. Effective plans, processes, and, of course, people do. All technology will do is make you faster and more efficient. If you are doing things wrong, technology will help you do more things wrong in less time. So focus first on the top priorities you really need to address; they will drive your technology requirements.

How about content: Documents, courses, job aids, and other explicit forms of captured knowledge? Getting the right information to the right person at the right time is a goal, you say? Well, you're going to need tools to capture that knowledge in a tangible form and tools to allow users to access that information when they need it.

Start where you are. I'll bet you're sitting on a treasure trove of PowerPoint presentations, Microsoft Word documents, and Excel spreadsheets. And you have a staff that already knows how to use these tools. Right now, you can slug these documents on your intranet server and make sure your corporate search engine can find them.

You say that not everyone has the programs to read these documents and you don't want just everybody mucking with the original versions? Why not use Adobe Acrobat to convert them to a sharable

---

The products mentioned here are examples and not meant to be a definitive list or imply any recommendation.

copy? Those who need to read or print the document need only the free Adobe Acrobat reader.

Want to create some formal e-learning courses? You could get authoring tools like ToolBook or Authorware. And if you also need to make the same information available as Web pages, paper documents, online learning, sales brochures, job aids, classroom courses, and other forms, I suggest authoring the basic presentation component in PowerPoint and then using a converter to generate the various forms you need. For example, you can create animated presentations in PowerPoint with voice and text notes, and then convert the result to Flash for use on your Web site and in online learning. You can convert the same presentation to Microsoft Word for use in documentation and sales brochures. As a plus, you still have the PowerPoint slides for use in classroom courses and sales pitches.

Want to buy some ready-made courses? Vendors like SkillSoft, NETg, Element K, and many others offer a full array of topics to choose from. Most are SCORM compliant (I'll get to this a little later), but be careful to answer two questions before you buy: "Are these programs any good from a learning perspective?" and "Do these programs fit my needs?"

Want to implement collaboration? People are already collaborating over the Web through e-mail and instant messaging, but you can go further. You have several choices here: a discussion forum, an online meeting tool, or a virtual classroom system. The basic discussion forum is an updated version of the venerable computer bulletin board. Users post notices, to which other users reply, to which other users reply, and so on. Though ancient in Internet terms, discussion forums are unsung heroes of e-learning and knowledge management. They are where people meet to ask questions, swap ideas, and gain attention. Discussion forums are inexpensive; some are even free. They are easy to administer, but you will need to get creative in ways to persuade people to use them. This is very important to the success of your collaboration efforts.

Next, you might consider a general-purpose online meeting tool, such as Macromedia Breeze, Centra, WebEx, Elluminate, or Microsoft LiveMeeting. These are available as software you run on your own server or as a subscription service. Participants log into a meeting where they hear the speaker, watch the speaker's slides, and watch the speaker demonstrate software, make drawings, or conduct polls. Some tools allow participants to talk back or make presentations of their own.

Next up the collaboration food chain is the virtual classroom system. These systems are like online meeting tools with special features to make them more like schools. Some, like WebCT and Top-Class, include features familiar to teachers: grade books, homework drop boxes, and test administration tools.

If you have a budget over five figures, I bet somebody has been trying to sell you a management system. There are four types, known by their utterly confusing initials: LMS, LCMS, CMS, and CMS. (Those last two are not a typo; I'll explain later.)

LMS stands for *learning management system*, and it manages the process of formal learning. A pure LMS handles registration and tracks which students have completed which courses. Most LMSs launch and track online courses, as well as track classroom courses and other off-line forms of training. Some have special features that help people decide what courses they should take.

LCMS stands for *learning content management system*, and it manages the integration of lessons, topics, modules, tests, and other objects of individual courses. It typically tracks completion of individual learning activities as well as answers to specific test questions. LCMSs offer the possibility of reusing components in multiple courses, lessons, or topics. Some even come with their own authoring tools.

Confused about the difference between an LMS and an LCMS? An LMS, like Saba, Pathlore, SumTotal Systems, GeoLearning, and others, manages people involved in learning (the participants), and an

LCMS, like Outstart's Evolution, Aspen, KnowledgeBridge, Centre-Learn, and others, manages computer files. An LMS manages things down to the level of a course. An LCMS manages things from the course level downward. If you don't understand the difference, don't worry; most people don't. Some products and services marketed as LMSs contain LCMS features and vice versa.

But what about a CMS and how is it different from a CMS? The abbreviation CMS is used for two completely different systems: a *content management system* and a *course management system*. Course management systems are used by universities and school systems to manage academic programs. Unless you're in that market, you probably don't need one of these.

You may want a content management system, however, which is a general-purpose tool to assemble documents and Web sites from a vast library of text, graphics, sounds, animation, and video. A content management system, like Documentum or Interwoven, makes sense if you publish forty-three versions of a document and revise the document every few weeks. It is one of the core tools of knowledge management.

Still confused? Don't worry. You may not need one of these expensive tools. Ask yourself one simple question: Is managing content or participants a big problem yet? If not, look for a simpler approach. If your efforts are modest, use a spreadsheet or a simple database until that becomes too painful. Then consider buying a less expensive system that will get you by for the next year or so. Or consider a hosted (ASP) solution where you simply subscribe to a Web-based service. This can mitigate some of the risk until you decide when or if you need your own internal system. And don't forget to look around your own company. Maybe your IT organization (or another organization in your business) is also considering a system or already has one in place.

Do not fall prey to the notion that the first step in a learning strategy is to implement an LMS or LCMS. One company I am familiar with budgeted $1 million for its learning initiative: half for a LMS and half for content. Two years later, it has spent $1.2 million getting the LMS working. The company has no content to manage, and the CEO wants to know who is to blame. Strategy comes first, then technology.

Perhaps you have heard about open source tools and that they are free. Nothing is free. Open source tools are relatively inexpensive but not free. Open source refers to the fact that you get access to the source code for the program. Having the source enables you to adapt the system to do what you want—if you are a programmer or have a staff of programmers. Open source tools are for people who like it when the box says "some assembly required." What you save in license fees you may make up in time and effort installing, configuring, and maintaining the system.

What about standards? Perhaps you have heard of IMS, SCORM, AICC, or Section 508. Forget about all of them but SCORM and Section 508 for now. SCORM stands for Sharable Content Object Reference Model, which is gobbledygook for "here are some rules so that content created by different vendors using different tools can run on different management systems." SCORM is the hip, happening standard, and it incorporates the best parts of IMS, AICC, and other standards. But remember that these are standards for interoperability, not quality. If you're not careful, you can create learning programs that meet all the standards but don't teach much.

Section 508 is a U.S. government regulation that requires information technology be accessible by people with common disabilities like less-than-perfect vision and hearing. Outside the United States? You're not off the hook. Your country may have similar or even more stringent regulations based on the World Wide Web Consortium's Content Accessibility Guidelines.

Still baffled? Get to know your organization's IT manager. Even if you are not baffled, get to know him or her. Your success may depend on this individual. If you're unsure if your organization has an IT manager, your odds of success are close to zero. But if you know the pets and the birthdays of all the children of your IT manager, the odds for success are in your favor.

And keep learning. Read books, take e-learning, search the Web, and ask experts. The more you know, the better you can lead.

◆ ◆ ◆

William Horton is a consultant and author of *E-Learning Tools and Technology*, *Designing Web-Based Training*, and several other books on using electronic media and technologies (www.horton.com).

4

Knowledge Management
in Action

Share your knowledge. It's a way to achieve
immortality.

—*Dalai Lama*

There are many ways to manage knowledge in an organization. You
can focus on codifying and preserving important information, you can
focus on supporting collaboration or access to experts, or you can do
both. You can use sophisticated technologies, start with simple tools
like e-mail and instant messaging, or focus primarily on knowledge
identification (where is or who has your most valuable knowledge?).
You can support large departments or a few small work groups. You
can do some of these things or all of them, but if you don't do anything, if access to the intellectual capital in your organization is fren-
zied, if people can't get the information they need when they need
it, you'll never realize your new vision for learning and performance.

In the smart enterprise, knowledge management (KM) is about
creating information order out of chaos and turning business smarts
into real business assets. The level of sophistication and extensive-
ness of your solution, and where you start and how fast you scale,
are less important than keeping your eyes on this important goal.

In Chapter Three, KM was introduced as a key component of
the learning and performance architecture. In this chapter, KM's
potential in achieving smart enterprise goals is explored more
deeply. Applications and benefits, as well as some misunderstandings common to KM, are discussed. Finally, this chapter provides an

overview of a process for building KM solutions and introduces a framework for thinking about KM projects.

How Is Knowledge Management Used and Abused?

If only H-P knew what H-P knows.

—*Lew Platt, former CEO, Hewlett-Packard*

Knowledge is useless unless it is shared. The fact that you have a documented process is of little value if no one knows you have it. If some people in your organization are experts in a specific procedure, that expertise goes unused if no one knows who those experts are or how to reach them. This goes to the heart of what KM does: make information known and available to all who need it.

In any work setting, there is lots of knowledge in lots of forms. But if you don't know where that information is, you're as much in the dark as if that information didn't exist. This is *undiscovered* knowledge, and it represents a challenge to any business. A new cost-saving process that sits in a binder on a shelf, a product improvement no one sees, an innovation that goes unnoticed, or a new idea that's lost in thousands of e-mails all represent knowledge that might greatly benefit the organization if more people were aware of its existence. Sometimes undiscovered knowledge stares you in the face but you can't see it. Other times it's buried in complex patterns of work activities and communications, seemingly requiring a detective to ferret it out.

Your goal with KM is to turn undiscovered knowledge into *common* (or organizational) knowledge—knowledge that everyone who needs to know (or know about) actually does. KM enables the easy and systematic creation of knowledge and facilitates its dissemination so that it is commonly known. It creates opportunities for collaboration that bring undiscovered ideas to the surface, where they have value.

"Know How" and "Know Who"

Knowledge management is not just about identifying and using organizational "know how"; it is also about "know who." Finding the right people is just as important as finding the right document or Web site. By including collaboration through communities and networks or with experts, KM becomes a much broader field than content or document management, which deals only with building and maintaining information repositories. It is both a strategy to enhance learning and performance and a set of emerging technologies that are finding their way into many corporate infrastructures, large and small.

Communities, or communities of practice, are formal, and increasingly virtual, groups of individuals and teams with similar interests and needs. Knowledge networks are more informal relationships people establish with each other in the course of daily work. Experts and their expertise represent specialized subgroups in the overall organization, composed of people who, through experience, training, and other capabilities, are uniquely qualified to provide knowledge and advice to others. Collaboration with and between peers or experts makes use of new technologies and processes of social interaction, making it easier to find out who knows what. (The collaboration side of KM is discussed in more detail in Chapter Five.)

KM requires a sound process, meaningful management and organizational leadership, and unique software tools; like a three-legged stool, if you remove one of the legs, the stool (KM) collapses. KM should not be confused with training, which focuses on instruction rather than information. It is not simply a Web site or a search engine, although those are critical components. And it is not just technology, which should be viewed more properly as a critical enabler of KM.

Despite the name "knowledge management," knowledge cannot really be managed. It is exchanged, brokered, facilitated, shared, and leveraged. It is organic. Managing implies a top-down approach where a few people populate and organize everything. Knowledge needs to be managed jointly by everyone who uses it. Everyone in the organization plays a role in keeping knowledge fresh and accessible and ensuring its relevance, accuracy, and value.

Knowledge Management Traps

There has been confusion around what KM is and what it isn't. Some see it as primarily a technological solution to managing intellectual capital, while others simply use the term as an umbrella for a variety of other approaches to foster knowledge sharing and collaboration. There are those who don't like the term *knowledge management* and prefer *knowledge exchange*, *knowledge sharing*, or another similar term. But whatever you call it, the technical revolution of the information age, creating what Steven Johnson calls "near-infinite connectedness," has put KM strategy, processes and tools in the center of the conversation.[1] If it is to stay there, practitioners will have to be careful in avoiding the following eight KM traps:[2]

1. Believing KM is solely about knowledge storage
2. Implementing KM outside an organization's business strategy
3. Putting all your chips into technology
4. Thinking that KM projects must be huge
5. Using KM to overcontrol access to knowledge
6. Focusing on how KM works rather than what it does
7. Believing KM will be welcomed with open arms
8. Thinking KM will replace training

Believing KM Is Solely About Knowledge Storage. Archiving information is good but not nearly enough. To view KM as just about information storage and retrieval is to restrict thinking about how knowledge can be used to benefit the organization. KM systems are more than just large virtual filing cabinets; they are enablers of business activity. Initially most KM applications have focused on managing documented or codified knowledge. This is fine, but the collaboration, or knowledge exchange, side must also be part of your solution. Including collaboration—communities and networks, and experts and expertise—in your strategy is recognition of what most organizations already know: working together is a foundation for business success. Although creating successful opportunities for collaboration is tough, the rewards are worth it.

Implementing KM Outside an Organization's Business Strategy. KM systems must have a real business purpose, not one simply concocted to justify the investment. It is important to identify the specific value that the KM system will bring to the organization. What specific business problem or opportunities will KM address, and what will be its benefits? How will people use KM to become more efficient and competitive? Answering questions like these up front will generate initial support for KM and make it more sustainable over time.

> A knowledge strategy needs to have a broad base. It must be embedded in how the organization works and creates value.
>
> —*Hubert Saint-Onge and Debra Wallace*[3]

Putting All Your Chips into Technology. The rush to buy KM-related technology first and then figure out what to do with it confuses means with ends. This approach has sent many KM initiatives toward failure, jading lots of sponsors along the way. Understanding the learning, performance, and business issues for which KM might be a solution, and then carefully selecting scalable technology and tools that will help get there, is a far superior approach to successful KM implementation.

Many organizations that have been successful with KM have found, sometimes to their surprise, that the human element remains as important as the technological components, if not more so. For example, simply working to identify where knowledge is in an organization and whether that knowledge has value can be extremely valuable. Even when you look to technology for KM, providing for a knowledge broker, facilitator, or "managing editor" of a content domain ensures that information entering the system is highly accurate and relevant for users. This is similar to the role played by editors in a journalistic context: sorting through all the information coming in from the field to determine what to publish and where to publish it. This role is primarily performed by experts.

Thinking That KM Projects Must Be Huge.   Many KM projects overreach in terms of what can be accomplished with the resources (financial and human) on hand. A better way to look at KM projects is to think big but start small (with a supportive sponsor), and then be ready to scale up when the initial project is successful. In fact, some of the most successful KM projects stay small, focusing on a niche part of the organization.

Using KM to Overcontrol Access to Knowledge.   Some organizations institute a KM system to deepen control or restrict information access and exchange. A better alternative is to do the opposite: democratize access to critical business and technical content. Of course, there is always some information, such as financial, investor, and HR information, that must be restricted, but in successful KM systems, locking up information is done only when deemed necessary.

Focusing on How KM Works Rather Than What It Does.   It is tempting to get so involved in how the system will work that you forget to think about how the system will be used. While there may be strong arguments for a single KM platform, there will likely be even stronger arguments for finding ways to use that platform to meet divergent needs. Understanding and addressing the true performance needs of end users, and testing it with them, is very important. If using the system makes work harder than not using it, they will overwhelmingly reject it.

Believing KM Will Be Welcomed with Open Arms. If online training represents a major change in the way people are trained, requiring special care in bringing them onboard, KM will require even more work in this area. Comprehensive change management and incentive efforts are essential to any KM deployment.

Thinking KM Will Replace Training. Both are important and serve complementary purposes. Training is a more structured presentation of content than is KM and has more specific and likely narrower objectives. In many cases, a blend of the two will result in more efficient and effective long-term learning. Nevertheless, the role of training role will change, and while many instructors will continue teaching, some will move into more facilitative roles, helping people find the knowledge they need, supporting collaboration, and serving as knowledge experts within the KM initiative. In many ways, these new responsibilities represent the logical evolution of the instructor role. If you can help the instructor staff (and perhaps the developer staff as well) move to new roles and opportunities, there will be less need to downsize, and you can better maintain your team as opportunities for KM and other workplace learning solutions grow. Failing to prepare for these changes will likely be far more disruptive to your staff and capabilities. Another implication is that the role of the training organization shifts from that of course content provider to that of learning enabler or user advocate. The training organization identifies content, wherever it resides in the enterprise, and reorganizes or repackages it in the user's work context. This is a significantly different role from that of the traditional training organization.

> Knowledge will not attract money, unless it is organized and is intelligently directed through practical plans of action.
>
> —*Napoleon Hill, 1937*[4]

Avoiding these KM traps can significantly improve your KM success rate and the overall value of your KM solution. With KM as a part of your learning and performance architecture, you will be better able to maximize the impact of the expertise in your organization.

Course-Centric Versus Knowledge-Centric Viewpoints

A good way to look at the differences between training and KM is to look at how they both treat content. Online training catalogues, whether they are supported by a learning management system or not, tend to organize content by domain (like sales and marketing, IT, and leadership) and ultimately by curriculum and course. For the training organization, providing easy access to courseware is paramount. Figure 4.1 illustrates how parts of a hypothetical course catalogue might be organized for three simple domains.

Figure 4.1 Course-Centric View of Knowledge

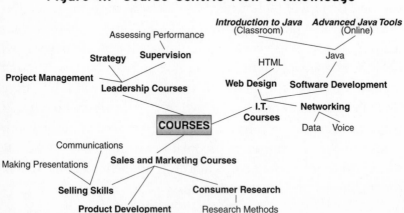

If you wanted to take a Java (software development) course, for example, you would search or browse the catalogue until you found what you were looking for. Perhaps you would take advantage of additional software tools to guide you, based on your role and job, level of competency, and predefined training plan. This is all fine, as far as it goes.

The problem is that navigating through a course catalogue, no matter how well designed and how comprehensive, usually serves up just one type of knowledge "container": courses. What should be apparent by now is that there are many other knowledge resources that are unsynchronized, and therefore go untapped, because they are either undiscovered or inaccessible.

Figure 4.2 shows a hypothetical knowledge-centric view, a far different picture of online content. The knowledge base is far more robust than that of an online course catalogue. The Java courseware is still there, but so is a wide array of additional resources: experts, information repositories, live events, and virtual communities, all of which can be accessed through a common user interface. When a user queries this knowledge base to learn about Java, the amount and variety of resources served up is much more comprehensive.

Figure 4.2 Knowledge-Centric View of Knowledge

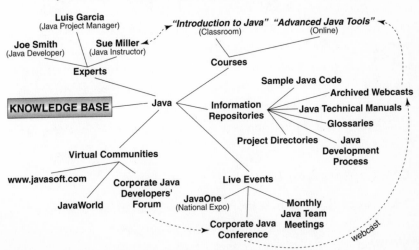

What is even more interesting is the ability to see interrelationships between knowledge assets (dashed lines). Notice that "Sue Miller," a Java instructor, is also positioned as a Java expert. Also notice this possible scenario: Java developers' virtual forum can meet live, perhaps once a year, at a corporate Java conference. Conference activities can be Webcast to those who could not attend. Then the Webcasts can be archived in the information repository for future reference and may also be used as a resource for the online "Advanced Java Tools" course. That's an example of how KM supports knowledge sharing and reuse. A knowledge-centric, rather than a course-centric, approach embraces the expanded and more inclusive definition of e-learning and adds more value by systematically bringing more content to the surface where it can be found.

Knowledge Management Applications

Knowledge is sticky. Without systematic processes and enablers, it won't move.

—Carla O'Dell, president, American Productivity and Quality Center[5]

Opportunities for KM abound in all types of organizations and in all types of functions. Whenever people need to share information, work in teams, or improve the efficiency of projects, KM can be a valuable tool. Sometimes KM reduces the need for training; other times it augments it. The key is considering all KM approaches as viable options when making design and implementation decisions. Here is how KM can be applied across several organizational functions.

Call Centers and Customer Care

KM is at work when hotel rooms are reserved, users get support for their computers, or customers seek product information for a possible purchase. Call center representatives certainly should be well trained, but training can't possibly keep up with the almost daily changes in product specifications, prices, and schedules. Today the expectation is that a representative provides customers with information from multiple databases and certainly does not recite it by heart. When service levels decline, it is usually because the rep takes too long to find the right information, supplies incorrect information, or says those dreaded words: "I don't know." Good KM systems provide better organization and delivery of information to call center reps in ways that make customer interactions more consistent and helpful. The results are often manifested in better service in less time, quicker responses to new promotions, more up-selling opportunities, and improved call center efficiency.

Here's an example of how KM supported a group of call center supervisors who were having difficulty with some representatives who were technically competent but had problems dealing with irate customers on the phone. Frustrated that the examples in the reps' training program could not cover every new or unique contingency, the supervisors began to share their current experiences and lessons learned—first by telephone during monthly conference calls. This soon evolved into more frequent e-mails and ultimately into a community of practice. One recommendation that came out of these interactions was the establishment of an online repository of suggestions and case studies around handling irate customers. As a bonus, as supervisors submitted new situations to the repository, the training group was able to incorporate them into their programs.

Customer Relationship Management

Customer relationship management (CRM) systems collect a vast amount of customer data, from initial transactions to overall buying habits (past and predicted). But this knowledge is useless unless it gets to the right person at an opportune time. Training alone could never keep up with changing customer demographics, buying patterns, and interests. KM takes a more real-time approach, asking questions like, "Who should get this information, when should they get it, how is it different from yesterday's information, and how should it be structured?" KM systems collect CRM information, structure and parse it into appropriate categories of knowledge, and distribute it rapidly to those who need it, in a format they can use. This creates better, real-time customer intelligence. For example, being able to get customer buying behavior to the right marketing managers at the right time creates tremendous competitive advantage for inventory management, product design and placement, and sales.

E-Commerce

With the Web firmly established as a core piece of almost every company's market strategy, KM is playing a more important role beyond the sale. Customer satisfaction with after-purchase support is consistently cited as a major factor in a customer's decision to purchase additional products from the same company. As customers become increasingly comfortable with e-commerce, businesses are responding with online access to user manuals, product demonstrations, troubleshooting and support resources, user communities, online training, and other knowledge-rich environments that help build customer loyalty. The KM principles of content organization, searching, and personalization can be applied to create a high-quality user experience (as opposed to a chaotic one) that strengthens the customer bond. And when customers get more information and help from a company's Web site, the more costly calls to a call center or help desk tend to decrease.

The success of e-commerce overwhelmingly demonstrates that people are willing to move to the Web for a wide variety of services and support, including features that help them better learn how to use the products they have, as well as about new products. Given that access to information and other types of online support is intuitive and time saving and that the content found is valuable, users quickly become comfortable with a Web-based model. Creative Labs discovered this when it implemented a KM-based customer support strategy. The results were 300,000 unique customer hits per month, a two-thirds reduction of calls to the call center, and an overall increase in customer satisfaction, which, in many ways, is a direct reflection of how well they learned from the site.[6]

Government

Serving a diverse citizenry is as important to government as serving diverse customers is to corporations. The challenge is to provide access to reams of public information without overwhelming the user. Good KM practices help meet this obligation, thus helping government agencies better serve their constituencies. In the United States today, most state and local governments provide an extraordinary amount of information on the Web. The U.S. federal government is moving quickly to do even more, especially at the agency level. But the biggest user of KM is undoubtedly the military. The U.S. Army's information needs are so voracious that its KM system, Army Knowledge Online, had more than 6 trillion documents in 2003, making it one of the largest online repositories in the world. Imagine managing all that information without a disciplined KM approach!

> AKO (Army Knowledge Online) is the Army's strategy to transform itself into a network-centric, knowledge-based force.
>
> —*Major General Steven W. Boutelle, U.S. Army*[7]

A regional first responder agency had to make sure that all its agents and specialists across the region were always up to speed on a wide variety of issues and topics, including security and public safety, disaster recovery, health, and law enforcement. The agency established an online information repository of critical content, demonstrations, protocols, and contact information that was available wirelessly to first responders wherever they were. After each drill and simulation and after any real emergency, after-action reviews were conducted to capture lessons learned, which were incorporated into the growing knowledge base. These first responders spent a lot of time in training, as they should, but there came a point where information was so volatile and so situation specific that much of it could not be taught on a regular basis. Instead, the first responders were trained how to access the information in the field. This has the added benefit of reducing some of their training needs and increasing their time on the streets.

Human Resources

Human resource departments were early users of online information. As the Web emerged in the 1990s, HR was quick to see the potential of putting benefit information online, allowing employees to manage their pay and medical claims over the Web in a self-service mode. Now, internal (and external) job searches and performance management systems are on the Web. And it's not just the forms and the process, but associated tools and training as well. Employees naturally value this type of information, and they have quickly become comfortable in the online world, making it easier for the business to "Web-enable" additional business functions.

Information Technology

Perhaps nowhere else in an organization is there more complexity and more risk than IT. Today no organization can succeed without significant support technology. It is vital to keep track of a company's substantial IT investment, from facility, network, hardware, and software assets, to the process documentation, administrative manuals, and training that keeps it all running. If and when technology fails, quick and reliable access to accurate information for disaster recovery, system restoration, and troubleshooting can mean the difference between a short service interruption and closing down the business.

The IT department of a major company, headquartered in New York City, wanted to be sure everyone had consistent and reliable access to key methods and procedures. The firm built a secure knowledge repository around critical IT procedures, including disaster recovery. After September 11, 2001, the firm was able to recover its operations faster because this KM system was in place. In order to ensure the right response (that is, the right performance), the corresponding training had to be blended with access to critical business and technical knowledge. Besides ensuring that employees were knowledgeable, training focused on how to use and rely on the KM system, which contained key information that no single person or group of individuals could master.

Partner-Supplier Relationships

As companies create stronger ties with partners and suppliers, a symbiotic relationship develops, and the need to share information becomes essential. Through KM, businesses can share important knowledge with partners and suppliers, while restricting information that should not be shared. For example, a company can share its procurement processes with suppliers to improve the supply chain. It can share marketing materials with resellers to enhance sales. And these partners and suppliers can feed product and service performance and cost and customer data back to the business. In these ways, and others, a vibrant knowledge exchange improves productivity as all parties learn how best to use mutually created and shared information to the greatest advantage.

Dell Computer uses KM to share customer buying patterns and preferences with its partners and suppliers, which then tweak their production schedules and product mix to precisely match Dell's market demand, which keeps the supply chain humming.[8]

Professional Services

Consulting and other professional services firms rely on the expertise of their employees as their primary, and sometimes only, asset. With consultants spending most of their time at client sites, their ability to access information, collaborate, and learn would be severely restricted without KM. Tapping into information databases and using technology to support collaboration at a distance overcomes the physical separation that consultants often feel. When executed well, KM enables individual contributors to call on the collective wisdom of the organization as if they were just down the hall rather than across the country or around the world. And they can represent that collective intelligence to clients, which significantly increases their value.

Sales

Salespeople spend most of their time with customers, and they often see office work and classroom training as unproductive. Many sales organizations are discovering that KM can keep distributed sales teams up to speed on customer characteristics, product specifications, competitive intelligence, proposal status, and other key topics without reducing customer "face time." Furthermore, as salespeople learn more about a customer or industry, they can feed that information back to a small KM core team that republishes the information to everyone else. This transforms the savvy of a single salesperson into common knowledge as the information spreads throughout the sales force.

Here's an example of how KM can transform learning in a sales organization. At a global technology company, every sales support, product management, and marketing organization had its own Web site on the corporate intranet; it became impossible for salespeople to find any information quickly. And when information was found, much of it was out of date. More sales training would not have helped here. This was a case of an inability to find information. Each support area reflected its own perspective rather than contributing to a unified perspective for the salesperson. The organization aggregated all the critical information into a common knowledge base, making content much easier to find. Within a short time, most of the old dated content was removed and replaced with current information. By using new publishing, shelf life, and analytical tools, feedback to knowledge providers was enhanced, and content accuracy could now be maintained as the number of knowledge assets and users grew. Once a critical mass of users and resources was reached, the KM system began to define the knowledge culture rather than fight it, and the system was expanded to support additional product families. In many ways, the new KM system helped shift the organization to a more collaborative culture, and the unified view made its intellectual capital much more valuable. The KM system became a central component of much of the company's sales training program. New salespeople began interacting with the system even before they went into the field.

> Rapid deployment of technology, coupled with rapid changes in the work patterns of large (and small) companies, has provided a fertile ground for weaving knowledge management and organizational learning into the fabric of the enterprise.
>
> —The Conference Board[9]

Knowledge Management Benefits

There are many ways KM can be beneficial to organizations. From the business perspective, KM enables faster response times through faster access to information. It reduces costs by surfacing and eliminating information redundancies. It leverages internal expertise by using technology to distribute that expertise to an increasingly larger and global audience (creating more common knowledge) and provides opportunities for new ideas and innovation to surface, be captured and shared, and ultimately refined into best practices (reducing undiscovered knowledge).

From a strategic perspective, KM creates a scalable knowledge infrastructure to help the business grow at a more rapid pace, without bursting at the seams. It affects productivity to the level where it becomes a differentiating factor in a competitive marketplace, and ultimately creates a knowledge base that will become an independent, capitalized asset of the firm.

Finally, from the employee or HR perspective, KM improves employee satisfaction and retention by building a greater sense of community online, enabling people to work with cutting-edge technology, and reducing frustration caused by an inability to navigate a growing organization and its associated knowledge requirements. KM reduces ramp-up time for new employees (enhancing productivity), supports employee career development, and preserves expertise when people leave the firm.

Building Knowledge Repositories

The approach to building knowledge repositories is systematic and replicable. It borrows the best from other processes, including training design and development, information design, human factors, software development, library science, and social systems, to name a few. As illustrated in Figure 4.3, there are three primary stages in the process:

1. Knowledge capture: Identifying and gathering the right content
2. Knowledge convergence: Organizing and storing the content
3. Knowledge access: Providing user access to knowledge

Figure 4.3   Building a Knowledge Repository

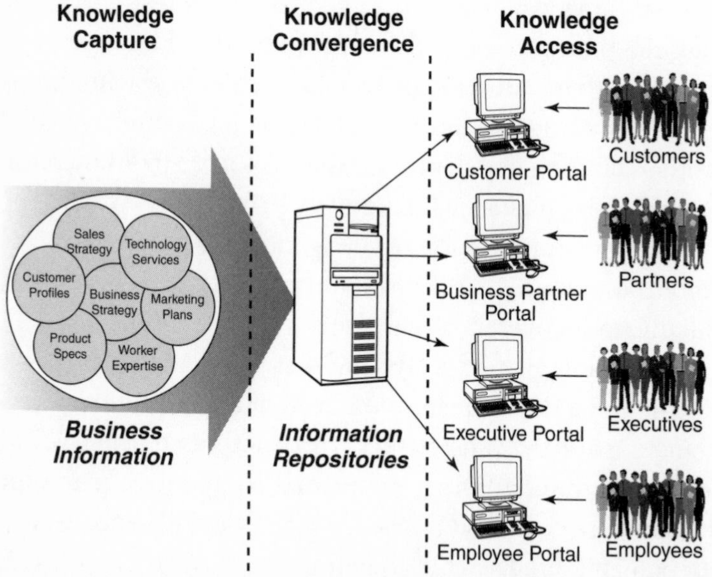

Knowledge Capture

A successful KM strategy must be based on capturing the right content that will provide the most value to those who use it. There is much information in an organization that is explicit or codified already. That is, the content is already in some documented and accessible format. Examples of codified content include product information, research, customer service information, troubleshooting guides, training materials, recommended resources, marketing collateral, policy and procedures, best practices, and competitive intelligence.

Other knowledge is more tacit. This knowledge is characterized by elusive but valuable heuristics and ideas, often embedded in people's experiences and life's work. In almost any situation, the amount of tacit knowledge far exceeds the amount of explicit knowledge, but it is much harder to capture and codify. Think of tacit knowledge as the two-thirds of an iceberg that is underwater, where it can't easily be seen.

Doing knowledge capture work is challenging. There are several key considerations to take into account if you are to do it well. First, you must pick the right content sources. It is important to cover all appropriate knowledge sources, internal and external, human and documented. If the information is explicit, great care must be taken in choosing what content goes into the system. Not everything that can be published should be published. The system can become worthless if it contains so much of the marginal, outdated, or unstable content that the information people truly need is lost. Do not make independent decisions; a group of experts and users can best determine what is and is not valuable. In many cases, less is more. Prioritize the content based on value; put fewer knowledge assets into the system (that reflect the highest priority knowledge needs) and then, over time, work to identify knowledge gaps (through user and expert feedback) and fill them. If the information is in tacit form, the first step is to pick the right experts: people who not only have the knowledge you need but can talk about it or demonstrate it in a way that will enable you to capture it through an interview, focus group, or performance observation. There are many questions you can ask; each situation is different. Here are some that are fundamental:

- What precisely is it that you do? (Try to break this down into discrete steps, tasks, and decisions.) How often do you do it? How important is it?
- How did you learn to do what you do?
- Can you demonstrate what you do?
- What tools and resources do you use to do what you do? (Ask to see them.)
- Can you or have you ever taught others to do what you do?
- If you had the time and the proper support, could you document what you do so that others could do it as well?
- What have you learned by doing what you do (recommendations, advice to others, lessons learned)?

Many knowledge capture techniques come from other forms of systematic analysis, including training needs assessment and performance analysis (see Chapter Ten). There is often a tendency to minimize, postpone, or avoid knowledge capture, especially the decision-making process about what content is valuable and what is not. This is dangerous, because without some type of quality check, your KM system may soon be overloaded with drivel.

Knowledge Convergence

Once you've selected the right content for your repository, you need to bring it together. Some people argue that it is okay for knowledge to be stored in multiple and divergent places, such as multiple databases, e-mail, online documents, hard-copy print materials, in the heads of experts, and Web sites on the intranet and Internet. But if the user has to first know where the information is in order to get to it and then figure out how to assemble the pieces before any real value is delivered, the experience is likely to be frustrating and wasteful. Knowledge convergence eliminates this problem: the user can access knowledge without precisely knowing where it is located.

In order for users to locate knowledge or expertise in a repository, that knowledge and expertise must first be organized in a way that enables easy and logical access. This organizing scheme is called a *knowledge architecture*. This is one of the most challenging and important tasks in building a good solution and is giving rise to a new class of professionals: knowledge architects.

One way to build a knowledge architecture is by content domain. Think about your high school subjects. You took math and you took science. Each is a content domain. Within science, you find additional domains, like chemistry and biology. Each of these has subdomains as well, and you can continue down this level of specificity road as long as it helps rather than complicates your understanding of the depth and breadth of the domain. Encyclopedias represent an excellent example of how content domains can be organized. So do many Web sites, such as WebMD (medicine), Expedia (travel), and Edmunds (automobiles). In addition, most content domains intersect with other content domains. For example, math and physics have points of intersection, as do health and athletics.

In a business, there are many ways to organize knowledge. Content domains can be structured by product line, geographical regions, core technology, market segment, or business unit. Knowledge can also be organized by performance domains: what you expect users of the system to do (see "Performance-Centered Design" in Chapter Six). And there are certainly intersections across many of these areas. A basic example is provided in Figure 4.4.

Figure 4.4   Simple Knowledge Architecture

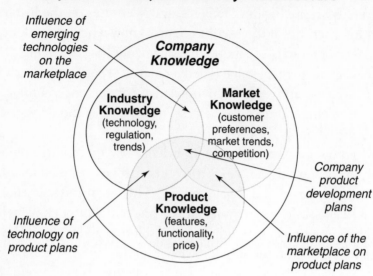

In this example, three content domains are illustrated, along with multiple intersections. In order for this hypothetical company to develop products that satisfy its customers, it will have to draw on multiple knowledge disciplines.

In any organization where knowledge is managed, you will first need to establish a knowledge structure that works for you. You will develop a taxonomy (categorization) of the content that reflects its unique nature, as well as the way people in the organization think about and use the content. There is no hard and fast rule; the key is logic and consistency and avoiding ambiguity, so that future content can be placed in its proper place and then easily accessed by users. Once your taxonomy is set, you will develop unique descriptors, called *metatags*, which define what the content is and where it can be found. Metatags are essentially data about data. It is a coding scheme that tells you about the knowledge asset, including, but not limited to:

- Media: document, Web site, audio/video
- Subject matter: math, science, technology

- Business purpose: finance, technical, management, sales
- Level of complexity: novice, expert
- Publication data: date published, author, language

Every knowledge asset is assigned appropriate metatags. When knowledge seekers are searching for it, they will use the metatags as filters to narrow their search and make it more efficient. The Dewey Decimal System in libraries uses one of the most successful tagging schemes.

Using taxonomics and metatags significantly increases the likelihood that people will find what they need rather than simply getting hundreds, or thousands, of hits from their searches. The process provides additional contextual and descriptive information that enables people to qualify the relevance of the content to their particular need. It provides a way to add and organize large numbers of knowledge assets (sometimes referred to as knowledge "objects") and reuse them appropriately, without overloading the system. It also facilitates accountability for the content's accuracy, timeliness, and thoroughness (for example, who created the content, who approved it, and who is currently responsible for it).

> It's not about searching; it's about finding.
>
> —*Anonymous*

Knowledge Access

Naturally, the ultimate goal of any KM system is to provide easy access to information. But simply searching and browsing one or more repositories of information will not be adequate. Anyone who has ever searched using a common term will understand that getting lots of hits, while important, is not the same thing as finding the information you need. Portal technology can make the KM experience more efficient, personalized, and valuable.

Portals

> Knowledge is of two kinds. We know a subject ourselves, or we can know where we can find information about it.
>
> —*Samuel Johnson*

Portals are Web-based gateways to valued online resources and services. Many individuals use commercial portals like "My Yahoo" or "My MSN," among others, to personalize and manage Web-based information that's most important to them. In much the same way, businesses use portals to provide a scalable, consistent approach to finding, sharing, and managing information across an organization. Portals are highly reusable and customizable. Essentially an organizational portal can be a simple front end to a stand-alone knowledge management system, or it can be extended to building a company's next-generation intranet where the existing and sometimes chaotic collection of Web sites is replaced by a consistent portal strategy with KM features and functionality.

Businesses use portals to support three primary groups: customers, business partners, and employees. For customers and business partners, portals provide a single access point to all the resources they depend on. From technical support to product training and from new features to fresh ideas on how to use a product or service in new ways, the portal can serve as the primary link to the company. By providing value through a comprehensive portal, the bond with customers and business partners is significantly strengthened, an essential ingredient to a strong and enduring relationship.

Employee portals don't create knowledge or applications or products or services. They aggregate them, creating a single view into the organization's intellectual capital, its service offerings, and its overall capabilities. In providing a window through which the resources of a firm can pass (such as training, documentation, or expertise), a portal enables employees to better manage the information they need to do their jobs with greater speed, responsiveness, and acumen. This makes for more satisfied employees and a more agile business, enabling it to alter course as the marketplace dictates, leverage new ideas and products faster than the competition, and generate new ideas faster through businesswide knowledge sharing. Employee portals can be further subdivided depending on user group or task to be accomplished, each with different, customized content and services. Sales force portals, executive portals, and technical support portals are just some examples.

Employee portals create easy-to-use, easy-to-navigate self-service capabilities that allow people to control a bigger part of their relationship with the firm. They bring together a variety of information, tools, and applications that allow work processes to be streamlined, as employees from across departments or across great distances collaborate and execute business plans more effectively and more cohesively. Portal functionality is likely more powerful than the individual tools and services it integrates. In many cases, portals can reduce or eliminate specialized staff by transferring work to the employee using a set of Web-based services. Portal self-service features enable employees to manage their own paycheck deductions and benefits, training, and career advancement. Portals can also support corporate services such as travel, purchasing, and technology support.

Employee portals provide a user-centric front end to complex businesswide applications, including sales, customer care and marketing, enterprise resource planning (for example, Oracle/PeopleSoft, SAP), and complex technical systems like those typically found in manufacturing. The common functionality makes it easy to master and scale as new features and users are added.

In addition, the personalization features of a portal enable a firm to use a single-technology platform to create almost limitless customization, each providing common corporate features as well as features selected by individuals that strongly relate to their role, organization, or geographical location.

Finally, by providing easy access to a wealth of reliable information, a portal elevates the knowledge of its users. It can reduce training requirements and shorten the ramp-up time for new employees. It can replace the watercooler as the primary source for company news and serve as a firmwide suggestion box, where new ideas are generated and shared.

Portals represent a new and fast-growing segment of the IT and KM industries. The primary goal of greater access, common platform, ease of use, and scalability promises to make them a central feature of a company's business strategy.

No two portal solutions are the same; they reflect the uniqueness of the organization and its culture. Through this approach, a portal can be configured for different users, roles, and purposes by varying the features that are used, as well as the information and functionality provided to each user. In this way, each portal is both a personal and an appropriate view into the business for each constituency.

Portals organize and deliver the right knowledge to the right people at the right time and at the right level of detail. Because of this, they make finding information more efficient and reliable. This is a powerful aid to learning. When people no longer have to figure out where content is or guess at its accuracy or relevance, they become much more productive and comfortable using it.

Additional information on KM features, functionalities, and challenges is provided in Appendix B.

> The most important contribution management needs to make in the 21st century is to increase the productivity of knowledge work and knowledge workers. It is on their productivity, above all, that the future prosperity—and indeed the future survival—of the developed economies will increasingly depend.
>
> —Peter Drucker[10]

Bristol-Myers Squibb Gets High Value Out of People-Centric, Low-Tech KM

Technology can be very useful to KM efforts, but there are many situations where, at least at the start, it can get in the way. Bristol-Myers Squibb (BMS), a global pharmaceutical and health care company, faced two such challenges where the value of personal, people-centric, low-tech KM was just right.

The first challenge surfaced when BMS acquired DuPont's pharmaceutical business and needed to get scientists and researchers on both sides to engage in a conversation about the best product and human assets to incorporate into the new company. The second challenge became apparent when several BMS medicines failed to get regulatory approval. Considering the massive investment and time needed to bring a new drug to market, the company had to discover what was going wrong and fix the problem fast.

Melinda J. Bickerstaff, vice president of knowledge management at BMS, immediately recognized that these two challenges represented opportunities to implement a people-centric, low-tech approach to KM to solve two important business problems that were also important learning problems.

The DuPont Acquisition

When the DuPont acquisition was announced in 2001, BMS established a fast-paced timetable to get the two businesses together. Once the deal closed, BMS would have several months to select all the appropriate product and human assets to bring into the new company. "Everyone knew that one of the significant risks to this $7.8 billion acquisition was the potential for knowledge loss," Melinda noted. Indeed, BMS knew that unless it selected the right products and human assets, the planned synergies of these combined businesses could suffer.

To avert this problem, Melinda and her KM team, working in close partnership with R&D business leaders, developed a strategy and plan for knowledge capture that would enable BMS to quickly understand and specifically assess the R&D assets and people resources within DuPont. By first implementing a knowledge capture training effort, BMS scientists learned to ask key questions, in a thoughtful, compassionate manner, of their DuPont counterparts—for example, "What is your role with this asset? Who else knows about it?" and "Where is the knowledge that supports this asset? What form is it in? A document? Embedded in technology? In a process? Or in a person?"

Too often, when an acquiring company makes wholesale decisions on what to keep and what to jettison from an acquired business, the results are often hurt feelings and a brain drain. Not here. An extra effort was made to let DuPont people know that they were valued and that everyone would be given an opportunity to tell their story. So skilled were the scientists that BMS was able to quickly understand DuPont's value in a matter of weeks rather than months. This resulted in the fastest corporate integration in the industry and retention of the right assets and the right people. A number of these assets are progressing forward into BMS's rich portfolio. In the future, they hope to see several enter into the marketplace and thus into the hands and lives of people who need them. That is, after all, the ultimate measure of success.

Understanding Regulatory Failures

When a new medicine fails to get to market, it is an enormous problem. The cost of developing a single drug is estimated to be about $1.7 billion. So when two drugs in a row got mixed reviews from regulatory agencies in late 2001, BMS wanted to know why. Were the failures related solely to regulatory problems, as was the initial suspicion, or was it something else? What worked well in the submission process, and what needed to be improved? The company used its well-tuned knowledge capture techniques to help answer these questions.

The company identified six drugs—some that failed and some that succeeded—and with specially trained facilitators (from the

KM team, learning and development, HR, organizational develop-ment, and the corporate library) conducted an intensive root-cause analysis. Once again, this process was supported and implemented with a strong partnership with key business leaders within BMS. The knowledge gleaned pointed to a number of causes, not a single, simple one.

The team wanted to ensure that their colleagues would truly buy in to these findings and the ensuing recommendations. Presenta-tions of mountainous data, backed by hundreds of PowerPoint slides, were rejected, even though they were common in the culture. Instead, the team engaged senior leadership in a six-hour "lessons learned" conversation. The changes that were recommended and implemented, backed by strong leadership commitment, contributed to an impressive string of three drug approvals in the following six-teen months, a record unprecedented in the industry.

> The hardest piece of KM, but perhaps the most impor-tant one, is transferring what people know how to do, to people who will do it next.
>
> —*Melinda J. Bickerstaff, vice president, knowledge management*

Learning from These Experiences

For Melinda and her KM team, these two experiences, and others like them, have generated their own lessons learned:

1. **KM will not work unless it is tied to solving a real business problem.** This provides the opportunity to create a close part-nership with the key business leaders who have a huge stake in finding a solution.
2. **Be courageous.** Step up to the challenge, and the rewards will be there. But also be honest; speak up if KM will not be of help.

3. **Look for partners to help you execute your KM strategy.**
   KM took the lead in these projects, but Melinda and her team
   could not have been successful without the aid of HR, learning and development, IT, organizational development, the
   corporate library, and other resources.

4. **Figure out a way to embed what you do directly into the
   fabric and processes of the business.** That's where the true
   value is.

5. **Never forget that KM activities can help to create a learning
   organization culture.** Organizations that are open and willing
   to learn from both their successes and failures can adapt more
   quickly to changing circumstances and are most likely to be
   around and thrive in the future.

KM in a Decentralized Company: The DiamondCluster Experience

Organizations are more virtual than ever before. Even small companies can have employees in different cities or countries. More
people work from home or at customer locations than ever before,
and the trend is growing. Nowhere is this more evident than in professional service firms, where consultants work almost exclusively
at client sites or home offices. Intellectual capital is the competitive
currency of these firms, yet, paradoxically, the structure of these
businesses makes it competitively disadvantageous to bring people
together to learn.

Such was the challenge at DiamondCluster International, a
global management consulting firm. In its forming years, everyone
knew one another. Personal relationships were the key to knowledge sharing. Want information? Just call or e-mail the person who
had it, and a copy would be sent to you. But as the firm grew, it became increasingly difficult to find information, and when it was
found, it was increasingly difficult to determine if it was the right
information. As a result, too many versions of the content were in
circulation; no one really knew which was the most accurate or

complete. Although DiamondCluster had a training program, the content focused on consulting competencies rather than client and industry knowledge, and the firm knew that it could not bring everyone to its Chicago headquarters each time this knowledge changed, which was quite often. In addition, much of this information was specific to a unique consulting team, client, or industry, making cost-effective classroom delivery even more problematic. Furthermore, speed became a driving force of the business. Consultants working on client projects could ill afford to wait for critical information. This would slow the project, with adverse impacts on the timeliness and quality of the deliverables. So in addition to maintaining its investment in training, a significant amount of effort was put into a knowledge management system known as the Knowledge Center (Figure 4.5). DiamondCluster's Knowledge Center portal allows consultants around the globe to access the firm's intellectual capital in the same way.

Figure 4.5 DiamondCluster's Knowledge Center Portal

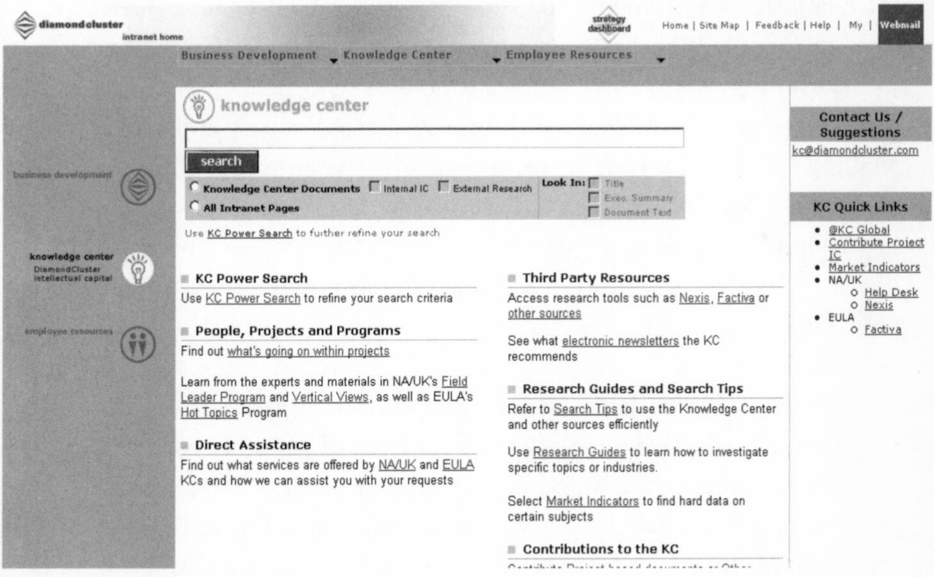

Source: DiamondCluster International.

DiamondCluster's Knowledge Center was developed to address three fundamental issues:

• **How will the firm support knowledge sharing, and information protection and preservation, within and across project teams?** The first challenge was to provide virtual repositories where project work (research, proposals, presentations, deliverables, assessments, and so forth) could be stored securely and still be shared across distributed teams. Project-centric virtual "rooms" were built on the Web where all forms of project, client, and relevant industry documentation could be stored. Each room was organized and managed locally by the project team itself, so that team members would be able to retrieve the information, maintain version control and project-level security, and contribute new content as easily as possible. These project repositories were maintained outside the Knowledge Center so that it would not be overwhelmed with interim reports or project work that would not be relevant to the rest of the firm. At key points in an engagement, and especially at its conclusion, major deliverables (reports, presentations, and research, for example) are uploaded to the Knowledge Center and made available to all.

With project and client information well managed, operational costs fell as accessing accurate knowledge became easier and faster. Making key information assets available to other groups through the Knowledge Center reduced redundant efforts and improved the firm's business responsiveness. Over time, this online library of major project documentation provided the firm with an extremely valuable preserved history of all its work, a key competitive advantage for the business.

• **How will the firm create, disseminate, and manage new intellectual capital independent of individual project work?** In addition to project-specific knowledge, the firm wanted to generate or identify new knowledge across clients and industries, and ensure that this information was available to all who needed it. Depending on the requirements of the business, DiamondCluster uses two approaches to accomplish this. A small core research staff manages a variety of external information resources, such as subscriptions to proprietary research and business intelligence services, and makes them available to the field. In other situations, consultant field teams, organized around industries and service offerings, such as cellular technology, IT management, customer service, and product marketing, contribute critical information, such as white papers, articles, and presentations, grouped and organized for easy access in the Knowledge Center. These collections are used to support specific consulting engagements or business development activities. Key knowledge assets can be tagged as "recommended" by the field team as being of particular interest or value. This facilitates faster searches and ensures that the best resources are at the top of the list.

- **How will the firm balance information and message consistency with the need to serve diverse clients and industries?** One of the most daunting tasks DiamondCluster faced was how to allow individual project teams to use the Knowledge Center in ways that served their particular client and industry and yet ensure that the firm continued to speak with one voice. With information that was corporate in nature, such as credentials and capabilities statements, the firm selected specific individuals to "own" the knowledge and maintain the most up-to-date information on the Web. For industry and service offering-specific content, the field teams not only developed new knowledge, but served as a gatekeeper as to what information was deemed accurate and valuable enough to include in the knowledge repository. This kept the library from being overrun by marginal or inaccurate content. These teams, which soon became known for their expertise, provided a critical quality assurance function for each client, market, and industry the firm served.

Over time, DiamondCluster took a vast array of disparate tools and technologies that supported these three goals and integrated them into a more seamless KM approach. But it took a lot of work. The initial challenges were primarily in organizing the system to make the Knowledge Center valuable from a content perspective as well as easy for people in multiple locations to use. In the early years, the system was inundated with too much content: incomplete or draft documents, outdated information, or content that was too narrow in focus to be of use to anyone but the author. Today much of this information has been removed from the main repository. Extensive upgrades in portal technology, search, authoring, and information management capabilities made finding and organizing content easier and faster, a far cry from the cumbersome, inaccurate, and frustrating processes of the past.

> We continue to focus on ways to help users better filter through the increasing number and variety of knowledge assets, whether it's through more comprehensive tagging of the documents (for example, richer taxonomy) or additional qualifiers for the documents, such as recommendations by recognized experts in the field. The trick is getting the right document to the right person at the right time.
>
> —Linda McKula, Knowledge Center director

More challenges remain, not just for DiamondCluster, but for all other organizations that try to manage their intellectual capital better. As information access grows, there is an increasing need to weed out less valuable knowledge assets and bring the most valuable ones to the surface. Balancing official, sanctioned content with interim or experimental work is important. Naturally, all good KM systems must protect the reliability and validity of its most important knowledge assets, but it must also provide a "sandbox," that is, a private and secure area where individuals can develop and manage their own content contributions, nurturing them until they are ready to move to the main firmwide library. Recruiting and empowering field experts and getting them to submit high-quality content is a continuing struggle, especially when the demands of the business draw them away from their expert support role. At the opposite end, encouraging people to use and trust a KM environment is also critical, and helping them to believe that using the KM system will make their work life easier and more successful is the key. Justifying the expense of dedicated KM staff, even if part time, can be daunting unless you demonstrate the business return on the investment. Finally, managing back-door knowledge sharing, where content is shared outside the system to meet unique needs, can be challenging as well. You want to allow people to share content freely, and sometimes bypassing the process is appropriate. But over time, you want people to increasingly trust and rely on it.

How you balance these often conflicting demands, and how well you use carrot and stick motivators will, in a large sense, determine the success of your KM efforts.

The DiamondCluster experience is useful for several reasons. It shows that the development of a successful KM system is iterative and evolutionary, not a one-shot deal. There will be setbacks and frustrations, which can be great learning opportunities for moving forward. As DiamondCluster discovered, it is never how much content you have, but how valuable the content is that you have. The firm's KM system got much better once it got rid of marginal or dated content. Great technology alone will not create great KM; getting people to participate—users and contributors—will ultimately determine the success or failure of your efforts. Finally, the benefits of KM are not limited to consulting firms. Rather, they extend to any diverse, virtual, or complex work environment, including sales, service, health care, teaching, call centers, manufacturing, and retail.

The Knowledge Management Development Framework

One way of looking at KM development is through a framework that brings many key activities together. The framework is a matrix of activities bounded by four steps to an overall systematic process and five KM components that results in twenty primary KM development activities (Figure 4.6). Each is essential as you develop your KM system; together, they ensure that you are solving the right problem, using the right tools, and creating the right environment for success.

Figure 4.6 Knowledge Management Development Framework

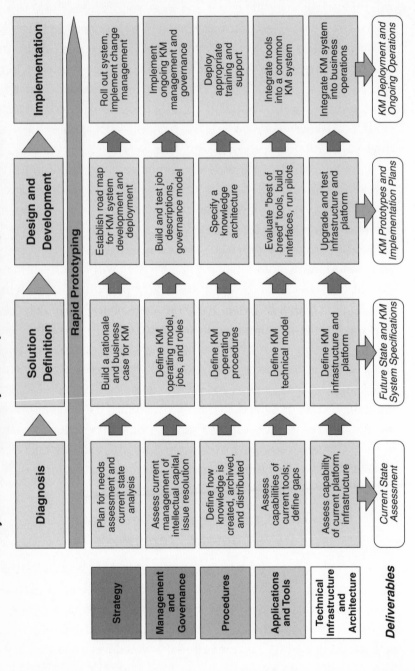

Systematic Process

The process to follow in building a KM solution is not unlike other systematic processes. It has four major phases: diagnosis, solution definition, design and development, and implementation.

Diagnosis. Here you define the current state: an accurate depiction of how knowledge is currently managed in the organization. You might assess the organization's strengths and weaknesses, as well as the opportunities and risks associated with solving the problem, or leaving it alone.

Businesses are replete with solutions looking for problems to solve. If your KM effort falls into this category, you are in trouble. Ignoring diagnosis may lead you toward some assumed solutions and away from others before the evidence is in. This may lead you to develop the wrong solution or address the wrong problem. If, however, your first step is to define the problem clearly from a business performance and a human performance perspective, you are much more likely to end up with a solution that is both accepted and works.

Sometimes there isn't a problem, per se, but rather an opportunity for doing something better. For example, you might want to explore a new market or improve operations because you know your competition is always looking to do so. It is important not to overlook these opportunities, as they can put you in a more proactive, rather than a reactive, role, using KM to innovate rather than to fix.

Almost every organization has some form of KM. The good news is that there is growing recognition of the importance of KM, even if the term is never mentioned. The bad news is that poor practices may be ingrained in the culture, with lots of work-arounds and money spent to maintain a less-than-effective system. It will be important to identify both the positive and negative aspects of the current state from how the organization creates, archives, and distributes information to how people collaborate and how experts are used.

It will be important for you to identify all key stakeholders—potential users, sponsors, and partners (especially other departments with expertise you need, such as IT)—so that you can get their viewpoints regarding the problems or opportunities to be addressed and, later, regarding support for implementation.

Solution Definition.   In the solution definition phase, you articulate your specifications and requirements clearly and fully. By doing so, you are more likely to end up with the solution you envisioned. If you are not clear in defining your solution—your future state—you may incur significant waste in time and resources before you discover you are heading in the wrong direction. Even worse, you may not notice that you are on the wrong path until it is too late and you have deployed something that people find less than useful.

It is here that you define what your KM system will look like across each KM component. This blueprint serves six purposes:

- When compared with the current state, it helps to identify the gaps in your KM strategy, which enables you to pinpoint key weaknesses more quickly and with less guessing.

- It provides a first look at the solution and allows key stakeholders to provide commentary and suggestions.

- It generates an operating model that outlines the organizational, staffing, and other management structures that will be needed to run the system.

- It lays down a set of criteria that drives your tools and technology decisions. This "technical model" can be supplied to vendors, software developers, system integrators, and other key members of the team so that all components of the solution are built as designed and are compatible with each other.

- It defines the infrastructure and platform requirements for the KM solution. This enables the IT organization to add the system installation and maintenance requirements to its work plans.

- It provides an early look at what it will take to implement the system, including training, support, and change management.

Most important, the solutions definition phase of the process should generate a sound business case and verify your value proposition for the KM system. Once you have defined how the system will work, the problems it will address, and the value it will bring to the business, you are ready to build.

Design and Development.   Here is where you configure and test your KM system, including both technical functionality (for example, search engine, content management) and organizational processes (for example, content publishing procedures, rules for protecting proprietary information). This is where you also build and test your knowledge architecture.

Implementation.   Finally, you deploy your KM system according to plan. This is accompanied by a training and support strategy that extends far beyond the initial rollout. This phase is not much different from what you might do when you launch any new software application. However, since KM may represent such a new way of learning and supporting performance in the organization, as well as a new emphasis on user-initiated and user-defined knowledge searching, particular attention should be paid to change management (which is covered in Chapter Eight). Implementation and evaluation are covered in more depth in Chapter Seven.

Rapid Prototyping

Throughout the project, you have the opportunity to test small pieces of the solution with users and stakeholders to get early feedback when changes are less disruptive and less costly. A series of rapid prototypes enables users to react to the solution iteratively as it takes shape and provide feedback on its usability and its value at each stage of development. Early prototypes may be nonworking representations of the system designed to get initial user reactions to design, features, and navigation issues. Later prototypes might be rough working components of the system that will enable developers to make changes to functionality before those changes become too costly. Final prototypes might be working models of the complete system that are introduced to small pilot groups to see how the system works in its intended setting. The last prototype, which is likely to be very close to the final system, is tested from a technical standpoint to make sure that it will function to its specifications in the organization's IT infrastructure. All of this ensures that the end product is in line with expectations and effective in addressing business needs.

None of the systematic process phases should be overlooked. Addressing the process in its entirety can result in a number of important benefits. The systematic process can serve as a quality assurance checklist to ensure that you are covering all the major activities and deliverables of your KM project. It can help you define key checkpoints and milestones that aid in project management and program assessment. The rapid prototyping approach generates increased user and stakeholder participation earlier, which can translate into a stronger buy-in later. And finally, the systematic process will help enable easier transitions—from the project team to the operations team, for example.

Knowledge Management Components

In building a successful KM solution, it is important to work across five key components of the final system: strategy, management and governance, procedures, applications and tools, and technical infrastructure and architecture.

Strategy. Too often, systems are built before a strategy is articulated or verified. When this happens, you can be way down the wrong road, and have spent the bulk of your resources, before you realize you are trying to solve the wrong problem or achieve the wrong objective. Sample questions (provided at various levels of depth, but by no means inclusive of all the questions you may have to ask) to answer include:

- What are the business objectives for the company that have an impact on, or may be affected by, a knowledge strategy? How can KM contribute to the success of that strategy and the achievement of those business objectives?
- What changes are under way in the company's product and service offers, marketplace and channel management approach, competitive landscape, and others areas that may have an impact on, or may be affected by, KM?
- What should the scope and objectives of the knowledge strategy be? Is the value proposition clearly defined, especially in terms of specific business objectives?
- What business functions or operations will change as a result of this initiative?
- What employees, partners, suppliers, or customers are the specific targets, users, or beneficiaries of this initiative? Do you know enough about them and their performance requirements?
- What is the level of senior executive support for this strategy?

Management and Governance. This gets to the heart of any leadership, political, cultural, and change issues that may block deployment of your KM system or impede its sustainability. When management and governance issues are swept under the rug, they don't go away; they linger until they become insurmountable and cause the entire effort to crash. Sample questions to answer include:

- How is knowledge managed across the business? How should knowledge be organized and managed? How centralized or decentralized should it be?

- What decisions are required to get specific knowledge into the hands of employees, partners, suppliers, or customers?
- How hierarchical or collaborative is the culture of the company?
- How will problems or disputes about KM be resolved?
- How well coordinated are all the knowledge sources: product and service teams, marketing and sales, customer care, operations, R&D, manufacturing, training and HR, and others?
- Are the job descriptions for key KM roles adequate? What new roles should be created to support an enterprise knowledge strategy more effectively?
- What new skills are needed to implement the knowledge strategy?
- How are users encouraged to contribute knowledge and use knowledge? Is it easy or difficult? Are there ways to improve knowledge sharing?
- How should the effectiveness of the company's knowledge strategy be measured (in support of business objectives)?
- What support do the KM initiatives need related to change management and training?
- How will users learn to use the system?

Procedures. Here, the focus is on the operational effectiveness of the system. Everything from help systems and training to features and functionality are considered. It's one thing to deploy a KM system and quite another to enable people to use it easily, effectively, and willingly. That is what the procedural component is all about. Sample questions to answer include:

- How does knowledge flow across the business? Who has it, and who do they give it to? What bottlenecks and detours exist in the knowledge flow?
- How easy or difficult is it to access needed information when and where it is needed?

- How much knowledge is already codified and up-to-date?

- How much is more difficult to pin down or out-of-date?

- How will information security be maintained?

- How accurate is customer, product, business, or technical information, and how easy is it to get information updated and distributed?

- What levels of access to information (entitlements) are appropriate?

- How easy is it to get access to specific experts and their expertise or to identify key resources?

- How is knowledge organized (by product, customer, industry, "spend" level, or something else)? How should knowledge be organized, and how flexible should that structure be?

- How are decisions made regarding what to publish, when to publish it, and when to remove content from the system? Are publishing processes clear and easy to follow?

Applications and Tools. Of course, you need to select the right KM tools. From search to document management to collaboration, there is an increasing array of sophisticated tools and applications that make KM systems work. Choosing the right tools and combinations of tools can make the difference between a system that is easy to use and highly valued, and one that is too painful work with. Sample questions to answer include:

- How easy is it to find needed information (about customers, products, services, markets, finance, HR, IT)? How well organized is this knowledge? How effective are the search engines and methodologies that are in place?

- Does the platform support a systematic, coordinated approach to the distribution, sharing, archiving, and purging of information from its knowledge repositories?

- How can KM better integrate the business and technical communities inside the firm?

- Does the system provide identification of experts and access to their expertise?
- Does the system provide periodic evaluation and removal of dated or inaccurate content?
- What file types are supported?
- What portals and Web services are supported?
- How is new information entered into (or removed from) the KM system? How are people notified when it is?
- Do current knowledge platforms allow collaboration and community building by groups with similar interests or needs?
- What other KM systems or initiatives are under development or deployed in the organization? Are there technical or business conflicts resulting from possible redundancies?
- How well are training (classroom and online) and KM integrated?
- How do users deal with an overload of information? Are filters or other tools available?
- Can knowledge from the system be personalized or configured depending on the level of user expertise, type or level of complexity of the customer interaction, nature of a particular product, and so on?
- Does the system provide analytics on its use and effectiveness?
- Is the user interface intuitive and easy to use, enabling users to move through the system efficiently and with confidence?

Technical Infrastructure and Architecture. Finally, you must determine if the KM system can run inside your business using the networks, servers, and other technologies that the organization uses to run its mainstream operations. If your KM system is totally internal, it will likely run on your corporate intranet. If outside partners and suppliers are going to access it, you're likely going to have to create a special extranet capability that allows authorized users to access the system from outside your firewall while keeping everyone else out. If customers are involved, you will have to be sure they can access the system over the public Internet. You will also have to determine how to support virtual and mobile users (from home, hotels, client sites, and other places). Care must be taken to ensure that you don't have to overhaul your entire IT strategy or replace your installed base of hardware and software just to get KM to work. Involve IT people early in the effort, not just to be certain that the technology will work but so the IT organization will embrace and support it as their own. Sample questions to answer include:

- Will the company's current technical infrastructure support the proposed KM system? If not, what modifications are necessary?
- Are the business platforms (employee desktop, mobile, customer care, technical) able to support a unified KM system?
- Does the system provide adequate backup and recovery to protect against lost data?
- Is the infrastructure robust enough to support the distribution of rich media (such as streaming video)?
- Does the system provide adequate data and operational security?
- What other infrastructure or platform projects are under way or planned? How can they add value to this initiative?

It is important that none of these five components be overlooked or shortchanged. If they are all considered appropriately, you can expect to reap five benefits as you move forward with your KM initiative:

- You will ensure that your KM initiative is tightly coupled with your business strategy.

- Your management and governance structure will reduce friction and increase cooperation, participation, and overall support.

- You will create a seamless approach to content contribution, access, and collaboration rather than multiple, disjointed efforts.

- You will establish procedures that not only work but can be upgraded as the business changes and your KM efforts evolve.

- You will ensure that the most appropriate tools and technologies for your situation are used and that the system works in harmony with the rest of your IT infrastructure.

Each of the twenty primary KM development activities is discussed further in Appendix D.

A Team Approach to Knowledge Management

Knowledge management solutions, whether they are just information repositories or include more extensive collaborative communities, cannot be built by training departments alone. Most training organizations, including corporate universities, do not have the charter, sponsorship, reach, resources, or expertise to provide a complete solution alone. But neither do most business units or HR or IT organizations. The fact is that KM is interdisciplinary. It involves a deep understanding of how people learn and use information, a sharp focus on business objectives, and extensive technological prowess. It is a team effort.

Knowledge management development teams may not be experts in the knowledge that is captured, the content that will populate the repositories, or the domains that will constitute the communities of practice, but they should understand the business problems the organization is trying to address. The KM team may not be the ultimate users of the system, but they should know what the system will look like and how it will perform from a learning and usability perspective. They may not be the funding sources for the initiative, but they should be able to advise and advocate KM with those who pay the bills. And they may not actually build the system, but they should know how to work with system architects and how to express their requirements and goals clearly.

Beyond leading efforts to create KM solutions, these teams are stewards of the value of knowledge in the organization. In building KM solutions, it is vitally important to keep learning and performance, not search engines and chatrooms, at the forefront of the discussion. Rather than focusing on how well the system works, the essential question is how well people work with the system. And just as in online training, where it matters less how many courses you have online than what those courses are accomplishing, in KM, it matters less how much knowledge you are managing than how valuable that knowledge is.

Don't even begin to develop a KM solution if you don't know how you will use it to accomplish specific business goals. Building KM solutions just in case a use pops up for them in the future will never be enough justification to sustain the project, and you'll find yourself losing technical, financial, and leadership support quickly. But if you can carve out a specific and valuable role for KM, even if it is in just a small part of the organization, it is much more likely that the solutions you'll build will have a real impact without traumatizing the organization in the process. And learning and e-learning professionals can make significant contributions to the effort.

A little knowledge that acts is worth infinitely more than much knowledge that is idle.

—*Khalil Gibran*, The Prophet

Notes

1. Johnson, S. (2001). *Emergence: The connected lives of ants, brains, cities and software.* New York: Scribner, p. 113.
2. Adapted from Rosenberg, M. (2002, August–September). The seven myths of knowledge management. *Context Magazine,* pp. 12–13.
3. Saint-Onge, H., & Wallace, D. (2003). *Leveraging communities of practice for strategic advantage.* Burlington, MA: Butterworth-Heinemann, p. 15.
4. Hill, N. (1937). *Think and grow rich.* New York: Ballantine Books, p. 75.
5. O'Dell, C. (2002, September 12). *KM in action: Looking back and looking ahead.* Human Capital Live! Webcast presented by SABA.
6. Favilla, E. (2004, November). Global knowledge must be multilingual. *CRM Magazine,* p. 53.
7. Boutelle, S. (2003, June 4). *Information and knowledge management: Enablers for transformation.* Presentation to the 2003 Conference on Knowledge Management and Organizational Learning, Conference Board, New York.
8. Sviokla, J. (2001, February 15). Knowledge pays. *CIO Magazine.* http://www.cio.com/archive/021501/new.html.
9. Hackett, B. (2000). *Beyond knowledge management: New ways to work and learn.* New York: Conference Board, p. 24.
10. Drucker, P. (1999). Knowledge worker and productivity: The biggest challenge. *California Management Review, 41*(2), 79–94.

Who Owns Knowledge Management?

Steve Foreman

A training organization that attempts to implement knowledge management (KM) sometimes finds itself in conflict with the information systems organization. Some business leaders view advanced, workplace-based learning interventions, such as KM, as a radical departure from the training organization's traditional role.

The charter of the information systems function is clearer. It lays claim to anything having to do with technology. Since every role, function, department, and organization in business uses technology, the role of information systems is ubiquitous. Business leaders have little trouble associating KM with the information systems charter.

But a similar claim can be made by those who are responsible for learning and performance improvement. Since KM is designed to support these goals, there could be an equal argument that it belongs there.

As businesses face greater competitive and economic pressure, the training and information systems functions are being held more accountable to demonstrate business productivity gains. Gone are the days when broad-based learning solutions and enterprise technology systems were justified without a clear return on investment. An effective partnership between information systems and training is critical to the business success of any KM solution. Ultimately training and information systems have nothing to gain by competing for ownership of KM. They have everything to gain by collaborating. So what is the problem?

In many organizations, each of these functions has little understanding of the motivations, values, culture, and jargon of the other. They certainly approach technology differently.

Groups responsible for learning tend to experiment with technology, searching for new models to support instruction and performance.

They seek to make rapid changes to content and features in response to pilots and feedback from users. To learning professionals, the ability to make system changes quickly is central to their iterative approach to solving human performance problems.

Information systems groups tend to slow things down in order to ensure the reliability and security of technology. They introduce rigorous procedures, authorizations, and forms to be completed before any changes can be made. To information systems professionals, system changes must be carefully controlled.

Learning professionals often push the envelope, employing some (or all) of the most complicated Web-based technologies: Webcasting, Webconferencing, streaming media, voice over Internet protocol (VoIP), instant messaging, application sharing, browser plug-ins and players, and more.

Information systems may attempt to rein in these diverse bandwidth-intensive learning applications. They see the wide array of learning software as a maintenance nightmare. The more complicated these systems are, the more that can go wrong.

Frankly, when it comes to technology, the training operation presents a huge, unwieldy challenge to the information systems organization. And the information systems operation presents a giant, immovable obstacle to training. So how do they overcome their differences and work together to implement KM?

It is important that each function understand and appreciate the value the other brings to the table. Both functions share a common view of KM as a repository where tools, resources, and information can be collected from across the business and made accessible to all. They both see KM as a platform for workers with common goals and challenges to network and collaborate with one another. So where is the disconnect?

The key difference is one of focus. Learning professionals view KM as a just-in-time intervention to support employee learning and performance. For them, the employee's job performance is the central focus. Information systems professionals view KM as an enterprise technology to manage the knowledge assets produced by various departments. For information systems, enterprise technology requirements are the key focus. This distinction has a critical impact on how KM solutions are formulated and implemented.

Employees use KM systems to solve problems, research, analyze, assess, decide, recommend, organize, and communicate. When planning a KM solution, learning professionals identify what employees need to be able to do, what knowledge is needed to be successful, and who are the sources and providers of that knowledge; organize knowledge according to the employee's work context; identify and fill gaps in the knowledge base; collect employee feedback; and use the data to continuously improve the knowledge base.

Information systems approaches KM planning from a technology perspective. It determines the publishing and distribution needs of each user group; identifies read and write permissions, user authentication, and entitlements; defines requirements for data storage, content tagging, file archiving, and purging; specifies hardware, software, and network requirements; and determines end user system training and help desk requirements.

Neither of these approaches is more or less valuable to the business, more right or wrong than the other. Both are important. But unless the two viewpoints are combined, the impact of the resulting KM solution will be significantly diminished.

To be successful, the two functions should start communicating early. Training professionals may identify a need for a KM solution, perhaps one that targets a business process and provides support to the job functions most critical to that process. The information systems organization should be consulted early on, to determine the technical requirements and feasibility of a KM solution.

Conversely, information systems professionals may identify a need for a KM solution, perhaps one that addresses the Web publishing and distribution needs of a geographically dispersed sales organization. The training organization should be consulted early to identify critical problems and opportunities that are important to salespeople and sales support functions.

Since information systems professionals tend to focus on technical requirements and learning professionals tend to focus on human performance gaps, the two groups must establish a governance process and agree on how to collaborate on roles and responsibilities, terminology and communications, processes, and milestones.

After implementation, information systems and training continue to share responsibility for KM. The information systems group ensures that the KM technology is fast, reliable, and secure. The training group works with the client organization to ensure the continuous improvement, relevance, and sustainability of the solution. By working together from conception through implementation, training and information systems ensure that KM results in real productivity gain for the business.

The fact is that neither function owns the complete solution. The training and information systems organizations each share responsibility for KM, the success of which can be achieved only by working together.

◆ ◆ ◆

Steve Foreman is president of Q Innovation (www.qinnovation.net), which offers a new generation of KM and performance support products, and InfoMedia Designs (www.infomediadesigns.com), which provides instructional systems analysis, design, development, and implementation services. He can be reached at steve@qinnovation.net.

5

Learning Through Online Collaboration

I get by with a little help from my friends.
—*The Beatles*

Knowledge sharing is a hallmark of the smart enterprise; the more ways organizations can do it, the better. Although sharing knowledge through training, even online training, is effective in many ways, it doesn't support informal learning. Knowledge management tools, in contrast, greatly enhance informal learning by facilitating the delivery of information at the moment of need and in the context of work. To be most effective, KM systems must also support collaboration among individuals and groups, peers and experts alike. Collaboration changes the knowledge management dynamic by shifting information sharing from "one to many" to "many to many."

Organizations that focus most of their resources on building massive knowledge repositories and ignore the collaboration side of KM miss out on tapping the huge reservoir of talent and expertise inside the business. When collaboration is not supported and rewarded, new ideas and innovations are slower to emerge, redundant efforts proliferate, and practices tend to stagnate. Nevertheless, simply deploying tools that support collaboration, such as chatrooms, threaded discussion, or instant messaging, does not guarantee that your organization will be more collaborative if you don't have a supportive, knowledge-sharing culture.

If in years hence, people remember anything about the TV game show, "Who Wants to Be a Millionaire?" they will probably remember the contestants' panicked phone calls to friends and relatives. . . . What people probably won't remember is that every week, "Who Wants to Be a Millionaire?" pitted group intelligence [polling the studio audience] against individual intelligence, and that group intelligence won.

—*James Surowiecki*[1]

The value to be gained from the collaboration side of KM is so great that the benefits clearly outweigh the implementation challenges. When people willingly share what they know and volunteer to serve as experts and when the organization recognizes their contributions, smart enterprise thinking turns into smart enterprise reality.

This chapter is about collaboration—through communities and networks and through experts and expertise. It looks at how collaboration works, the role of technology in making it happen, and the critical success factors to consider in making it succeed. When you need to know something, there's nothing better than being able to find the right person, with the right answer, right away.

Communities

More than any other way, people learn not from courses or Web sites but from each other—not in formal training presentations or online delivery of programmed instructional sequences but through dialogue. Many of these conversations are informal watercooler or lunch table talk. Others are more formal, taking place in department meetings, project work, and brainstorming sessions. In all of these situations, learning is taking place. So it makes sense to augment access to training and access to information with access to people.

> Many ideas grow better when transplanted into another mind than in the one where they sprang up.
>
> —*Oliver Wendell Holmes*

What Is a Community?

Communities, or **communities of practice,** are trusting groups of professionals united by a common concern or purpose, dedicated to supporting each other in increasing their knowledge, creating new insights and enhancing performance in a particular domain. They are people who need to work, learn from, and help each other achieve business goals.[2]

Sometimes these groups are referred to as "knowledge communities" or "learning communities," but for the most part, they are synonymous terms. Etienne Wenger, a thought leader in this area, notes that most communities serve four key functions:[3]

- **They are nodes for the exchange and interpretation of information.** Because members have a shared understanding, they know what is relevant to communicate and how to present information in useful ways. As a consequence, a community of practice that spreads throughout an organization is an ideal channel for moving information, such as best practices, tips, or feedback, across organizational boundaries.
- **They can retain knowledge in "living" ways, unlike a database or a manual.** Even when they routinize certain tasks and processes, they can do so in a manner that responds to local circumstances and thus is useful to practitioners. Communities of practice preserve the tacit aspects of knowledge that formal systems cannot capture. For this reason, they are ideal for initiating newcomers into a practice.

- **They can steward competencies to keep the organization at the cutting edge.** Members of these groups discuss novel ideas, work together on problems, and keep up with developments inside and outside a firm. When a community commits to being on the forefront of a field, members distribute responsibility for keeping up with or pushing new developments. This collaborative inquiry makes membership valuable because people invest their professional identities in being part of a dynamic, forward-looking community.

- **They provide homes for identities.** They are not as temporary as teams and, unlike business units, are organized around what matters to their members. Identity is important because in a sea of information, it helps sort out what to pay attention to, what to participate in, and what to stay away from. Having a sense of identity is a crucial aspect of learning in organizations and characterizes the smart enterprise. If companies want to benefit from people's creativity, they must support communities as a way to help them develop their identities.

> Line managers must make sure that people are able to participate in the right communities of practice so they sustain the expertise they need to contribute to projects. Knowledge managers must go beyond creating informational repositories that take knowledge to be a "thing," toward supporting the whole social and technical ecology in which knowledge is retained and created. Training departments must move the focus from training initiatives that extract knowledge out of practice to learning initiatives that leverage the learning potential inherent in practice.
>
> —*Etienne Wenger*[4]

Vertical and Horizontal Communities

Communities can be organized vertically, the way people are organized in a business, or horizontally, spanning departmental bound-

aries. Vertical communities are more common, generally representing an organizational structure, usually based on reporting relationships. Organizational charts are reasonable illustrations of a vertical
community structure. Business units and departments are all vertical communities. Each member of the community has a specific role
to play in supporting the larger group. Dialogue will likely center on
achieving the specific short- and long-term goals of the group. Software developers, for example, are members of an application development department, which is one of many departments in the IT
organization, which itself is one of the major business units of a
company.

Horizontal communities are relationships between people with
similar interests and needs, independent of reporting relationships.
Corporate executives, representing all parts of the business, can be
grouped into a horizontal "executive" community. There can be a
community of administrative assistants, technical specialists, or
project managers, for example. Horizontal communities serve to
provide opportunities for professional affiliation and development.
Conversations generally focus on knowledge sharing. This is not to
say that vertical communities don't learn as well; it's just that learning is the primary force behind horizontal communities. It is what
makes them so interesting and so potentially powerful in the smart
enterprise.

It is possible, and increasingly likely, that people will belong to
more than one community—both vertical and horizontal. Software
developers are in the vertical IT community, but individual specialties, like Java or Linux, offer horizontal community opportunities as well. Branch managers are part of a vertical sales community
that focuses on revenue and productivity measures, but they may
also be part of a horizontal middle manager or supervisor community that focuses on coaching and motivating issues.

The dynamics of communities can be quite robust. Community
membership can be short or long term, and the community itself
can be temporary or permanent. Individuals can join a community
based on a short-term work assignment and then leave when the

assignment is over. Other communities might have longer-term membership. Chemists in the pharmaceutical industry, for example, are likely to be lifelong members of horizontal scientific communities of their peers both inside and outside the company (universities, professional associations). Here is where they learn about new advances in their field and in the knowledge domains of chemistry and pharmacology. They are also likely to be part of vertical corporate departments, like R&D or product development. Here, they learn about specific business and project activities related to their role. There may also be special communities set up for specific reasons, for example, an experiment or clinical trial. When the activity is done, the community may disband or take on another similar role. The new knowledge generated from the temporary community, be it a new insight into a chemical compound or a new way to manage a project budget, is taken with members back to their other communities. That is how learning and knowledge spreads in the business and how best practices are born.

Four Successful Communities

Despite the relative newness of the concept on communities of practice, they have been flourishing in organizations for some time. Here are four brief examples.

PlatoonLeader.army.mil and CompanyCommand.com! These two online communities, available only to active and retired military personnel, began as grassroots efforts to help soldiers and officers in the field with practical advice and knowledge sharing that was often ignored or too late in coming through formal military communications channels. Everything from the type of candy that won't melt in the desert to how to armor a truck was included. Almost all of this information comes from online conversations between soldiers who, as they say, have "been there, done that." These sites were so popular and effective that they now receive official support from the military.[5]

Amazing things happen when committed leaders in a profession connect, share what they are learning, and spur each other on to become better and better.

—Home page, CompanyCommand.com

Xerox's Eureka! Repeat customer visits and added service costs became an unfortunate reality when Xerox service technicians began to encounter unique technical problems at customer sites that were not addressed in online technical manuals or taught in training. Over time, individual technicians developed solutions to individual problems through trial and error. The challenge was communicating these tips and fixes to the entire technical workforce. The company developed Eureka! a collection of online communities that allowed technicians to share insights and ideas worldwide, in near real time. In addition to accessing information, technicians can contribute new knowledge, which is then validated, managed, and distributed to all.

ExxonMobil's BestNets. When technical problems crop up in refineries or other facilities around the world, ExxonMobil often had to send specialists to the site to help solve the problem. More important, there was no way to capture and reuse the experience. With BestNets, a community of practice network that allows engineering employees to share knowledge, collaborate on problems remotely, and capture best practices, business and technical challenges are addressed far faster and at less cost, and the solutions that come out of each incident can be preserved.

St. Paul Companies' Knowledge Exchange. In 2001, KM was an initiative owned by St. Paul Companies' corporate university. But after cost cutting dramatically reduced the size and role of this standalone training function, KM became an initiative on its own. As the number of traditional training programs declined, the company's

Knowledge Exchange, featuring multiple business virtual communities, dramatically grew in size to fill this gap, and it quickly became one of the most important ways people share information and collaborate on work projects. Learning continues, just in a different and more efficient way.[6]

Critical Success Factors

Sharing knowledge is an unnatural act. You can't just stand up and say, "Thou shalt share knowledge"—it won't work.

—Hubert Saint-Onge, collaboration guru and principal, Saintonge Alliance[7]

More communities fail than succeed. They don't get the participation that was expected or don't achieve the results for which they were formed. Getting people to collaborate is problematic, like the proverbial chicken and egg. The community must offer sufficient value for members to become engaged, yet people must participate in order to create value. You have to find a way to get to critical mass, after which the community takes on a life of its own. People must be motivated to contribute not just their knowledge but their time as well. It is the sharing of information, not simply its publication, that matters. If all anyone did was put their content online, you might have the beginnings of a good knowledge repository, but you would not have a successful community.

For communities to succeed, that is, for members to value their participation and for the community to be valued by the organization, it is important to focus on ten critical success factors.

Peer Identification. Group members by common interest or need. Make sure that each member sees the other members as kindred spirits because of their shared knowledge, role, or task ahead. This enhances the bond members need to feel with each other to begin sharing and learning. You want members to feel that the people they interact with in the community are like them.

This doesn't mean that all participants are alike. Some are deeply involved as content contributors, individually or in groups; facilitators or moderators, who may not necessarily add content but serve to keep the community functioning and vital; and observers, who may participate quietly but get value out of the content and dialogue that is taking place.

Content Value. Make sure the content and conversations inside the community are valuable. Experts do not want to spend all their time with novices, and novices will get little value trying to keep up with experts. Fresh, relevant, and authentic content, at the right level of detail, focused on the needs of members, will keep them coming back.

Incentives. Encourage members to participate, especially on the contributions side. Make it rewarding for them to share what they know. This very much goes to the culture of the organization. When knowledge sharing is not valued, it is likely that community participation isn't either. When potential members ask, "Why should I get involved?" or "What's in it for me?" be sure you have a strong and convincing answer.

No Pain. Remove punishment and risk to participation. No one will spend time in a community if it takes away from their work (without value) or is too difficult to be worth it (for example, making access to or navigation around the community too time-consuming). If members are penalized for spending time in a community, especially if they feel it merely adds to their already heavy workload, they will check out and never return.

Make It Special. While many communities are open to all, sometimes it will be important to make entry and membership something that has to be earned or approved. This creates a sense of exclusiveness that can be a badge of honor. This is not elitism; rather, it is recognition to those in a community, and to those outside, that membership is unique. Not everyone can join.

Community Leadership. Communities don't run themselves, and although it might be nice to think that the membership can collectively run things, it is likely that good and frequent facilitation will be necessary to keep the community vibrant. This is especially true for large communities. Sometimes facilitators can come from outside the group, and at other times, they can be chosen from the member ranks. Instructors who are familiar with the knowledge domain of the community or subject matter experts who have good communications skills often make excellent facilitators.

Take care when you select facilitators; you want them not just to lead the discussion but to motivate the participants as well. Malcolm Gladwell's principles are particularly applicable to forming, facilitating, and sustaining successful communities.[8] For example, the three types of people who spread messages—"salespeople" (great persuaders), "mavens" (great teachers), and "connectors" (great networkers)—probably have the characteristics you would look for in people you would recruit for active participation and facilitation in a community.

Support from the Top. Communities are more likely to flourish when there is real leadership support. Executives who say they support the activities of a community, and the time commitment required of its members, may be a good start, but more active participation by the executive, as well as financial support, is better. The best type of support is when organizational leaders model collaborative behaviors as a foundation of how they run their own shop.

No "Big Brother." Nothing will kill a community faster than using it for ulterior motives. Spying on community activity or other inappropriate actions will negate all the benefits you might have received and will quickly turn all of these ten success factors into negatives. There is a fine line here; certainly effective management oversight of communities is warranted, but not so much as to give the perception of extraordinary monitoring.

The Right Environment. Avoiding "big brother" activities is the right start, but you must go further. A culture of trust for knowledge sharing is not built overnight. People need to feel that community participation is a positive activity. There are many techniques that can be used to build the learning and knowledge-sharing culture that is necessary for community success (this is explored in more detail in Chapter Eight).

Tools. Naturally the right tools and technology are essential. These are discussed in more depth later in this chapter.

> Communities tap the power of the many.
> —*Rosabeth Moss Kanter, Harvard Business School*[9]

Sun Microsystems' Java Developers Community (www.java.sun.com) is a good example of a commercial online community. It offers documentation, peer collaboration and support, code samples, tutorials, and "code camps" among other things. Forums are monitored by a couple of Java experts who seem to step up and get into the conversation only if and when it is heading down the wrong path, incorrect information is being shared, or no one is replying to a cry for help. Several efforts to duplicate a Java community inside other companies have failed because Java developers rely so much on this resource, a true test of how well it meets its constituents' needs.

Unilever Uses Online
Communities to Develop Leaders

A lot rides on corporate leadership programs. The immediate and long-term success of a business depends on creating the next tier of leadership talent. Nobody can be trained to be a leader. Rather, leadership development requires profound changes in core personal behavior and belief systems. Potential leaders must be challenged and molded through intense real-life, hands-on experiences. Given that, it seems almost counterintuitive to make an online community the backbone of an innovative leadership development program. It is much safer to go with the perfunctory team exercise of building a rope bridge or rappelling a rock wall. Right?

Not for Unilever, a worldwide enterprise of over a quarter million employees and maker of famous global consumer brands like Dove, Lipton, and Slim-Fast. To fulfill its growth strategy, Unilever requires decisive leaders to fight constant and ever fiercer competitive battles every day.

To meet these challenges, Unilever realized it was time to overhaul its traditional leadership program, Previously, new directors or vice presidents were enrolled in a two-week classroom course consisting of the traditional fare of case studies, professors, and guest speakers in a highly academic experience. Although the program presented excellent content and was well regarded, its participants were unable to demonstrate the type of sustainable leadership behaviors that Unilever required. Yet repurposing leadership content was the lesser of the challenges faced.

The greatest challenge was changing the core beliefs of new leaders. Having spent most of their careers in the company, these individuals rose in a corporate culture that had admittedly become inward looking, bureaucratic, and slow. According to David Coleman, global learning manager, many of these new leaders "had very little belief that this could change, and as a result felt personally powerless in attempting to do so." But what Unilever needed in its next generation of leaders was take-charge individuals who showed the highest degree of commitment and authenticity.

A new leadership program was born. Leaders into Action (LIA) consisted of two alternating virtual and residential sessions. The virtual sessions were conducted through an online community provided by Communispace, a Watertown, Massachusetts–based company. LIA began with a six-week virtual session, facilitated by an online community to amplify the impact of the learning experience.

Online communities provide an essential infrastructure for participants and coaches to interact, conveniently accessible at any time and any place. Communal sharing motivates participants to dig deeper into themselves, yet at the same time provides private space and pace. Coleman described the phenomenon of positive peer pressure: "The participant is thinking, 'Hey, that person shared, so I guess I can share a little more.'" He believes that the virtual environment's unique combination of individual isolation plus knowledge sharing accelerates the learning process, likening it to "a penny dropped into a pool: the ripple effect is quite amazing. Without the online community, knowledge doesn't have the chance to ripple."

Individualized coaching is a vital element. The participants checked in with coaches during weekly telephone calls about a wide range of topics, and often the most important thing a coach did was just listen. These calls built trust and relationships, an essential element in communities. Says Andrew Waller, head of global leadership development, an LIA alum and coach, "Without coaching, the online portion wouldn't have succeeded. You have to find a way over the personal hurdles to participation."

The coaches had their own exclusive space within the LIA online community where they shared perceptions and insights from their coaching sessions. This enabled seamless rotation of coaches among participants, which occurred in the first module of the program. These practices, plus the ability to access all of the participants' online assignments, allowed the coaches a comprehensive picture of the entire group and enabled expert one-on-one coaching based on individual needs.

After the initial six-week virtual session concludes, participants met for the first residential session. For many, it was the first time they actually laid eyes on each other, although as Coleman points out, they already knew each other quite well. Recognizing colleagues from their photographs, they "made a beeline to people they had gotten to know online. It accelerated the group dynamic process hugely." LIA program members had already forged critically important professional relationships by the time the residential program began at a level rarely accomplished after a week or more in the traditional program. Not surprisingly, these relationships extended long after the LIA program concluded. This is one of the most important benefits of learning communities: they can become valuable business communities. If fact, introducing communities in a learning situation may be one of the best ways to instill community thinking and collaborative behavior in employees at all levels. It can truly be culture changing.

During a second twelve- to fourteen-week virtual session, dedicated to organizing a virtual small-team project, participants had already mastered the skill of online interaction, made the personal commitment to change, and forged important relationships. Now it was time to leverage this experience in action learning. Virtual teams of about six members formed around a key business objective like expanding a brand, and the entire group of about twenty-five people formed around a community project, in one case, extending a small hospital building in Brazil.

The results were truly amazing for both the business and the community. One team took a new product concept and had it on the shelf in eight weeks, an outstanding achievement compared with the usual product development cycle. In the case of the Brazilian hospital, the group accomplished this project, including raising the funds and using their personal influence to secure supplies and services, in just twelve weeks. These are dramatic results from individuals who had felt powerless just months before. In fact, 70 percent claim to have significantly raised the impact of performance in their professional and personal lives.

An online community can be an essential ingredient of a broad-based learning and performance architecture. Unilever's success demonstrates that such communities, combined with strong coaching and a focus on real-life problem solving, can produce truly breakthrough results and increase the collaborative way people learn and work going forward. Incorporating communities into learning is essential, according to Coleman, because, "e-learning needs support; it doesn't look after itself."

Knowledge Networks

> No man is wise enough by himself.
> —*Titus Maccius Plautus (254 B.C.E.–184 B.C.E.)*

Like communities, knowledge networks bring people together virtually. However, knowledge networks are much more informal. Everyone maintains some form of knowledge network: collections of people you call on for information, feedback, problem solving, and other needs. Your e-mail or instant messaging list, your online or personal digital assistant (PDA) telephone directory, and even the stack of business cards on your desk or the sticky notes on your wall represent networks of people and resources you call on on a regular and not-so-regular basis. Knowledge networks can be vertical, horizontal, or a combination of the two, and are enhanced by the increasing ability of people to connect with each other regardless of where they are, what they are doing, or the device they are using (computer, telephone, PDA). Over time, as people build their own personal networks, they tend to increasingly value and protect them; they are often a source of pride and a true enabler of higher performance. It is not uncommon to hear people say something like, "Whenever I need something, I call on my network," or "When I have an idea, I use my network to get feedback I can trust."

Knowledge networks grow organically, from the ground up, are usually based on the needs of individuals, and are formed through individual relationships. Communities need much more cultivation and are more goal or process oriented. Technology can be the fertilizer for both.

Collaboration Technologies

Managing formal communities of practice or informal knowledge networks would be much more challenging without technology. The increasingly virtual and global workplace makes getting together face-to-face increasingly difficult. Collaboration technologies allow people to participate asynchronously, contributing to the group at a time of their own choosing and, when warranted, synchronously, in virtual teleconferences or Web conferences. Many of the technological tools contribute another important aspect of community: the capturing and archiving of the work of the group in discussions, documents, work products, and other ways.

> Sharing knowledge may seem to be a touchy-feely goal, but not doing so can result in lost product development time, unnecessary consulting engagements, ineffective project teams or misdirected marketing campaigns.
>
> —*Sarah L. Roberts-Witt*[10]

Collaboration technologies, sometimes referred to as groupware, run the gamut, from specialized tools like Web conferencing, to general everyday tools such as e-mail. Many of these tools also come under the banner of "social software," which enables people to organize themselves into a network based on their preferences.[11] It embodies technology that builds connections between people and a purpose for those connections that has value; both are necessary and should not be confused. The purpose of social software is to enable a dynamic exchange of ideas, knowledge, and viewpoints among participants, making their collective wisdom greater than individual wisdom. Here are six common technologies that can be used to support collaboration:

- **E-mail.** Billions of unique knowledge assets are transported over e-mail every day, but as a collaboration tool, e-mail is lacking. Using multiple e-mails to string a conversation together is often cumbersome. In addition, although many people use e-mail files as places to store documents, the danger is often too great that critical files can be misplaced, lost, or deleted.
- **Instant messaging.** This is a much more real-time approach to electronic conversations. However, too much instant messaging can quickly overwhelm, if not annoy, users. Also, IM conversations normally cannot be saved without extra effort.
- **Discussion threads and chatrooms.** These work for seeing the history and relationships between contributions, and the conversations are storable and searchable. However, it is often difficult to get people to use these tools without considerable motivational efforts and facilitation.
- **Web conferencing.** This refers to real-time sharing of applications and presentations over the Web. Scheduling and technological barriers can get in the way of spontaneous usage.
- **Knowledge network building tools.** These are new technologies that try to find affinities among people by looking at the work they do. They try to answer the question, "Who else is working on the same things I am?" One concern about this approach is that some form of work surveillance or monitoring may be needed to identify network members.
- **Weblogs (or "blogs").** Weblogs allow almost anyone to "author" and instantly publish information, ideas, suggestions, and other content for all to read and comment. The templated format allows knowledge creation without any knowledge of HTML or other Web publishing languages and tools. It tends to democratize knowledge sharing and collaboration, but can be difficult to weed

through to get at the best "knowledge nuggets."[12] A variation of a weblog called a *wiki* allows multiple authors to collaborate in the creation of a Web site, including adding and modifying content, and the actual organization of the site itself.

Additional details on each technology are provided in Appendix C.

Communities don't always function using technology. Local teams often meet in conference rooms or at lunch, for example, and still behave as communities. However, technology can expand community participation for many more workers. Ideally, a blend of technical and nontechnical approaches to fostering collaboration is usually best.

Finding "Birdman"

Sometimes you have a problem that you can't solve on your own. You've asked the people around you, but you're still stumped. You know the answer is out there somewhere, but you just don't know where. That's the situation Joanna Miller faced.

Joanna is a training specialist at Tufts University near Boston and a member of a team implementing a new online account management tool to support university fundraising. This advanced Web-based system requires new skills and new ways of working for the professionals who use it to raise money for the institution. Because the tool can be used remotely, and knowing that people abhor carrying around big user manuals, Joanna set out to create an online help system geared to the needs of her organization. Certainly training would be offered as the university moved to the new system, but once people were in the field, online support would be critical.

The design of the online help tool—essentially, an integrated KM resource—required that a user open the help system in its own window without any impact on the application itself. Unfortunately, because this particular software uses lots of open windows, the in-house programmer could not make it perform independent of those other windows. Joanna was not willing to accept that what she wanted couldn't be done, so she turned to her research training and a search engine. She needed to find an expert.

Logging on, Joanna entered the search string, "how to open a new browser window." The results were instantaneous. One of the first hits was an online forum on Javascript issues that appeared to be precisely what she needed. Upon searching the forum, she found one member, "Birdman," who seemed to have the right expertise. She posted her question and received a response within an hour. At first, Birdman requested several lines of code and then quickly provided a solution that the programmer was able to implement without problems.

Of course, not all Web queries are so successful, but more and more are proving fruitful all the time. Even so, Joanna had to overcome some concerns before she was willing to rely on Birdman's help. First, of course, Birdman was a stranger and was not willing to reveal his true identity. Joanna determined that this wasn't an issue, because in examining the history of the forum, Birdman seemed to have a strong and positive reputation as an expert. This trust factor is less sophisticated, but not unlike similar approaches eBay uses to build buyer confidence. Second, she had to overcome her own uncertainty about using the Web in this way. She found the experience similar to making her initial online purchase; it's unnerving at first, but after you submit your credit card information and hit "purchase" and it works, you quickly come to realize that it's easy. And finally, Joanna had to be convinced that accessing knowledge in this way was easier than trying to find it locally. After Birdman solved her problem within a day, she was convinced.

Instead of using the Web just for resources like e-mail, we need to look to it as an enormous repository of wonderful information. As for the credibility of the information you find, I think people who use this resource will quickly learn how to discriminate between high-value knowledge and expertise and junk.

—Joanna Miller, training specialist, Tufts University

Finding Birdman has been an eye-opener for Joanna and her colleagues. They now understand that there are lots of expert resources available to them, even in the somewhat chaotic realm of cyberspace, if they are simply willing to seek them out. Now Joanna is establishing her own online expert forum to help members of her target audience collaborate with and learn from each other. She knows it will take a long time for her online forum to build credibility, but she is confident that her own "Birdmen" will emerge. Together with her online help system, she is well on her way to building a unique learning and performance architecture.

Working with Experts and Expertise

For most of human history, the way people predominantly learned a skill or a craft was through apprenticeship. They would spend years learning from a master and, after meeting the master's criteria for competence, would set out on their own, perhaps becoming masters to new apprentices themselves. Unfortunately, today there are too many knowledge seekers and too few masters. The challenge becomes how to leverage experts and expertise across a large and diverse population of nonexperts.

Although it is possible for experts to place their knowledge in information repositories so that what they know is accessible to large numbers of people (if this weren't the case, there would never be any textbooks), the fact is that the distinguishing feature of true expertise is an expert's ability to size up unique and often unanticipated situations and then provide the appropriate and specific guidance. Experts can be most valuable around knowledge that is not quite firmed up: cutting-edge research, new inventions, or an improved way to accomplish a task, for example. Thus, conversations with experts can often revolve around storytelling or descriptions and approximations of problems and solutions that, with experience and time, get closer and closer to the right answer. Once you get there and the expertise can be easily replicated and codified, access to the actual expert will be less necessary. Experts, more likely than not, have a larger information base to draw on when solving a problem. Once the problem is solved, it is no longer a solution that needs to be generated; rather, it is knowledge that can be shared. It's the difference between sharing an algorithm and creating one or demonstrating a rule and generating a higher-order rule. In other words, that which makes the expert most valuable is knowledge that is least definable. This is the expertise paradox: the more the expert is needed, the less is usually understood about the expertise.

Challenges

Expertise can be extremely valuable, especially when knowledge is changing at a rapid pace or the nature of work is around new and perhaps untested ideas. Experts can validate new ideas, provide sound and unbiased judgment, cut through data overload to get at what's truly important, and point people to additional, reliable knowledge resources. But locating experts and getting access to their expertise, especially when the need to know is urgent, can be daunting.

Expertise is everywhere but often difficult to find. The first thing you must do is identify the real expert. Often, finding the expert in the first place is near impossible. As illustrated in Figure 5.1, as you search the organization for experts, you will have to filter out two types of people: nonexperts and false experts.

When searching for expertise, you will likely come across the vast majority of individuals who are nonexperts. To weed through this group, which will likely be most of the organization, you will need some criteria for separating them out; otherwise, your search will take far too long and end up wasting a lot of people's time. Here, technology can play a role. If you can identify the certified expertise of everyone based on their online profile or bio, you can filter out many individuals who do not match your criteria.

You also have to filter out the false expert (circled in Figure 5.1). These are people who honestly claim expertise but in fact are

Figure 5.1 Finding Real Experts amid Nonexperts and False Experts

lacking bona-fide expert credentials or are not as knowledgeable as they think they are. Here is where the rigor of your certification and selection criteria matter. If you've done a good job, your "false positives" will be fewer, and if the system has some adaptive intelligence, it will learn, over time, how to do a better expert search.

Experts are often thought of as unique specialists who are masters of a particular knowledge domain. But expertise is more abundant than you might think. Help desks and call centers represent a common way organizations provide expertise to workers or customers. Some companies also establish "centers of excellence" that concentrate specific expertise around a technology, function, or product, for example, and then make that expertise available to all.

Peer-to-peer collaboration is often characterized by the sharing of expertise, and many good managers, who are also good coaches, have the ability to share expertise with their teams. This is not always the case, of course; just as often, managers find themselves supervising people in an area where their own knowledge is light. The hope is that they compensate for this by identifying others who bring expertise to the group.

There is an emerging category of software that supports expert identification and interaction. This can be very important in large, complex, and decentralized organizations. New profiling tools allow experts to enter their areas of expertise and other characteristics into a database that can be matched to user queries. Other tools scan work products to see what projects people are involved with and make deductions about their expertise from that. Similar programs scan e-mail messages to try to identify people who might be experts in one or more domains of knowledge. Office hour software allows experts to establish and manage specific times when they are available to answer questions. In many cases, users can subscribe to distribution and alert lists that will automatically let them know when specific information, and the expert who created it, is available. Finally, experts can be identified with the communities of practice they participate in. In many cases, finding experts is simply a matter of joining a community that is focused on the knowledge you are seeking.

Managing Expertise

Even more challenging is getting true experts to devote the time necessary to share their expertise. Chances are that your experts have a full workload and are already responding to requests for help in an informal way. If you make this more formal, without a support or incentive structure, you will get resistance from your experts and frustration from everyone else as they begin to compete, and maybe even fight over, this limited but extremely valuable knowledge resource. In many ways, making experts and their expertise available to all who need them is the most difficult KM challenge. Here are eight approaches that can improve your chances of success.

Reduce the Workload. Often people are willing to fill the expert role, but they honestly do not have the time. When experts are bombarded with questions or requests for advice in addition to their regular workload, they can resent the extra burden they have to carry. If the situation gets too stressful, something will give, and most likely it will be their willingness to share what they know. Over time, their overall work quality will suffer. In worst-case situations, they may quit, and their expertise will be lost to the organization. To avoid this, be sure to build expertise sharing directly into the job description and role. Allow time for true experts to respond to questions and give advice. Make sure they know, and everyone else knows, that this is part of their job

Use the Right Incentives.   In addition to time, you need to add the right incentives to encourage experts to share what they know. But before you do, be sure that you are focusing on real experts rather than nonexperts or false experts. If you don't distinguish the right people, the incentives you use will spread to the wrong people and will lose their meaning. Certainly money, promotional opportunities, and workplace perks can be used, but don't discount incentives around professionalism, like the opportunity to attend professional conferences and mingle with peers across the industry. In some cases, the opportunity to teach more advanced courses or be a guest lecturer in a class is a good professional incentive for an expert. Allowing experts some freedom on what projects they work on can be highly rewarding to them. Make "expert" a career-defining role. Build it into your management or technical leadership career path so that the role is considered a "must-have" developmental experience, and use role models to help people see how it is done. All of these incentives and others will motivate the experts and play to their ego in a positive way. This will encourage them to continue developing and sharing knowledge.

Rotate Your Experts.   If you do a good job of defining the expert's role and then motivating experts to serve in that role, chances are you will find many people wanting to step up to it. Naturally you will want to qualify each person to identify your true experts, but even then, you may have more qualified people than you can use.

Consider rotating your experts so that more people get a chance to serve in the role. Not only will this keep the knowledge fresh, but it will create an increasingly large cadre of people across the business who believe in and practice knowledge sharing.

Manage the Demand. No matter how well you plan, you always have to protect experts from being inundated with requests, especially if many of the inquiries are for the same information. Setting up virtual "office hours" is one way to manage the demand. In addition, give experts the ability to post responses online so that those making future requests for the same knowledge can get it without actually communicating directly with the expert. FAQs (frequently asked questions) are an excellent way to do this. So are publishing short documents and presentations that deal with hot issues. Experts can also develop e-mail lists of people who would benefit from their knowledge and insight and can send content to the list, which will reduce demand later.

Publish Expertise as It Becomes More Stable and Repeatable. Publishing expertise reduces the time demands on your experts, but it does not reduce their importance. By setting up companion knowledge repositories, experts can publish content that is frequently requested or that they believe will be useful to their constituencies and then alert everyone that the content is there. The expert becomes not just a person with the answers, but someone with a wide array of information resources to offer. This is how a small number of experts can support a large number of people. However, care must be taken to ensure that the way the information is posted is up-to-date and easy to find and use. Otherwise the expert can expect even more calls and e-mails than before.

Point to Where the Information Can Be Found. Sometimes the value an expert brings to the table is knowledge of where information can be found. Encourage experts not only to answer questions, but to point people to the sources of information they are seeking so that the next time they need help, they can go right to the source instead of repeatedly asking the expert.

Use Different Knowledge Capture Techniques. Capturing expertise is not easy. You will likely find may situations where experts are unable to organize, let alone publish, their own knowledge. In many cases, the nature of their expertise is such that it would be difficult to get your arms around it. Can your best salesperson, with thirty years of experience, really articulate in explicit terms what makes him or her so good at this work? Can your chief scientist really spell out exactly how to make the next great discovery? Sometimes getting the right knowledge out of an expert requires a long-term plan. Detailed interviews and observations are certainly useful, but even then, you might not get it all. Sometimes having experts tell a story (captured on video) helps, because they can provide anecdotes and insight in their own words. Apprenticing "future experts" to your best people for a period of time is another way to transfer expert knowledge. In any plan to capture expertise, you must always weigh the value of the knowledge with the cost of harvesting it.

Bring in Your Trainers. By definition, your classroom trainers should be subject matter experts. In many ways, a training assignment is a natural career step for your best experts. Similarly, training professionals can often go on to fulfill an expert role. You can use a training assignment as a way to help experts learn to communicate with their constituencies, a skill that will benefit them greatly in the future. This benefit is enhanced as you bring in increasing numbers of experts for rotational training assignments and assign instructors to expert roles after their training assignment is concluded.

Pinging Experts at Accenture with Instant Messaging

Eren Rosenfeld is an expert in performance simulation at Accenture Learning. Throughout her career, people have wanted to learn from her; they've picked her brain for information and advice. In the beginning, she got calls; more recently, she got e-mails. Now it's instant messaging (IM). In a world where e-mail isn't fast enough, people are resorting to IM to get answers to questions, confer with peers, and learn from each other.

At Accenture, IM has become a dominant, albeit informal, learning strategy. Eren has a "buddy list" of experts and team members whom she relies on every day. She has confidence that she can IM anyone on her list for information and know that she'll get an accurate, complete, and quick response. And when she's "pinged" for her expertise, she helps others learn by responding in any number of ways, including:

- Providing the information in a text message
- Sending the requester a link to where the information can be found
- Sending the requester an e-mail, perhaps one she's prepared in advance because she knows she'll get multiple requests
- Suggesting a telephone conversation if she believes the response is too complex for IM

In some ways, Eren has become a personal search engine for those who need her expertise. Over time, she has learned what most people want to know, and she maintains links, documents, and other resources to quickly send that information to requesters.

> The most powerful people in the room are those with the most powerful IM connections—people you can ping for immediate advice and expertise.
>
> —*Eren Rosenfeld, general manager, performance simulation, Accenture*

What Eren says almost never happens is that an IM request for information is returned with a course recommendation. "The whole purpose of IM," says Eren, "is that it is fast. While you aren't going to get the depth of knowledge you would receive in traditional training, you'll get answers to a specific question in real time."

IM has become so popular because it is so easy to use. Unlike discussion groups that require searching, posting, and constant review, which makes them far less used, IM is right there, on the desktop. And the users control whom they "speak" with.

This is not to say that IM is a perfect learning tool. People still need training and experience in order to know what to say in an instant message. IM is great for collaboration, but not for detailed content or long-winded explanations. In addition, people identified as experts, either formally, or informally through the grapevine, can quickly become overtaxed with information requests. For Eren and others, this means protecting and respecting her IM list. It means knowing who is the right person to ping and managing the relationship so that it benefits everyone involved.

IM still has some security concerns, however. Although it is a great collaboration tool, it is not secure from a data-sharing perspective. Thus, another important consideration is the sensitivity and confidentiality of the information being shared. For this reason, at Accenture, files are prohibited from being sent using IM. Employees are also required to use more secure methods in the communication and sharing of information that might be deemed private. In those cases, the policy is to use the telephone or Accenture's internal, and more secure, e-mail system.

As with any other new technology, there is a learning curve to using IM effectively. At first, people spend too much time "talking" on IM. They also tend to use it as e-mail, with messages that are too long and detailed. As users mature, they tend to get it right and use IM for what it's best at: quick chats and instant help.

There are three other important implications of instant messaging. First, people use IM as a "backchat" channel. For example, on a conference call with a customer, salespeople often use IM to communicate with each other while the call is taking place. Although opportunities for abuse exist, with experience, people can use backchats to improve the overall group presentation, respond more quickly to unanticipated developments, and plan next steps before they are suggested. In a sense, such a team is learning from each other as they work, in real time.

Instant messaging can be linked into other online tools, including KM systems. For example, at Accenture, when consultants are working in an online "e-room" document repository, the software shows them all the other people also "in the room" at that moment and allows people to IM one another.

Even more important are the social aspects of IM. As social software, IM helps people, especially those who work at a distance, keep in touch, maintain stronger relationships, and establish peer groups that they can rely on over time.

IM can also be used in support of formal training. For those taking a classroom or an online course, IM can be used to connect them to others who are also taking the course (or those who recently completed the course). Such learning communities can endure far past the end of the training experience and provide added value to the training experience. Today, more than a decade after her first training course at Accenture, Eren still IMs the colleagues she met in her initial class.

Opportunities for Learning and E-Learning

Why should the training function take note of collaboration through communities and networks or of experts and their expertise? What does this mean for learning and e-learning in the smart enterprise?

Most training, even within a curriculum of courses, is primarily event driven. When people come to class, they form a short-lived community with their peers; when they leave the class, the learning community dissolves. Training can do better. It can use courses as a forming ground for longer-term communities. It can make membership in learning communities transcend the classroom. Of course, such communities will have to be managed over the long term, and this represents a new responsibility for the training function. But the benefits of taking the collaborative learning that characterized the class and extending it to the workplace are worth it. These types of communities reinforce learning, helping employees transfer what they have learned to their work, and foster collaborative knowledge networks among practitioners who have taken the same class. As Jay Cross points out, when you get right down to it, learning is the optimization of those networks.[13]

Even more important, communities of practice can be powerful and independent forces for learning. In a flourishing community, where people learn from one another, the work context in which they operate is likely much more closely tied to real, immediate, and emerging learning needs—the kind of situations formal training is hard-pressed to serve because of the lead time necessary to put the course together.

When a community of practice becomes successful and valued, it often becomes an employee's first choice for information. Training becomes a reinforcer of the community rather than the reverse. Where appropriate, peer-to-peer workplace-based learning replaces instructor-led classroom training. The community becomes the class.

Most training is packaged expertise. The early stages of the instructional systems design process usually include interviewing or observing subject matter experts and transforming what they know, or what they can do, into a coherent instructional program designed to transfer that expertise to rank-and-file employees. It is argued that a training course is a very efficient way to impart complex knowledge and skill to large numbers of nonexperts; if it is done right, it provides opportunities for people to practice and test their new capabilities, in addition to receiving the content in an easy-to-understand and easy-to-use format. This is often the case, but there is an increasing realization that if the expertise itself could be made more directly accessible and if experts themselves were more available to respond to questions or solve problems, the learning could be even more efficient. If it were possible to blend classroom or online training, when necessary, with experts and their expertise, when available, the result would be more immediate learning at lower cost.

Collaboration and communities will create great opportunities for new forms of learning in the future. David Grebow hits the key points pretty well:

> We will include the idea of community into the act of learning so that the separate, isolated learner, struggling along in what we today call "self-paced mode," will become a relic. Instructors will morph into facilitators and coaches. Mentors and experts will be available in a variety of ways, outside the course or class, to guide learners through their education. A course will be considered the beginning, not the end.[14]

The technologies of collaboration, in communities or with experts, expand the notion of e-learning. They enable new sources of knowledge, that is, peers and experts, to share what they know in real-time work settings. These technologies can and often should be incorporated directly into training programs. But their real contribution to learning and smart enterprise thinking is in extending the opportunities to share knowledge long after the course is finished or actually replacing the need for some training altogether.

Notes

1. Surowiecki, S. (2004). *The wisdom of crowds*. New York: Doubleday, p. 3.
2. Hessan, D., & Vogt, E. (1999, November). Presentation at TechLearn conference, Orlando, FL.
3. Wenger, E. (1998, June). *Communities of practice: Learning as a social system*. http://www.co-i-l.com/coil/knowledge-garden/cop/lss.shtml.
4. Wenger. (1998).
5. Baum, D. (2005, January 17). Annals of war: Battle lessons. *New Yorker*. www.newyorker.com/printables/fact/050117fa_fact.

6. Thompson, E. J. (2003, March-April). Effective KM in a cost cutting environment. *KM Review*, 6(1), 12–15. Thompson, E. J. (2003, June 4). *Less is more—The St. Paul's knowledge management journey.* Presentation at the 2003 Conference on Knowledge Management and Organizational Learning, sponsored by The Conference Board, New York.

7. Paul, L. (2003, December 1). Why three heads are better than one. *CIO Magazine, 17*(5), 100.

8. Gladwell, M. (2000). *The tipping point: How little things can make a big difference.* New York: Little, Brown.

9. Kanter, R. M. (2001). *Evolve! Succeeding in the digital culture of tomorrow.* Boston: Harvard Business School Press, p. 19.

10. Roberts-Witt, S. L. (2002, March 26). Know thyself. *PC Magazine*, p. 89.

11. Kaplan-Leiserson, E. (2003, December). We-learning: Social software and e-learning. *Learning Circuits.* http://www.learningcircuits.org/2003/dec2003/kaplan.htm.

12. There are several blogs in the e-learning space; the longest-running and most robust comes from Jay Cross at the Internet Time Group, www.internettime.com.

13. Cross, J. (2004, November 17). *The human side of workflow learning.* Presentation at the TechLearn conference, New York.

14. Grebow, D. (2004). Looking back on technology to look forward on collaboration and learning. In M. L. Conner & J. G. Clawson (Eds.), *Creating a learning culture: Strategy, technology and practice.* Cambridge: Cambridge University Press, p. 101.

The Case for Learning Communities

Diane Hessan

When they hear the term *e-learning*, most people naturally think of an online course, designed and developed for an individual whenever and wherever he or she needs new knowledge or skills. In the past decade, there has been a tremendous amount of progress in the e-learning arena, and it clearly *is* better, faster, and cheaper than ever before.

What, then, does the future look like? Although online courses will continue to be more interesting, accessible, and efficient, we are in for incredible breakthroughs in the noncourse arena. Although training professionals focus on formal learning through courses, the statistics still indicate that 95 percent of learning is informal—in other words, not a course.

What do most people do when they don't know how to do something? To access learning informally, they typically use a search engine if they are looking for explicit information. If they are seeking advice or judgment or insight, that is, tacit knowledge, they tend to learn by reaching out to their network of colleagues, often by telephone or e-mail: "Here's my situation. Have you been here before? What did you do? What can I learn from that?" Such networks are in fact personal learning communities, or knowledge networks, and although some companies have been working since the late 1990s to enable communities to work online, people have been learning from their peers, on a fairly spontaneous basis, forever.

We define a learning community as any network of people who are connected because they need to learn something in common. It might be a global network of marketing people who need to share best company practices about how they will work effectively on a worldwide basis, or it might be a group of learning professionals

189

who are connected so that they can reduce duplication of effort, share vendor information, get access to proprietary company content, and so on. These groups tend to be valuable, and the primary rationale for putting them online is to accelerate their learning in the most convenient way. If you are in London, for example, and want to understand whether anyone else in your organization is working on the same project you are or has information you need, e-mail requests tend to be cumbersome. With e-mail, it's difficult to identify who can help; people get an overload of e-mail requests, and if someone does have the information you need, there is not much of a chance that the answer will be sent to everyone else who might need the information. It's also unlikely to be documented, so that the next person who has the same question can easily access the answer. Online communities provide one-stop shopping for groups of people who need to share and capture what they know.

A successful learning community requires both an attention to design details and solid implementation practices. A vibrant learning community has these qualities:

- **Common purpose.** People must have solid reasons for participating in a community in the first place. If an organization tries to create a community based on a past shared experience (a common training program, for example) that community will be short-lived. People will stick with a community only if there is a strong reason to work together going forward.

- **The right members.** People want to learn from others whom they believe are like them and who are on their level. A "sales community" isn't compelling if the experienced salespeople are in the same network as junior people because the issues they want to discuss are often vastly different. People in a community need to feel that there will be reciprocity: they will give information but also get information in return. Having the right profile of members is critical to success.

- **Strong facilitation.** Imagine a meeting where no one is in charge or no one is responsible for making sure that people get what they need. It might still be a meeting, but it would be incredibly unproductive and people would probably not want to hang around. Good facilitation means that someone is accountable for the value and vibrancy of the community, and thus it increases the chances that members will keep coming back.
- **Asynchronous design.** Although it would be fantastic if everyone were available precisely when we need them, today's world doesn't work that way. Synchronous technologies, like chatrooms and Web conferences, are useful but insufficient. Ask a group of people to meet at a certain time, especially across time zones, and you can be sure that half of them won't show up. Being able to communicate when and where people have the bandwidth to participate is crucial. Asynchronous technology also has an added benefit for facilitators: they do not need to be on the spot with a live group. Facilitators can take a breath and provide thoughtful responses that really engage people.
- **Integration with formal training.** One great application of a learning community is to prolong the impact of a formal course. For instance, you can plan to populate a leadership development program with people who can potentially be an ongoing community (people who need to work together well over the long term). You can invite these people into a community a month before the course to meet each other, find the prework, ask questions, handle logistics, and maybe even go through a few exercises. After the course is over, you can continue learning online through discussions of on-the-job experiences, additional exercises, new readings, chatting with the instructor, and so on.

Communities are truly organic entities; when they are nurtured, they can be a tremendous way to capture the collective wisdom of an organization and make it easy for companies to operate in an accelerated and agile way. Communities continue to evolve and have great value beyond traditional learning solutions. Right now, Communispace is intensely engaged in helping clients create communities of customers; the idea that companies can build their customer relationships through increased interaction and learning is compelling not just to learning professionals but to marketing executives as well. These lessons learned are not lost on other business leaders. As organizations become increasingly decentralized and global, communities, and the technologies that make them work online, can create a collaborative culture as if everyone was right next door.

◆   ◆   ◆

Diane Hessan is CEO of Communispace, a provider of Web-based software and services that help companies leverage the power of online communities (dhessan@communispace.com).

6

Learning and Performance in the Context of Work

When those who benefit [from technology] are
not those who do the work, then the technology
is likely to fail, or at least be subverted.
                                    —*Grudin's Law*[1]

Ultimately the hallmark of a smart enterprise is to make learning and work so indistinguishable from one another, so mutually beneficial, that learning becomes work and work becomes learning. This is a far cry from most of today's training environments, where the separation of work and learning often creates conflicting demands on people's time, priorities, and resources.

New advances in technology have contributed tremendously to workforce productivity. From the typewriter to the computer, from specialized publishing services to personal publishing software, from "snail mail" to e-mail, from paper calendars and rolodexes to personal digital assistants, from memos to instant messaging, and from individual desktop applications to enterprise networks, technology has changed the very nature of work. This emerging technological workplace environment creates new and abundant opportunities for integrated learning and performance solutions.

This chapter moves from unique but separate learning and performance solutions to solutions that are so infused directly in work processes that they often become transparent. It focuses on performance support, which provides assistance to people directly in the performance of a task or job; performance-centered design, which places—appropriately—performance goals ahead of learning goals; and finally on the seamless integration of learning and work.

Electronic Performance Support

> Performance support enables people who don't know what they are doing . . . to do it as if they did.
>
> —Gloria Gery, pioneer in electronic performance support[2]

Not too many people can track their investments or their personal budget on their own. They'll try and perhaps get parts of it done, but there is always room for doubt and error. Are the calculations right? Are there any mistakes? Is anything missing? Enter Quicken and other similar products that support personal financial management and planning. Now, the complexities of the process are simplified, the math is performed automatically, and the user is coached around possible scenarios and alternatives. The result is better-prepared investors with more realistic personal budgets and a better handle on their financial situation.

Not too long ago, it was impossible to book your own airline reservation, let alone a hotel and rental car. The schedules and pricing were too confusing, there was no way to process the documentation, and the entire effort was full of guesswork and uncertainty. Today the majority of travelers book online, so much so that much of the consumer travel agent industry has collapsed.

Want to know how your business is doing? You could ask around, or you can gather innumerable reports with massive amounts of data that you can weed through to try to get a picture of what's actually occurring in your business. Or you can develop a more intuitive dashboard that automatically pulls together key information from a variety of sources and packages it in a way that enables you to make more immediate and reliable business decisions.

What does each of these three scenarios have in common? They are all examples of performance support. More specifically, they are all examples of *electronic* performance support systems (EPSS). Where performance support was once manifested primarily in paper-based job aids, it is increasingly electronic, with software development and performance-centered design (discussed later in this chapter) as the overarching methodologies for building these products. In this chapter, the focus is on technology-based software solutions.[3]

Whereas the goal of training is to support learning, that is, impart new skills and knowledge for the end purpose of improving performance, the goal of a performance support solution is to guide and improve performance directly. With performance support, the desired outcome is performance. Any learning that may (and often does) take place becomes a secondary or, more precisely, incidental dividend of performance.

EPSS uses software to assist people in achieving a level of performance they would not otherwise be able to achieve. It reflects the context of what is to be done—monitor investments, make an airline reservation, or track business results—rather than just providing interesting and related content. Building performance support solutions requires a deep understanding of what people have to do or accomplish, that is, the performance, and the processes they need to go through to get there.

Categories of Performance Support

Gloria Gery breaks performance support into three categories:[4]

- **External support,** primarily stand-alone, requiring the user to break from the work in order to learn or access the support. A printed user manual is a good example. It supports job performance but is not actually part of the job routine.

- **Extrinsic support,** available within the performance system, but still requiring the user to break from the work task in order to obtain it. Most knowledge management and "help" resources fall into this category. This is more efficient than external support and is often more context based. That is, it is more likely to "understand" where you are in a work process and provide help and other resources directly related to what you are currently doing.

- **Intrinsic support,** completely embedded within the performance system, provides the needed support as part of the work process itself. Software "wizards" are good examples. Here, the support and the work coincide: you are being coached and supported in the accomplishment of your task while you are actually doing it.

Today most support is either external or extrinsic. In many cases, this type of support works well, is cost-effective, and is easy to implement. But the closer you get to truly transforming the work people do (making it easier and them more productive), the more you will want to investigate intrinsic support. This means working with system and work process developers proactively, and much, much earlier, as part of the design team. (This is discussed in more detail later in this chapter.)

Benefits of Performance Support

Performance support represents an additional expansion of the learning and performance architecture to a point where learning, while beneficial, may be a secondary goal. In the performance support world, getting the job done is what matters; internalizing the why's and how's are less important.

Why is this so valuable? Here are five key benefits of performance support.

Makes Work Simpler.   Performance support can take the complexity out of work processes and tools. It can reduce the level of skill required to perform a task. Salespeople, for example, can use a performance support tool to prepare a proposal for a client that suggests different types of proven pitches, gathered from past successful efforts and placed in a repository for easy downloading. Handheld devices that can receive medical information in the field, at accident scenes or natural disasters, for example, provide up-to-date support and step-by-step emergency procedures to already highly trained rescue workers. This enables them to perform faster and more effectively.

Configurable.   Users can format an EPSS to their own needs. They can use it for support in areas where they may be weak and bypass parts of the tool in areas where they are already competent. The ability to personalize your own help menu is a good example of this. For bigger service areas, such as technical support, help desk personnel can configure their technical support systems to provide themselves with information related to solving unfamiliar problems, and they can make sure the system doesn't get in their way when they are working on well-known or routine solutions.

Provides High Scalability.   As software, electronic performance support can be quickly rolled out to a few people or to thousands. Using the Web and increasingly fast wired and wireless networks, updates in both content and features can be distributed quickly and securely. For example, an IT organization can try out a new desktop application in one part of a company and when all is ready and the solution has proven itself, they can deploy it across the business with relatively minimal additional effort.

Fosters Performance Consistency and Reliability—to a Point. Performance support can reduce variability in the way people perform work tasks, which can be especially critical in technical or high-risk areas. New computerized tools that help auto mechanics (engine diagnostics), service technicians (troubleshooting tools), and pilots (automatic safety warning systems) improve their performance do not replace judgment or decision making. Rather, they improve the quality and reliability of the data on which those judgments and decisions are made (and may even suggest a recommended path to follow). The increasingly computerized operating room, for example, provides much more information and support to surgeons, improving the likelihood of a successful procedure, but the medical decisions are still left to the doctors.

Allows the Nonexpert to Perform Closer to the Level of Experts. This may be the most important benefit of performance support: allowing individuals to perform with similar speed and limited error rates as if they were more proficient than they actually are. In the military, no matter how much training soldiers get, it is a wonder that they can operate some of the world's most complex technology. Training can go only so far; the complex technologies must be made simpler to use in the field. So almost all high-tech weapons systems include sophisticated performance support tools and interfaces to guide the soldier. The systems are designed so that they enhance the competence of the soldier beyond the level of his or her training.

Performance Support and Learning

Increasingly, EPSS solutions are products of IT departments or even business units that invent their own new ways to approach their work. What should be clear to learning professionals is that EPSS, by focusing directly on the work or task to be done, mitigates the need for some training (and learning). In other words, learning may be a by-product of performance support, but it is not its goal. Turbo-Tax does not care if the user learns how to complete a tax return; it cares only that the user can do it successfully. If, over time, the user gains a better understanding of the intricacies of tax filing, that's a bonus. The factory worker who is doing quality control checks on a finished product may use a computer to check tolerances and other measurements essential to product quality. The fact that the worker does not know the math involved in the calculations is immaterial from a performance perspective.

There is sometimes confusion between knowledge management and performance support. In some ways, they are two sides of the same coin. Knowledge management solutions focus on making access to information, in all its forms and from all its sources, faster, easier, and more reliable. Performance support solutions focus on making specific work tasks faster, easier, and more reliable. It is not uncommon to see these two approaches combined in ways that enable information to be provided to workers precisely when they need it, and in the quantity and depth they need it, with the least interruption in actual work activities in order to get it.

When AT&T was a much larger global company, it invested tremendous resources into training. To understand the impact of this investment, extra effort was put into evaluation and testing. When a small group of learning experts wanted to find the best way to support training test developers in the field, they had three choices: classroom training, computer-based training (CBT), or a how-to manual or process guide. The group chose a new path, the Training Test Consultant, a performance support software package that combined CBT, a complete reference guide to test development and administration, and a set of tools designed to help test developers improve their products. What was unique about this was that the courseware, information repository, and online performance support tools were linked; no matter which part of the system a user was in, he or she could always access relevant content from the other parts. This made the product flexible for a wide array of users who had different levels of expertise at the start, and it provided a common, and inexpensive, approach to distributing test development knowledge and expertise across the company. By synchronizing so many different learning tools, the whole of the Training Test Consultant was more useful than its individual components. Interestingly, the CBT part of the tool turned out to be the least valued; over time, users gravitated more to the support components that helped them "do" rather than the training component that helped them "learn." The CBT part got them started, but the knowledge management and performance support parts sustained them.

Here's another example, suggested by Allison Rossett.[5] Since ancient times, maps have been essential in getting from one place to another without getting lost. Early maps were inaccurate, so knowledge of celestial navigation and the ability to use a compass helped. Later, maps came with legends and other job aids to make using them easier. Going a step further, the Auto Club created "TripTiks," customized maps and directions that travelers could follow without having to locate the road on larger, more generalized maps. This concept was taken a huge step further when Web-based mapping software, like MapQuest, came on the scene: all you have to do is input your departure and destination locations, and customized directions (sometimes not as usable as desired) became instantly available. Now these very popular tools are being challenged by GPS navigation systems that not only provide a personalized map but talk the driver through the trip in real time.

What do maps have to do with learning and performance support? The earliest explorers had to apprentice for years before they were qualified to use maps and other navigation aids to lead an expedition; the learning curve was enormous. Although that curve is drastically reduced today, even modern maps require some map reading skill. With TripTiks and MapQuest, and now with GPS navigations systems, far less map knowledge is needed. In fact, in some voice-aided GPS systems, actual maps are optional. In each case, as support for performance improved, results also improved: fewer people get lost, and travel is more reliable and efficient. The amount of map knowledge needed to be successful has been significantly reduced, but as in most other situations, old knowledge is replaced with new knowledge; you don't have to know much about maps, but you now have to be able to refresh your mapping software to keep it up-to-date, so the system won't guide you to a destination that no longer exists. Still, the knowledge required to find your way from here to there certainly has changed, from "how to navigate with a map" to "how to simply follow directions." This is the power that performance support brings to the learning equation. Think of all the potential that exists in your organization to improve performance by simply making the performance easier to accomplish, and thereby changing the entire learning dynamic.

Critical Success Factors for Performance Support

Building successful performance support solutions is challenging, especially if you don't think performance support is part of a learning strategy. So buying into the performance support paradigm is the first critical success factor. You will not be very effective in building performance support solutions if you can't focus on the performance outcome. To be successful here, you must let go of the belief that learning is always the end goal or is always essential in achieving performance. This may take time, but once you begin to think this way, you will start seeing the real potential that performance support brings to the table.

Another success factor is the recognition that building electronic performance support tools is primarily software development, not instructional development, and the role of software developers takes precedence over the role of instructional designers. Beyond software developers, your team should include usability experts who are skilled at testing software with actual users and understanding how it can be improved and made easier to use in the context of work. This testing strategy, probably using multiple prototypes, is critical in enabling you to discover flaws and improvement opportunities early on, when the fix is not just less costly but actually doable (before the software is too far along in its development to be deconstructed). Furthermore, your team will have a much greater chance of success if those who will use the tool—workers, managers, and even organizational leaders—are involved in its development from the start.

If you are about to introduce new processes or technologies into the workplace and want to support them with EPSS, you're too late.

One of the most critical success factors for performance support is to design the support directly into the new process. More than training, knowledge management, or any other intervention, getting performance support issues on the table early in the design of any new workplace process or technology is vital. If you wait until after all the investment of people, time, and money is spent and the process or technology is deployed, and then you try to incorporate performance support, the best you can probably hope for is to bolt it on to the application in a way that will be far less effective, and, in some cases, more annoying to users, than it is valuable.

The final and most important success factor for performance support is to make sure that the resulting tool actually enhances work, makes it easier, and contributes to productivity. That's what performance-centered design is all about.

Performance-Centered Design

> When designers have the point of view of the performer situated in a real work context, success is inevitable. If the point of view does not closely match the situation, usability and performance problems are inevitable.
>
> —*Gloria Gery*[6]

Coupled tightly with the concept of performance support is performance-centered design, an approach to developing performance support, and other learning solutions, where, once again, accomplishing tasks is the primary focus and learning is a secondary (albeit important) consequence of doing. Its focus is on designing an environment with explicit representations of the business process being supported by the work (for example, sales, customer care), integrating the software that supports the process in a natural way, providing just enough content needed to execute the tasks when it is needed (what the worker must know), and arranging other performance-enabling artifacts appropriately in the environment (the tools, resources, references, and decision-supporting materials). In addition, human factors—preferences regarding the complete user experience—are explicitly addressed and come to the forefront in performance-centered design.

A good example of performance-centered design might be the manual you received with your new video recorder or, better, a device like an iPod where the interface is so natural with regard to matching the task that no manual is required. A performance-centered approach would organize the interface or content around the specific tasks you do: hook it up, record a show, play back a show, and select and play music instead of listing the product's features in alphabetical order or the order in which the controls appear on the front of the unit, or, worse, just talking about what the recorder does rather than how to use it. Unfortunately, as most people can attest, too many manuals, guides, and other procedural documents were written by well-meaning experts and never tested with typical users. Still worse, the products themselves were designed so poorly that a detailed manual to compensate for the poor design is required.

Here's a great example from a business context, supplied by Gary Dickelman, which represents a usability problem that occurs far too often.[7] In the HR database of one enterprise resource planning system, in order to change the marital status of an employee, a user has to update sixteen data fields across seven different screens. The problem is compounded because the user has to know, in advance, which records to open, which fields and screens are relevant and mandatory, and what to do with them. There is no explicit support for this business process. All this contributes to making the change in marital status much more difficult than it needs to be.

Dickelman suggests that a performance-centered approach would have alleviated these problems. When confronted with such issues, he suggests a number of ways to increase performance in the absence of direct manipulation of the original software (which is seldom possible or practical). An alternative front end could allow the user to focus on only the data fields required of the process, perhaps on a single screen or window, and then populate all the screens automatically, without the user's having to retrieve them or even know where those screens are. Alternatively, an active, embedded guide could be used to prompt the performer and monitor performance as he or she moves through the updating process. This ensures more efficient completion of the task with far fewer errors, all without the need to train or learn in advance of doing. Even a contextually placed simulation that walks the worker through the process can be useful. Each of these solutions is possible today without the need to modify the core computer code, without the need to ask permission of the vendor or the IT support organization, and without extraordinary technical skills.

Performance-centered design transforms the notion of a passive help system to a task- and process-enabling system. It is what enables performers to encounter (rather than find) what they need when they need it, and it reduces or eliminates the burden around finding what they don't need (for example, a search of the term *e-learning* will reveal millions of hits; the challenge is finding the right hit in the right context). It enables performers to always know where they are, where they have been, and where they are going in a Web site, without getting lost in a myriad of convoluted links, or wasting time browsing for specific information only to find it isn't where it was assumed to be or is incomplete. Performance-centered design may reflect a creative or development process, but its focus is clearly on outcomes in context: what performers actually need to do.

Performance-centered design is essential for the successful development of EPSS, but it is also essential for good knowledge management solutions and even good instructional programs (since effective instruction should be performance centered). Unfortunately, many existing learning products are not derived from performance-centered design approaches. This can contribute to product irrelevance, user confusion, and, in many cases, rejection of technology-based approaches to learning. In the smart enterprise, workers want to get things done as easily and as quickly as possible, and they want assurances that what they are doing has value and will work. They have no time to figure out poorly designed software of any kind, and too much frustration will lead them to abandon these tools for something else—perhaps their old ways of learning and doing things. Using training or other interventions to help users cope with bad software is at best a short-term, time-consuming, and unnecessary stopgap, and could make the situation worse. This is why, if you are repurposing older content or programs for the online world, whether it is more traditional online training, a sophisticated EPSS, or something in the middle, or even if you are building from scratch, you will benefit greatly from using a performance-centered design framework.

Integrating Learning into Work

> The context of business learning is changing due to the no-time-to-spare pace of today's work environment. Event-based or "just in case" learning is no longer adequate; now, employees need knowledge, data and tools integrated into the workflow so that it is available at the moment of need.
>
> —*Gloria Gery*[8]

When moving from classroom training to online training, and then to knowledge management and collaboration, and finally to performance support, you are moving your learning and performance strategy not just to the workplace but to coexist with the work itself. This represents the future evolution of the learning and performance architecture, where the line between e-learning, knowledge management, collaboration and performance support, and work disappears.

Disrupting Work in Order to Learn

Initially most people think of work as a steady process, but in reality, work activities are disrupted all the time for many reasons, including social activities, meals, personal business, and training, where the disruption of work to take courses might look something like Figure 6.1.

Figure 6.1 How Training Can Disrupt the Flow of Work over Time

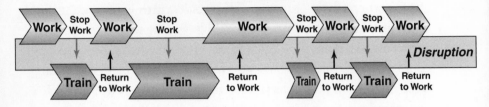

Sometimes the work stoppage is just a few minutes, as workers access a short instructional module on the Web. Other times, work may be postponed a week or more while the worker attends classes at a training center. Every work process and every training program has a different impact on work; Figure 6.1 is just a stylized representation of the key challenge: how to support learning without always relying on an approach that takes people away from work in order to learn. Since the productivity of a worker in training is basically zero, the goal must be to be as efficient as possible by reducing the amount of time work is disrupted for formal online or classroom training events to an appropriate minimum. This is where the other parts of the learning and performance architecture come into play.

The Seamless Integration of Work and Learning

> Think of workers not as users, but as co-creators of the workflow environment. Become a choreographer rather than a dictator, observe learning in action and seek to amplify it with technology.
>
> —*Jay Cross and Tony O'Driscoll*[9]

Accessing information repositories, a help feature within a software product or a Web site, or participating in a community of practice around a business process or product, or virtually asking for advice from an expert is less disruptive to the flow of work than is training. As more knowledge management, collaboration, performance support, and coaching solutions are blended into your strategy, and then implemented as much as possible within a work context, disruptions are reduced while productivity can be increased. There will still be a need to train, but as depicted in Figure 6.2, a more comprehensive work-based learning strategy will give you more options for strengthening performance directly.

Figure 6.2 How Integrating Learning into Work Reduces Work Disruption

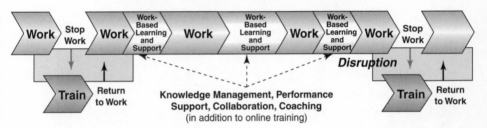

The Value of Integrating Work and Learning

Integrating work and learning becomes the ultimate goal for blended learning, where the framework for blended solutions will move not just to the workplace but to work processes as well. Instead of asking, "How can we incorporate components of the learning and performance architecture into our training program?" ask, "How can we use the learning and performance architecture to improve how work gets done?"

There are far too many instances where training is called on to compensate for poor processes, bad software, or poor documentation. When people have trouble working through a job routine or using a system, training is called on to help them. When they have difficulty understanding a technical or user manual, training is called on to explain it to them. What if, instead, the processes or the tools that people use were improved to make them easier? What if documentation was redesigned to make it more understandable?

To better address these problems, you might not want to lead with a training solution that will at best help employees cope with a bad situation. If, for example, you're confronted with a poorly designed process, first think about the ways to make the process itself more efficient or easier to use. This may be all that's needed, but if it isn't, look next into how you can support performers as they are using the process. If these two approaches aren't enough, *then* ask how training can better prepare workers to use the process more productively. Your training intervention, now part of an architecture of solutions, will likely be less costly and much more effective than if you attacked the problem with training alone.

Consider an alternative, where learning is a seamless component of the job and where learning professionals are called on not just to build training programs to help employees cope with their work, but to help support, supplement, and sometimes *redesign* work—to embed learning into the work flow—so that employees can do their jobs faster, simpler, and better. There might likely be less training, but there would likely be higher performance—a rewarding trade-off. That's the goal IBM set out to achieve.

IBM Integrates Learning into the On-Demand Workplace

Marketplace agility is one of the most important criteria for business success. At IBM, CEO Sam Palmisano says this requires organizations to be responsive, focused, resilient, integrated, open, virtual, and autonomic. For IBM, the only way to do this is to become an on-demand enterprise, an organization that, according to Palmisano, "can respond with speed to any customer demand, market opportunity or external threat."[10]

To accomplish this goal, IBM established the On Demand Workplace team, whose charter was to create a new online work environment that meets the requirements of this vision. That means providing real-time access to industry, customer, and product knowledge, as well as the ability to use business tools and collaborate with peers wherever they may be in a personalized and relevant way to key roles within the organization.

This On Demand Workplace team was essentially a four-way partnership within IBM. It encompassed work flow experts, who understood how to identify and characterize differentiating work practices and behaviors; IBM learning professionals, who contributed a deep understanding of how people learn; Corporate Communications, which understood how to communicate and distribute information over the Web; and the chief information officer's office, which provided the necessary technology strategy perspective.

The learning community could have responded with a traditional approach of classroom and online courseware. Instead, it embraced the partnership's much broader view of a learning and performance architecture—one that includes training where appropriate but expands significantly into knowledge management, collaboration, and performance support—with the goal of integrating all of these approaches directly into work so that the information and support needed to do a job were actually part of the job.

Traditional Training Is Important, But It Has Its Limits

IBM selected its large solution seller force, which represents one of the company's major touch points with customers, as one of the first groups to be supported with this new architecture. These professionals were extensively trained in the IBM sales process and general selling skills, among other topics. However, in the field, where competitive and product knowledge changes daily, training was insufficient. What the sales force needed, and what they told IBM that they wanted, was a reliable, on-demand way to access critical information, best practice, and expertise at any time and anywhere.

A performance analysis, using focus groups and "day-in-the-life" studies, revealed that solution sellers were spending too much time working with multiple systems and tools. They seemed to be required to know much more about how a system worked than they really needed to know in order to get the work done, and they had to navigate many unnecessary intricacies of each tool in order to move ahead. This stimulated demand to help the solution sellers cope with these systems, which were far from easy to use. Their pain was not about how to sell but how to use a wide array of resources to serve customers more effectively—a major productivity issue.

For example, solution sellers felt they were spending too much time inputting and pulling data from IBM's customer relationship management (CRM) system. Although classroom training provided the skills to use the system, it didn't decrease the time or improve the overall process. Thinking differently about learning and performance, IBM chose to leverage its WebSphere portal server technology to create an interface "veneer" to give people the ability to manage data in the CRM database without having to learn the entire system. By aligning the access to and input of CRM data to the key tasks that the solution seller was responsible for, the process became much more streamlined.

Another example is the IBM sales approach, Signature Selling Method (SSM), which has a wealth of job aids, tools, guidelines, and checklists accessible using a tools-based Web site. Most solution sellers downloaded the pdf files when needed, which was good, but not good enough. In order to increase efficiencies, dynamic online forms have replaced the printable pdf files. In addition, most of the existing online courseware was parsed into more manageable content categories (such as SSM steps, and business, industry, product, and technology knowledge) and combined with all of the other Web-based tools. Then all of these resources were embedded directly into SSM. Today, when a salesperson accesses a particular step in SSM, all of the associated resources they need to work successfully—information, instruction, expertise, and performance support—are dynamically served up.

Making Learning and Performance Improvement a Part of Work

IBM's intranet used to be seen as a giant library focused on getting vast amounts of information out to employees. Today, IBM uses portal technology to make the intranet less of a place to learn how to do work and more of a place to get work done. IBM's On Demand Workplace has three primary "entrances" into the company's knowledge, represented by tabs at the top of the screen:

- The Home tab is the standard productivity suite of tools, from e-mail to word processing and presentation software.
- The Career and Life tab focuses on the personal and personnel side of life at IBM.
- The Work tab opens the place where IBM applied performance-centered design practices to create "workware"— portal software that maps to work flow.

When individual solution sellers enter the On Demand Workplace, the system recognizes who they are from the personalized profile they created and populates the screen with information and resources that each individual needs for accomplishing her job: *her* clients accounts, *her* revenue metrics, *her* calendar, *her* tool kit, *her* learning plans. Other individuals and other roles (for example, financial specialists or general managers) would see the On Demand Workplace configured uniquely for them and their job.

Beyond access to information, IBM provides technological support to encourage and enhance collaboration and access to experts. By profiling each solution seller in the system—whether they are working on a particular account, preparing a proposal, or learning about a new client or industry—the system is able to identify subject matter experts and peers knowledgeable in these same areas and let the user know if the identified experts were currently online. This "presence awareness" software presents each solution seller with a customized yet constantly updated (and hot-linked) list of people who might be able provide real-time support.

Of course, even with all of these online advancements, traditional training still has a purpose. There are some topics and skills (for example, the unique approach to selling to a CEO) that are best facilitated in a formal training session. But over time, formal instruction will be reserved for specific, unique situations where it is warranted. However, it is important to remember that the content that was delivered in training didn't go away; it was redesigned, reformatted, and repackaged into more information and support rather than actual course work.

> Today workers have more learning options than ever before. More of them are now using Google to find the information they need versus using a course catalogue. In an era of increasingly powerful search technology, information in context is trumping instruction out of context as a primary learning channel.
>
> —Tony O'Driscoll, IBM learning strategist
> for on-demand learning

By using a broader learning and performance architecture, blending in a wider array of learning solutions, and synchronizing these solutions with actual jobs, IBM reports that an average of four hours of work are saved per person each week. Even more important than time saved is what the sales force can do with that extra time: call on more customers, manage accounts more effectively, spend more time building relationships with clients, learn more about an industry, increase their product expertise, and so on. IBM's On Demand strategy for its sales force was not based solely on learning improvements; it was also based on more critical productivity improvements and business results.

Lessons Learned

IBM has learned much from its rollout of On Demand learning that bears consideration for the smart enterprise. The creation of an On Demand learning strategy requires a fundamental paradigm shift in understanding how and where learning truly happens within an organization. It is in developing the capability to understand how learning happens organically within a system, and knowing how to leverage technology to amplify that naturally occurring learning process, that the ability to deliver on-demand learning resides. No matter how good the analysis, Web technology, work flow support, and instructional design, success is determined by having strong buy-in at every step of the way.

The seamless integration of learning into workware and workware into the work is key. By making the whole strategy work based rather than course based, there is a much higher likelihood that what is delivered is what is needed. Training organizations cannot accomplish this on their own; partnering with other key support functions and client organizations is critical for building long-term momentum. Getting useful tools out there quickly is important in building credibility and ownership with the end user community. The need for feedback from users and the ability to tune the workware system rapidly are critical to developing performance-centered workware. That's why this project used a rapid prototyping approach (consisting of several progressively more realistic versions of the system, where each new prototype was based in part on feedback on the previous version) to shorten the time between design, use, feedback, and revision. Cross-organizational initiatives like this require simultaneously managing multiple stakeholders, often with different needs. Building consensus and shared success is critical to transform a good idea into a valued way of doing business.

Perhaps most important, it is necessary to distinguish between "not useful" and "not usable." Tools, content, and courseware that are not useful, that is, have little value, should be discontinued;

similar products that are not usable, that is, difficult to apply, should be improved. They key is to be able to tell the difference.

Embracing New Opportunities

As IBM and other companies are discovering, the transformation of e-learning from just e-training to a broader array of tools and technologies that encompass information, collaboration, and expertise, as important as it is, is just part of the journey. Embedding learning not simply into the workplace but into the work itself expands the focus beyond learning to individual and organizational performance. It means there will be times when you will forgo training to help people use a process or system, and instead integrate learning and performance support directly into the system itself. Ultimately you will use your capabilities in this area to improve the system or process directly so that less training and support are needed. To some, this could be seen as putting the learning and performance improvement function out of business. More likely, it will open doors to many new opportunities.

> When one door closes, another opens; but we often look so long and so regretfully upon the closed door that we do not see the one which has opened for us.
>
> —*Alexander Graham Bell*

There is even more to do to ensure that these new approaches will stick in the organization. You must implement an effective change management and communications strategy to win the hearts and minds of workers and executives alike. Creating a leadership culture that values learning and performance improvement is also essential. Finally, you must recognize where nonlearning solutions are appropriate, to either reinforce a learning environment or address performance problems and opportunities where learning solutions, including e-learning solutions, will not work. For smart enterprise thinking to become integral to your organizational culture, these three areas must be considered (and will be considered in Part Three of this book).

Notes

1. Norman, D. (1993). *Things that make us smart: Defending human attributes in the age of the machine*. Reading, MA: Addison-Wesley, pp. 112–113.
2. Gery, G. (2004, July 23). *The moment of need: Providing on-demand resources*. Legends Series Webcast presented by SumTotal Systems.
3. In some cases in this book, the terms *performance support, electronic performance support*, and *electronic performance support systems* are used interchangeably.
4. Gery, G. (1995). Attributes and behaviors of performance centered systems. *Performance Improvement Quarterly*, 8(1), 47–93.
5. Comments made at The eLearning Guild's eLearning Producer Conference, San Francisco, March 16, 2005. See also Rossett, A., & Mohr, E. (2004, February). Performance support tools: Where learning work and results converge. *Training and Development*, 58(2), 35–39.
6. Gery, G. (1995). Handout for *Performance Support: Performance Centered Design* [workshop]. This handout is no longer available.
7. Dickelman, G. (2005, February 17). *Realizing performance centered design: Methods and technologies for competency and performance*. STEP (Systems for Training, Evaluation and Performance) Webinar. See also www.epsscentral.net.
8. Gery. (2004).
9. Cross, J., & O'Driscoll, T. (2005, February). A manifesto for workflow learning. *Training Magazine*, p. 32.
10. Palmisano says IBM will lead the way to the on-demand era. (2003, May 15). *Enterprise Innovator*. http://enterpriseinnovator.com/index.php?articleID=1750&sectionID=86.

The Business Singularity

Jay Cross

The structure of business, the role of workers, and the architecture of software are changing beneath our very eyes. Business is morphing into flexible, self-organizing components that operate in real time. Software is becoming interoperable, open, ubiquitous, and transparent. Workers are learning in small chunks delivered to individualized screens presented at the time of need. Learning is being transformed into a core business process measured by key performance indicators. Taken together, these changes create a new kind of business environment, a business singularity.

The Business Singularity		
Changes in Business	*Changes in Software*	*Changes in Learning*
Network model	Network model	Network model
Total integration	Transparent	Demand driven
Real time	Fully integrated	Performance-centered design
Sense and respond	User driven	
Flexible, adaptive	Ubiquitous	Individualized
Modular	Autonomic	Level 4/business process
Continuous improvement	Interoperable	
	Services	Collaborative
Process management	Grid	Capability
Unbounded	Loosely coupled	Small chunks
Bottom-out		Rich client

Business organizations are evolving into networks; what happens inside the corporate walls is nowhere near as important as the overall flow of value from raw material to customer. Internal boundaries are obstacles to be overcome. Networks shared among suppliers, partners, and customers integrate the business into a commercial ecosystem that is, no surprise, a larger network.

Software is evolving into networks. The network really is the computer, and the Internet is the new model for organization. Open networks that can talk with one another are far more valuable than yesterday's proprietary fortresses. As on the Net, enterprise software evolves with changing conditions, routes around damage, and reaches out to form new connections.

People are networks enmeshed in networks with one another. Our bodies are networks, and our minds are neural networks with built-in firewalls and filters. We network with one another. Outboard memory in the form of personal digital assistants and personal data stores supplements human wetware. The biggest factor in individual success is the quality of our social networks.

In any thriving network, tentacles reach out to snare new members like ivy climbing a wall, because the more active that members are, the greater is the value of the network. Growth begets growth until a tipping point is reached; then expansion becomes explosive. The rewards of membership become so high that everyone must join. In 1924, a business could live without a telephone; now, it cannot.

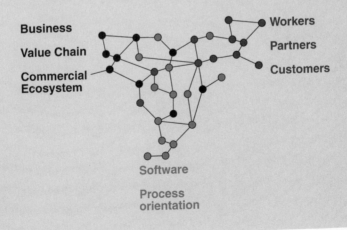

Business
Value Chain
Commercial
Ecosystem

Workers
Partners
Customers

Software

Process
orientation

We are about to witness a spectacular convergence of networks of people and businesses. Workers and their work are becoming synchronous and inseparable. Colleagues and customers collaborate seamlessly. Transparent software eliminates the business-IT divide. Organizations focus on what they do best, outsourcing everything else to the greater commercial ecosystem—sort of an eBay for business activities. Network efficiencies eradicate the largest drag on corporate performance: slack. The pace of business trends toward instantaneity.

The way people improve their performance in this business singularity is called *work flow learning*. It is what corporate learning can become three to five years hence. It takes place in a virtual workplace where workers interact, learn, and control the process of creating value in real time.

Networks are defined by the quality of their connections, and the measure of network success is its rate of error-free throughput. The successful business has high bandwidth and connections so good that value flows without friction. The successful software environment is one that connects so well with business, workers, and other computers that no one notices it's there. The successful worker is one so synchronized with the challenges of work that he enters a psychological state of flow while optimizing the flow of work under changing conditions.

Happily for us, when connections are working properly, we don't need to see them. Consider, for example, the Internet cloud—that vast interconnectivity of computers and networks across the globe. As far as the user is concerned, she has a direct connection to the site on her screen. In reality, the image she sees is probably the result of information being bounced through a variety of pipes both near and far.

Work flow learning is an aspect of a work cloud. As far as the worker is concerned, he is looking at the flow of work, making midcourse corrections, taking care of exceptions, communicating with colleagues, and learning how to improve performance. He doesn't take courses so much as drink from a stream of learning experiences flowing by.

Does this newcomer crowd out other forms of learning? No. Work flow learning is not a cure-all. It will supplement rather than replace current forms of learning such as pencils, cheat sheets, and workshops.

> Everything flows and nothing abides; everything gives way and nothing stays fixed.
> —*Heraclitus of Ephesus (536–470 B.C.E.)*

Look at things over a long enough period of time, and you'll see that nothing is permanent; what appeared fixed is actually fluid. When your time horizon is measured in eons, mountains, climate, and the position of the North Star all change. Everything flows.

The pace of time is accelerating. What once took months can often be accomplished in less than a day. Federal Express delivers a letter to the other side of the world in less time than it took the Pony Express to cross a state. Before the Industrial Revolution, few people needed a watch. In World War II, pilots synchronized their watches to the second. The computer on which I'm writing is running three thousand times faster than my IBM-PC in the early 1980s.

As time goes by more quickly, it becomes easier to see the flow of everyday things. MIT professor Tom Malone notes the evolution from rigid kingdoms to flexible democracies as language and then printing slashed the cost of communication. He charts a similar developmental path from stores to chains to networked business ecosystems.

The same progression appears in computing, where isolated, hard-wired mainframes gave way to top-down client/server, which is yielding to adaptive Web services network architectures. Corporate learning will soon follow. Individualized bursts of learning will replace fixed classes. Learning will more resemble the performance support systems of Gloria Gery than the classroom exercises of the old-time schoolmarm.

	State Changes		
	Isolated →	Fixed →	Fluid
Structure	Small group	Hierarchy	Decentralized
Human Society	Bands	Kingdoms	Democracy
Business	Proprietorships	Corporations	Markets
Computing	Mainframes	Client/server	Web/network
Boundaries	City, cottage, cave	Corporation	Ecosystem (none)
Learning	Apprentice	Schooling	Embedded

Ironically, in today's terms, embedded learning is neither work flow nor learning in their strictest sense. Some circles have usurped the term *work flow* to mean the flow of documents; what I'm talking about is the flow of products or services through a firm's value chain. Most definitions of learning predate the PDAs, laptops, and Internet access that supplement what's in our heads with knowledge and know-how from outside. Knowing where to find something is as valuable as knowing it. I have little vested interest in what we call this new learning phenomenon so long as we recognize that it is not business as usual.

Many training professionals won't "get" work flow learning, even though it's what they have long asked for: to be taken seriously as contributors to the bottom line. Learning will become a true business process and Kirkpatrick's evaluation level 4 (results) will be the only level worth looking at. The training department may disappear into the cloud as just another component of performance improvement.

The future of corporate learning is all business.

Jay Cross, founder of Internet Time Group and chairman of Ensemble Collaboration, coined the terms *e-learning* and *work flow learning*. Find him at www.internettime.com.

7

True Telecom's Story

Training professionals have typically focused on
developing brainpower more than managing it.
—*Allison Rossett and Kendra Sheldon*[1]

This chapter is a little different from others in this book. It is primarily the story of how Brian, a hypothetical account executive in a hypothetical company called True Telecom, used new workplace learning and performance resources to move himself and his customer to True Telecom's new business strategy. It showcases how knowledge management (KM), collaboration, and performance support can be delivered to the field, *not* as "the way" to do things but as an example of what can be done. It also demonstrates the blurring of the line between work and learning and how emerging knowledge and expertise can be captured, organized, and made available to users for immediate, on the job use.[2] After the story is told, the chapter discusses evaluation, exploring the many ways True Telecom can assess the value of its new learning and performance strategy.

Introducing True Telecom

For the past two decades, True Telecom built its reputation by selling the best hardware and software in the telecommunications industry. Now, its new CEO is taking the company in a new direction. She and her executive team want to move the business from selling products to selling solutions. The company has bundled its product line into four major business applications: customer relationship management (CRM), messaging, IP telephony, and switching. The goal is to be operating completely in the new model within a year.

For years, the sales force has pitched True Telecom's product features and capabilities to operations and technology managers. Now they are being asked to approach higher-level executives in a more consultative sales approach, where they learn enough about the customer organization to present the key financial and strategic benefits of True Telecom solutions that will be most compelling to individual customers. This fundamental change represents a major challenge to the sales force. The CEO has mustered all of the company's resources to make this transition successful. She charged True's chief learning officer (CLO) with providing as much support to the sales staff as possible, but, she cautioned, "we can't take people out of the field; we have to maintain our earnings and our customer relationships during this transition."

True Telecom's training organization offers some of the best training in the industry, both classroom and online. In fact, training for the sales force has recently been upgraded, with about 30 percent of all sales and product training available online, enabling True's account executives to refresh their skills and knowledge while remaining close to their customers.

The CLO had been rethinking the role of True Telecom's training organization for some time, and this new challenge was just what he needed to move the organization in a new direction. To support the sales force through this transition, the CLO recognized that the company had to move beyond training and beyond e-learning. A few months ago, in a conversation with the CIO, the topics of KM, collaboration, and performance support had come up. Out of that dialogue, the two departments, in cooperation with the national sales organization, implemented a system not only to deliver more learning and knowledge resources to the field sales force, but also allow and promote the growth and sharing of new knowledge, learning, and expertise as it emerges from the field. A number of account executives have been participating in a pilot for about a month now. Brian is one of them.

Planning for a Customer Call

Brian has been an account executive for True Telecom for just over two years, having moved up the ranks from customer service associate. He is very knowledgeable about True's product line and has attended many training classes on telecommunications technology and sales effectiveness. His sales manager noted that Brian is one of her best producers and has good relationships with customers at all levels of management, including some high-ranking executives.

Two weeks ago, Brian completed a one-week course on how to sell solutions rather than just products. The course included a briefing on the company's new strategy and extensive information and exercises designed to help Brian position the company to executive-level customers in a new light. At several points during the class, Brian was introduced to the new sales and marketing KM system, as well as several new sales-oriented and business case performance support tools. He was told that these resources can provide him with information, expertise, and support related to his job. He was also shown how he can input his own knowledge, learning, and expertise into the system's database, thereby defining Brian as not only a user of the system but a contributor as well. Two days after the class ended, Brian received an e-mail from the KM system administrator, informing him of his log-in and password; he now has access to this new resource through his laptop, at the office, on the road, or at home. Since then, Brian has been enthusiastically exploring the KM system.

Although Brian has participated in three previous sales calls where he was part of the account team, he will be calling on a new customer by himself in two days. It's a large retail company that is looking to True Telecom to enhance its CRM capabilities. This is one of Brian's specialties.

To prepare for the meeting, Brian accesses the KM system (Figure 7.1). The first thing Brian notices is that he's already been enrolled in two communities of practice. He makes a mental note to check them out later to see if there's any new information he can use on his sales call. He also sees that the system has recommended

Figure 7.1 True Telecom: KM System Home Page

several resources, based on his most recent searches. It seems that the system is smart enough to identify resources similar to those he is working with; this helps him make sure he is aware of all the relevant information in the system. Brian also notices that three other people are working in areas similar to his. He knows Janet, who works down the hall, but he didn't know Raj or Bob until now. It seems Raj is the contributor of several CRM knowledge assets Brian likes, so he makes a note to contact Raj to see if there's any other material he can provide.

At the top of the page, Brian notices a search tool he can use to find specific content. It's on every page of the system. He also notices four tabs representing the four new True Telecom business lines. Since he is working on a CRM solution, he selects that tab (circled on Figure 7.1). This takes him to the home page for the CRM content domain (Figure 7.2).

Figure 7.2   True Telecom: CRM Home Page

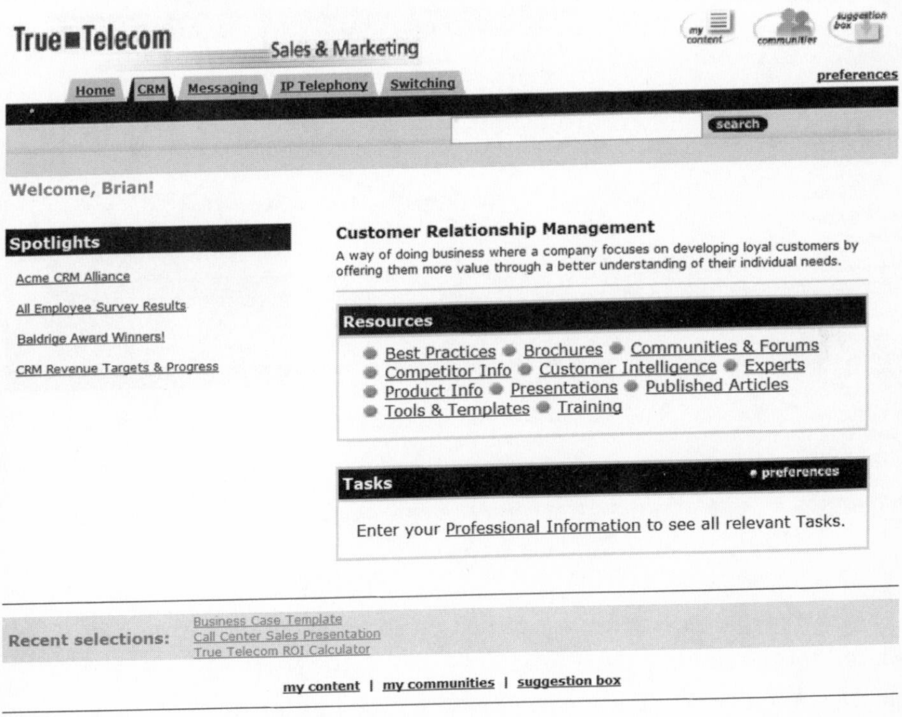

True■Telecom — Sales & Marketing

my content   *communities*   *suggestion box*   *preferences*

Home | CRM | Messaging | IP Telephony | Switching

search

Welcome, Brian!

Spotlights

Acme CRM Alliance

All Employee Survey Results

Baldrige Award Winners!

CRM Revenue Targets & Progress

Customer Relationship Management

A way of doing business where a company focuses on developing loyal customers by offering them more value through a better understanding of their individual needs.

Resources

- Best Practices ● Brochures ● Communities & Forums
- Competitor Info ● Customer Intelligence ● Experts
- Product Info ● Presentations ● Published Articles
- Tools & Templates ● Training

Tasks   ● preferences

Enter your Professional Information to see all relevant Tasks.

Recent selections: Business Case Template
Call Center Sales Presentation
True Telecom ROI Calculator

my content | my communities | suggestion box

Here, Brian finds a host of ways to access content about CRM. The managing editor of this tab has created a "Spotlights" feature that brings "hot" items to the surface, where Brian is sure to notice them. He can also browse the content by selecting the type of resource that most interests him (the "tasks" box will be discussed later). He begins by selecting two resource types: Tools & Templates and Experts. Each time he clicks on a resource, an associated content list appears (Figure 7.3).

Figure 7.3   True Telecom: Content Lists Organized by Resource Type

True■Telecom
Sales & Marketing

my content   communities   suggestion box

Home   CRM   Messaging   IP Telephony   Switching

preferences

search

Welcome, Brian!

Spotlights

Acme CRM Alliance

All Employee Survey Results

Baldrige Award Winners!

CRM Revenue Targets & Progress

Customer Relationship Management

A way of doing business where a company focuses on developing loyal customers by offering them more value through a better understanding of their individual needs.

Resources

● Best Practices ● Brochures ● Communities & Forums ● Competitor Info ● Customer Intelligence ● Experts ● Product Info ● Presentations ● Published Articles ● Tools & Templates ● Training

Tools & Templates

Title	Last Updated On	Language	Media	Resources
Business Case Analysis Model	June 2, 2005	English	Slides	Tools & Templates
Business Case Template	August 15, 2005	English	Document	Tools & Templates
Call Center Technical Assessment Survey	May 5, 2005	English	Document	Tools & Templates
Steps for Writing a Proposal	March 11, 2005	English	Document	Tools & Templates
True Telecom Call Center Configurator	December 7, 2004	English	Document	Tools & Templates
True Telecom ROI Calculator	March 11, 2005	English	Document	Tools & Templates

Experts

Title	Last Updated On	Language	Media	Resources
Dawn Leipzig, CRM Specialist	January 26, 2005	English	Email Contact	Experts
Patricia Seybould Group	November 20, 2004	English	Email Contact	Experts
Peppers and Rogers Group	May 21, 1005	English	Email Contact	Experts

Brian evaluates each list, noting that some assets have been updated more recently than others. Under Tools & Templates, he finds several resources he can use as he prepares for his customer call. Under Experts, he finds Dawn Leipzig, a CRM specialist who is available to him through e-mail or the sales hot line. She has volunteered to help field salespeople as they prepare to engage executive-level prospects, so Brian makes a note to reach out to her if he needs help. He appreciates the fact that the KM system provides real people to help him, not just documents.

After getting a pretty good idea of what resources are in the KM system, Brian determines that there is a wealth of data here, but he has a specific job to do right now, so he decides to use the system to help him accomplish his task at hand. To do this, he can take advantage of the system's flexibility to explore the content from a different perspective. He notices that the system can organize information based on what he is going to do, not just on what he needs to know. Brian thinks that this performance-centered focus can be very helpful and decides to try it. He enters his specific job function, Sales, into the system (Figure 7.4), and the system provides a customized set of tasks that are appropriate to him and the task at hand (Figure 7.5).

By providing his professional role, the system responds with a set of tasks related to solutions-based selling. Brian notices there are

Figure 7.4 True Telecom: Linking Role to Tasks

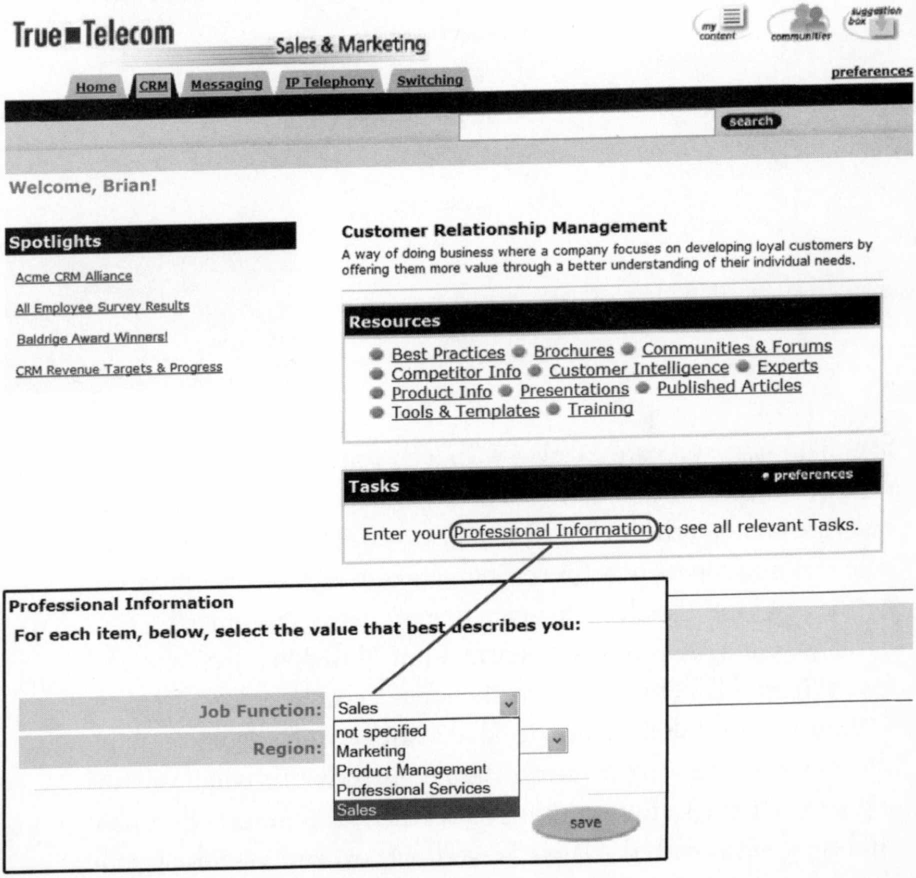

True■Telecom   Sales & Marketing

my content | communities | suggestion box

Home CRM Messaging IP Telephony Switching   preferences

search

Welcome, Brian!

Spotlights

Acme CRM Alliance

All Employee Survey Results

Baldrige Award Winners!

CRM Revenue Targets & Progress

Customer Relationship Management

A way of doing business where a company focuses on developing loyal customers by offering them more value through a better understanding of their individual needs.

Resources

● Best Practices ● Brochures ● Communities & Forums
● Competitor Info ● Customer Intelligence ● Experts
● Product Info ● Presentations ● Published Articles
● Tools & Templates ● Training

Tasks   ● preferences

Enter your Professional Information to see all relevant Tasks.

Professional Information

For each item, below, select the value that best describes you:

Job Function: Sales
                not specified
Region: Marketing
                Product Management
                Professional Services
                Sales

save

Figure 7.5   True Telecom: Displaying Tasks for the Sales Role

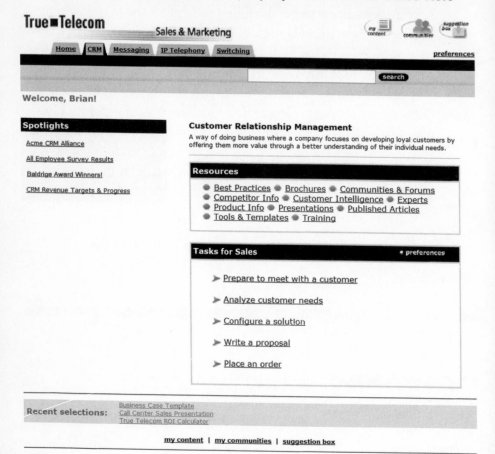

five main tasks: prepare to meet with a customer, analyze customer needs, configure a solution, write a proposal, and place an order. These tasks are familiar; they reflect the methodology he learned in his recent training experience. Since Brian is about to meet the customer for the first time, he selects "prepare to meet with a customer."

The system responds by helping Brian "drill down" to a specific task (Figure 7.6). He first selects the type of customer he is to meet (executive) and then selects from a number of specific tasks centered on this executive meeting. Brian knows that he will be giving a presentation to a high-ranking executive, so he selects that task and is provided with the latest PowerPoint executive sales presen-

Figure 7.6 True Telecom: Accessing "Making a Presentation" Content via Tasks

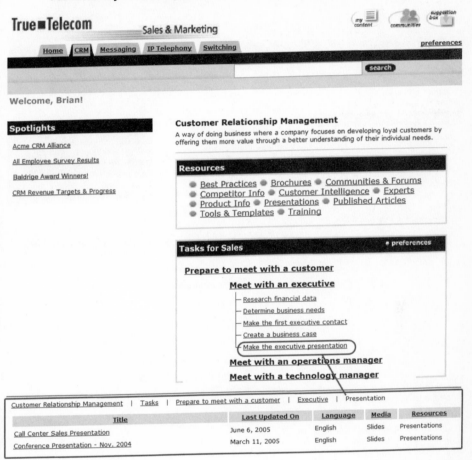

tation to download. He knows he can use this presentation and customize it so it is tailored to his specific customer.

Recognizing also that he will have to explain the financial benefits of True Telecom's CRM solution, Brian looks into "create a business case" (Figure 7.7). There he finds several valuable resources. One is a course, "Developing a Business Case 101." Brian has already completed this course, but is gratified to know that the system integrates the organization's course catalogue, so that whatever topic he selects, relevant training options will be presented along with other resources (if Brian were to select a classroom or online course, True Telecom's learning

Figure 7.7 True Telecom:
Accessing "Create a Business Case" Content via Tasks

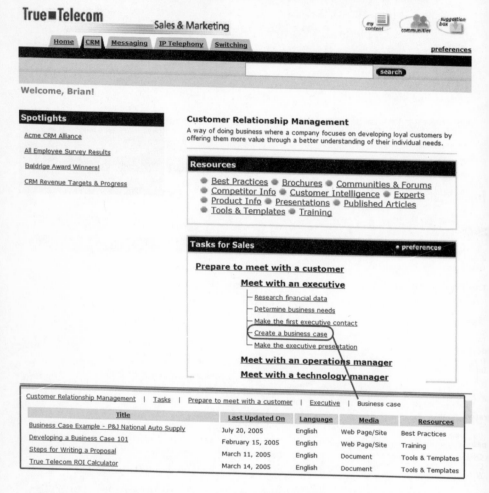

management system would take over and manage the process). He also makes a note to himself that once he has developed his business case, he may nominate it to be incorporated in the system; his "content contribution" may be useful to others in the future. In this way, Brian is moving across the boundary from user to contributor-provider.

Also in this list of recourses, the True Telecom ROI Calculator, a financial performance support tool, is intriguing. Brian knows that such a tool can help him run various rapid what-if scenarios to illustrate the solution's return on investment to the client. He believes this tool will add much to his capabilities, so he selects it to learn more and try it out (Figure 7.8).

Here Brian is presented with details about the asset he has selected. He finds information about who submitted it and when it was last updated. He can read a description to be sure it is what he is looking for. He feels that this tool will be worthwhile as another user (as denoted in the system) has rated it highly. So he opens up

Figure 7.8 True Telecom: Accessing the ROI Calculator Performance Support Tool

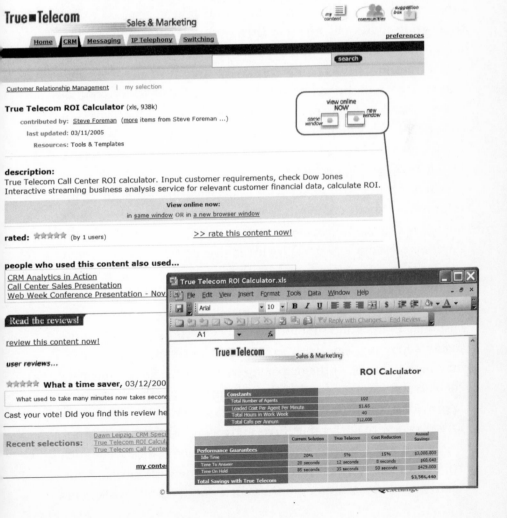

the ROI Calculator (in this case, an Excel spreadsheet) and downloads it to his laptop.

In the course of about thirty minutes, Brian has explored the knowledge base and identified several important resources that will help him prepare over the next two days for his meeting with the new customer. He found up-to-date documents about True Telecom's CRM product line, a performance support tool, a CRM expert who can help him with questions about the products, presentation materials, courseware around CRM, sales, and other topics, and more. He has also recognized that in doing his job, he is developing some of his own expertise that may be worthy of being shared with others who travel similar paths or have similar work goals as he. But there's one additional area that Brian must explore: he needs the most recent intelligence he can get about his competitors so he can respond authoritatively to any customer questions. Since this information is so fluid, Brian knows that any document he finds online may be useful, but only to a point. He needs to quickly collaborate with people who are up to date on the competitive landscape. So he enters the Competitive Analysis Community of Practice, where he is a member (Figure 7.9).

Here Brian can interact with colleagues and view the latest information about competitors in a private and secure environment. He can get advice and try out ideas within the community. After his presentation, he'll provide some feedback on how it went so that others can learn from his experience. Here again is where Brian can become a contributor to the system. In addition to participating with the community, Brian will write up a more detailed customer analysis and submit it for publication in the main information repository. One day after submitting his analysis, he receives an e-mail from one of the managing editors of the knowledge base thanking him for his contribution and advising him that it has been approved and published. It is now part of True Telecom's shared knowledge, with appropriate links and tags to other content.

In a smart enterprise, knowledge users become knowledge contributors and collaborators as they develop new information and insights and new resources in the course of doing their work. This

Figure 7.9 True Telecom: Community of Practice

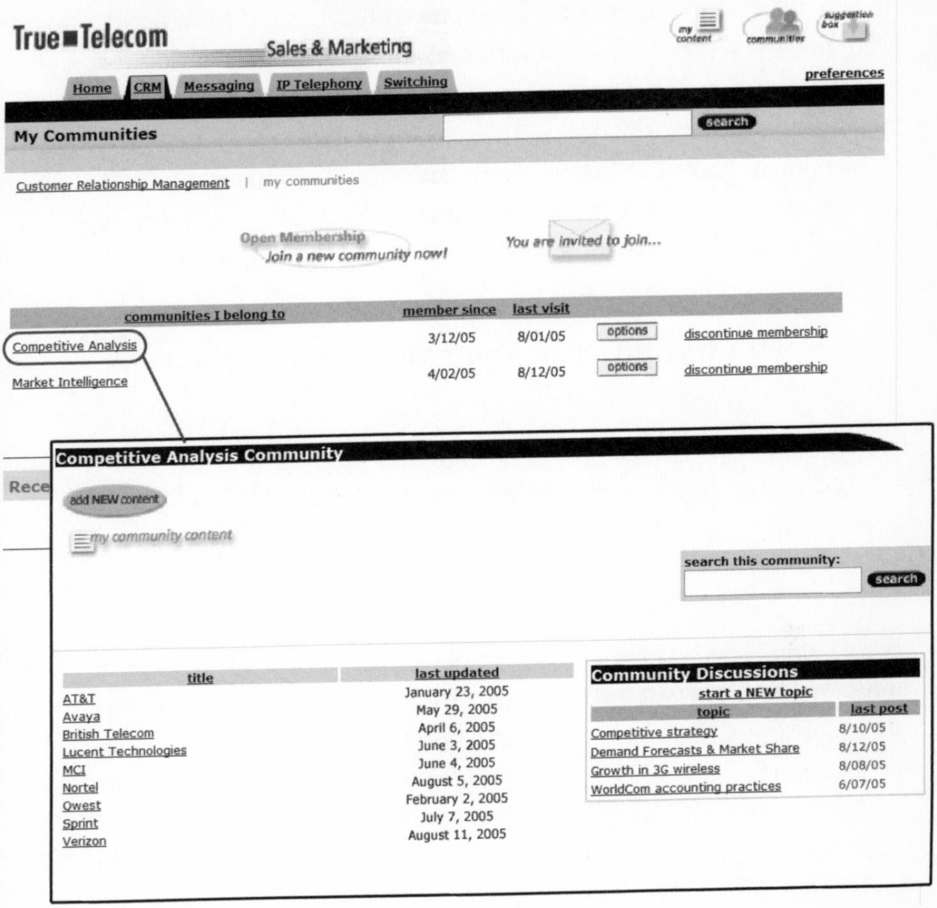

True■Telecom Sales & Marketing

my content   communities   suggestion box

Home CRM Messaging IP Telephony Switching   preferences

My Communities   [search]

Customer Relationship Management | my communities

Open Membership
  Join a new community now!   You are invited to join...

communities I belong to	member since	last visit		
Competitive Analysis	3/12/05	8/01/05	options	discontinue membership
Market Intelligence	4/02/05	8/12/05	options	discontinue membership

Competitive Analysis Community

Rece

add NEW content

my community content

search this community:
[search]

title	last updated
AT&T	January 23, 2005
Avaya	May 29, 2005
British Telecom	April 6, 2005
Lucent Technologies	June 3, 2005
MCI	June 4, 2005
Nortel	August 5, 2005
Qwest	February 2, 2005
Sprint	July 7, 2005
Verizon	August 11, 2005

Community Discussions

topic	last post
start a NEW topic	
Competitive strategy	8/10/05
Demand Forecasts & Market Share	8/12/05
Growth in 3G wireless	8/08/05
WorldCom accounting practices	6/07/05

is an important point. These are the kinds of systems you jump-start and then they build themselves with user input. They are constantly changing. The provider gets them started and sets the initial direction they will follow, to be sure. But they can, and often do, grow way beyond the providers' initial boundaries or intent. With these types of systems, you are not building new, complete, or static workplace learning and performance tools. Rather, you are constructing incomplete systems and setting them in motion—in a sense, following their own line of evolution. And with the active participation of users, they evolve along a path that is most valuable to them.

Some might see True Telecom's system as too basic, while others may see it as too advanced. Everyone's situation is different. For True, however, it is the right solution for now, and a foundation for continuing to evolve, experiment, and experience new approaches to learning and performance. If True's solution looks the same a year or two down the road, that would be unfortunate. This is the most powerful lesson about moving beyond e-learning: you can never be satisfied with what you are. It's where you're going that matters.

Evaluating True Telecom's Solution

> Not everything that can be counted counts, and not everything that counts can be counted.
>
> —*Albert Einstein*

Before your KM, collaboration, or performance support system is implemented, or even in its design, prototype, and trial phases, you should define an approach to evaluate its effectiveness. Then you will be in much better shape to assess its value when it is deployed. Ideally, each evaluation approach is matched up to selected performance and business metrics to determine worth. Your client or customer should be heavily involved in determining the appropriate success metrics.

Multiple Metrics

In most cases, True Telecom wouldn't use just one measure, but a variety of measures to give its evaluation strategy a well-rounded perspective. As with most corporate initiatives, True could use measures related to business impact (for example, increased sales, lower costs, customer satisfaction), individual productivity gains, and Brian's own assessment of the system itself (as well as the individual assessments of his coworkers). There are a variety of approaches the company can use, from internal surveys, interviews and focus groups, and performance observations, to outside independent audits, benchmarking, and more sophisticated balanced scorecard techniques, where the organization looks at a variety of interrelated measures to get a more holistic picture of how it is doing.[3] For example, True could look at these key metrics together: Brian's behavioral performance and job satisfaction, the customer's satisfaction with Brian and the company, and Brian's overall revenue production (his financial contribution). Here's how True Telecom might look at evaluating the solution just described.

As True Telecom deploys its information repository, it can measure how much or how often people like Brian used it to explore new knowledge domains to prepare for new challenges and responsibilities. Getting feedback from the sales team on the value of the knowledge in the repository is just as important as, and perhaps more so than, getting the same information from experts or executives. It would be relatively easy to observe and interview Brian and other salespeople in the future to determine if they keep using the system and how they use it. Running analytics of how people access specific knowledge assets, which assets are most frequently accessed, and real-time user asset valuations can also be useful in pinpointing which content is most used and valued and which assets should be removed from the system. In addition, you can determine where collaboration might be helpful by looking at the knowledge assets people are using in common, as well as their patterns of interaction. What people are working on might be a good indicator of whom they would benefit working with.

User Satisfaction

> A hundred objective measurements didn't sum the worth of a garden; only the delight of its users did that. Only the use made it mean something.
>
> —*Lois McMaster Bujold*, A Civil Campaign[4]

Measuring user satisfaction is a different but equally important way to evaluate the system. Satisfaction can run from comfort with the system to satisfaction with the quality and usefulness of the content and collaboration that comes out of it. Allowing users to review and rate content (similar to what is done on Amazon.com and other e-commerce Web sites) and adjusting search results so that the highest-rated content is displayed first is an excellent way to assess content value. This bottom-up approach to determining the most useful knowledge is a good balance against too much top-down pushing of content. This is especially true as the system gets bigger, with more knowledge assets and more users, as it provides another way to manage and filter the expanding repository.

Satisfaction surveys, observations, and other qualitative techniques should be employed on an ongoing basis to help spot problems before they become major user "turn-offs." Also, it is important to get the feedback of senior managers (who may not be users or contributors) on their perception of the impact of the system, as well as from those, like Brian, who use it on a day-to-day basis. In addition to internal users, customer impact is vital. From True Telecom's perspective, customer satisfaction surveys can tell the company if customers' opinion of Brian has improved, perhaps because he is more knowledgeable or performs better in the field.

It is almost always more cost-effective to retain valued workers than to replace them. Access to high-value information, ease of getting work done, and perception that a company is on the cutting edge may all enhance retention and recruitment. Do True Telecom's new tools create a positive impression in Brian's mind about how the company supports him? Does he feel the resources he has in the field are state-of-the-art? Incorporating questions related to workplace learning and support in employee attitude surveys and in exit interviews is a good way to begin to look for a positive relationship.

From User Performance Metrics to Business Metrics

Defining the question is a whole lot more important than figuring out the answers.

—Roger Schank[5]

At the end of the day, what any business really wants to know is much more than, "did learning occur"; it wants to know, "did any of this make a difference?" This is where moving up to business metrics matters. It is possible to correlate how people are learning with selected True Telecom business metrics. If the use of a new learning and performance system improves True's productivity, that has important business value. If, for example, Brian's productivity increased by as little as 5 or 10 percent, that might be significant if this benefit was widespread across the sales force. Assume that Brian has 400 colleagues and each reports saving about 1 hour a week in productivity; that's more than 20,000 hours of work time saved in a year. Assuming that each salesperson's loaded compensation is $100 per hour, the initial value to True Telecom is more than $2 million in savings due to productivity enhancements alone.

Reduction of redundant efforts is another good measure of the impact of any initiative. By using communities, True Telecom can store and cross-reference the work that multiple teams are doing, making it far more likely that groups working on similar projects will be able to identify each other and collaborate more effectively, even at a distance. By not reinventing the wheel, True can assess how well it is allocating its resources and reducing operational costs. This may have a direct impact on such business indicators as R&D contributions to new product development and time to market.

Speed is vital to a successful business, and the ability of Brian and the rest of the sales team to learn and share knowledge quickly is a fundamental capability that's essential for higher performance. True Telecom's goal might be to reduce knowledge access and sharing time from days to hours, or even minutes. Perhaps the amount of training Brian must take can be reduced or redirected to more complex tasks. These would all be important productivity indicators that might have a direct impact on the sales closure rate.

Although the evaluation strategy employed by True Telecom is hypothetical, it points to a wide array of approaches and techniques that can be employed in many situations. The ultimate goal of any workplace learning solution is to strengthen business performance. Does it help salespeople like Brian close more deals? In other parts of a business, the same questions can be asked. Do new approaches to call center representative learning enable them to handle more calls without a loss in customer satisfaction? Are these new learning and collaboration tools helping the IT department keep systems up and running through better allocation of human and technical resources? Do they help the business become more innovative and responsive in the marketplace? These questions go to the heart of why new workplace learning and performance initiatives are implemented. If these questions are asked up front, before an initiative is even conceived, designed, or deployed, and kept at the forefront of company strategy, they will be easier to answer once the system is implemented. If they emerge as an afterthought, there could be trouble; the new learning and performance systems may not have been designed to address the problems reflected in the evaluation questions you are now trying to answer. That's why, for True Telecom or any other business, it is always better to know what the success criteria will be before getting started.

Scaling True Telecom's Solution

A good way to understand the power and flexibility of True Telecom's (or any other) solution is to look at how it can be scaled across three key dimensions:

- Constituencies: Who will initially benefit from the solution, and how will it expand to serve additional users?
- Content domains: What categories of knowledge and performance will the solution address initially, and how will those domains expand?
- Channels: What features and capabilities will the solution use to deliver knowledge to users in the short and long terms?

Constituencies

The system built by True Telecom could not be all things to all people, at least not at the beginning. To attempt to do so would place the entire effort at risk by biting off too much at the outset. Instead, True's planners thought about who needed the solution the most and who would be able to use it to create the most value. Often, early efforts are pilot or even prototype solutions that seek to learn the strengths and weaknesses of the plan and the technology before full-scale implementation. That was True's approach.

Perhaps True looked first at frontline salespeople, like Brian, for the initial deployment phase. Getting support out to those who have primary sales and customer relationship responsibilities was likely of primary importance. Later, with more experience with how the system is best used, the company might expand access to all customer-facing teams, including customer care and technical support personnel, to help these groups move in unison in approaching each customer, providing a more complete and harmonious set of services. The learning that results enables the business to be more responsive and flexible—much more so than if all of these key people had to wait to get the information in a training session.

Implications for Your Learning/E-Learning Strategy. Don't rush to serve everyone. Focus on those individuals and groups with the most urgent need to learn and improve their performance. The information side of your architecture is more scalable than the instructional side (especially classroom training). Today you reach a dozen people; tomorrow you can reach hundreds or thousands.

Content Domains

If True Telecom had initially positioned its system to be a broad encyclopedia of all types of content for all types of users, it may have risked being too detailed for some and too light for others. Initial efforts are better focused on developing a few key knowledge content domains, establishing an organizing scheme for them, and then building on the same scheme for additional content areas. By approaching the solution in this way, you not only create a consistent view into the knowledge, which aids searching and overall information management, but you learn just how deep into each domain you need to go.

The initial system that Brian used focused only on the company's four most important service lines: CRM, messaging, IP telephony, and switching. In each of those areas, and in others that might follow, experts would monitor what content and tools are most useful and adjust the mix and depth of information as needed. Brian, as a CRM expert, probably doesn't need as much technical information as he needs competitive information and presentation and proposal tools. Later, as more people begin working in CRM, more in-depth technical content will likely be added.

Implications for Your Learning/E-Learning Strategy. When you build a knowledge management, collaboration, or performance support solution, you are going to spend a lot of time up front defining how your solution is designed. You will need to understand the depth and breadth of the content to be covered, to ensure that the needed information is provided at the right level of detail. And you will have to incorporate just the right tools, at the right level of complexity, that will make the work of people like Brian easier, not harder. Technology can help you establish your baselines for content, collaboration, and performance support, and then help you to refine them as you move forward. One of the benefits of these resources is that you can "kick-start" them, getting them roughly right, and then refine and improve them as you observe and track how people use them, making them more useful with each iteration.

Channels

Once you know who (constituencies) you will serve, in what order you will bring them onboard, what content will be provided, and you have organized the resources you will start with, the final step is to determine the channels you will use. How will knowledge be shared? As documents, Web sites, or training? As "conversations" between experts and team members? What collaboration tools and techniques will work best? How can experts be made available without overwhelming them? How will people in the field access new performance support tools?

True Telecom might have started with basic repositories, building its capabilities to identify and disseminate increasingly reliable documents that are easy to find and read. Its initial goals might have centered on ensuring that everyone is working from the same information and that content redundancies are reduced. Then the company might augment its document repository with access to experts and their expertise. Once experts are brought into the mix, salespeople like Brian can find the expert who created the content, instead of just the content alone. Ultimately the company's goal will be to create a knowledge-sharing culture, where collaboration, online and off-line, is the rule rather than the exception.

Implications for Your Learning and E-Learning Strategy. You may start with one or two channels, usually ones that have a good initial fit with your culture. Ultimately, however, using multiple channels to share knowledge and expertise firmwide will enable new ideas and innovation to surface and develop into best practices. This contributes to a smart enterprise where what is known by one person or group is willingly shared with everyone else. At this point, your new workplace-based resources become the heart of your learning and performance strategy, not an appendage to it.

Expanding the Scope

Carefully considering constituencies, content domains, and channels helps you manage your solution deployment so that it is most digestible for users and the organization as a whole. Of course, you will want to scale the system to serve more constituencies and content domains with a richer variety of features. Figure 7.10 illustrates the important choices you have when considering expanding your scope.

Figure 7.10 Expanding the Scope of a Learning and Performance Initiative

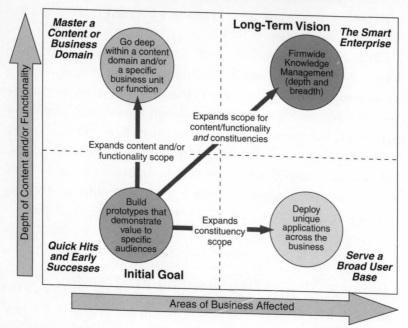

Your early goal should always be an early success. You may begin with some quick hits that meet the needs of a specific part of the business. As you scale, you can focus on either identifying new constituencies to serve a broader user base or expanding the content covered (more domains or diving deeper into existing domains). You can also add new functionality and channels (for example, adding communities of practice to a system that was previously supporting just knowledge repositories) as you move forward. In some cases, you can move in multiple directions, but be careful you don't do too much or get too big too fast. When cities get too big, services tend to focus on neighborhoods. Your solution should be managed the same way: when a single system gets too large (which can be at different points in different organizations), you may have to create smaller subsystems to meet the unique needs of increasingly diverse users.

Keep in mind that the costs for learning and performance solutions and technologies are front-loaded: you will likely spend much more to design, build, and deploy your system than you will to run it over time (for example, productivity gains don't kick in until after deployment). The real benefits and return on investment accrue over time, so you must take a long-range view. Most learning and performance systems, including most enterprise e-learning initiatives, cannot be fully built and implemented in a single fiscal year, and having to go back to ask for money each budget cycle can be risky. Therefore, it is wise to build your rationale, project plans, teams, budgets, benefit projections, and commitments based on a multiyear strategy—almost like a start-up or new venture, with milestones along the way.

Integrating Workplace Learning and Performance Solutions with Existing Training Programs

Using KM tools, including information repositories and collaboration strategies, as well as performance support systems, ultimately makes access to critical business and technical information not just easier, but a preferred way of learning and performing, anytime and anywhere. What does all of this mean for training programs? While approaches like True Telecom's can be powerful learning and performance solutions on their own, you may not be ready. Instead, you may first be interested in how they can be integrated with existing training programs, classroom or online. This isn't where you want to end up, but you can certainly start here.

There are several reasons that you might want to take this approach. First, if you are getting your feet wet with these new alternatives, you might not have the resources to embrace them as independent approaches. Testing them within the confines of a training program is often a good way to get comfortable. You may also not have the support or authority to deploy these alternative strategies as separate initiatives, but as part of a training strategy or an initiative solely within your department or business unit, you maintain control and can move forward faster. Working within familiar confines allows you to perfect your skills around new non-training strategies, giving you opportunities to try things out and learn from your experiences.

Working within a training framework allows you to use these new tools to enhance your training program in ways that make interactions with original company resources easier and more powerful. Because critical business and technical information is increasingly more reliable and accessible online, workers have opportunities to use these materials in class to a far greater extent than before. This reduces reliance on secondary sources, like student guides, that tend to become dated quickly, and compels the training organization to incorporate workplace tools and documentation as primary learning materials. Doing so adds tremendous authenticity to the course by getting people in training to interact with the same knowledge resources they will use on the job.

If you want to incorporate some KM into your classroom training programs, you can require participants to access information from the corporate intranet (or the public Internet, if appropriate). This can be done as a course prerequisite (such as researching a topic that will be discussed in class), during the course itself (perhaps as part of a case study or simulation), or as a follow-up activity (action planning or enrichment, for example). This not only teaches the participants to be better information researchers; it brings more authentic content into the training program. Again, this reduces the need for information to be rewritten into student materials that have a short shelf-life. Using actual company documents and other resources that are constantly updated lends more realism to the learning experience. If you want people to access information repositories during a class, be sure there is Web access available, either by allowing participants to bring laptops to class or having networked computers available in the classroom. If you are working in a virtual classroom environment, consider having breaks in the presentation where individual participants visit one or more Web sites (internal or external), or use one or more tools that you have provided, and then come back to the virtual class to discuss what they have learned and accomplished.

Training materials themselves can be stored online. Participants can download the latest materials right before they come to class, making it easier for the training department to keep everything and everyone up-to-date. As a bonus, where appropriate, course graduates can have access to updated materials long after the class is over, thereby keeping their training binders fresh and continuously useful.

You can easily integrate collaboration activities into formal training programs in much the same way. People come for a week of training, then go back to work for some time before they get back in the classroom. Online training is the same way. Learners log on, take a course (or part of a course), and then log off. If the program is good enough, they may repeat this process many times. But what happens between these events? A well-managed community of employees who have shared a common educational experience (and instructors) can be a powerful way to continue learning even when they are not in a formal class. You can prescribe a precourse assignment and ask participants to discuss it virtually prior to coming to the formal class. More important, when the class is over, you can maintain this community of employees who can keep in touch with each other, back on the job, as they apply what they've learned.

If new performance support tools are being introduced into the workplace, you can integrate them into the class. In this way, employees can try out the new tool and the processes that surround it in a low-risk environment, where they can get coaching on how to use it and provide feedback to instructors (who pass it on to the tool developers) on how the tool works for them. In fact, introducing performance support into a training environment first may be a good way to gauge early reaction to it. The bottom line is that instead of teaching people about what they will be doing that's new on the job, you can have them actually experience it.

Impact on Your Training Program

> There are many reasons to be pleased about this increased access to knowledge. . . . Having knowledge available at one's fingertips enables one to do research, to answer questions, to explore new relationships never before possible.
>
> —*Don Norman*[6]

When you are successful in blending KM, collaboration, and performance support solutions into your courseware (and into your business), you shouldn't be surprised when your target audience jumps to these resources rather than going to class. And although not every course is going to be replaced by a KM system, a community of practice, or an EPSS, once people get used to working with these new ways to learn and work, your formal training program will no doubt need some restructuring.

You may find that these alternative approaches will negate the need for some of your training programs, just as you did when an online course replaced your classroom course. This is inevitable, and as you grow into KM, collaboration, and performance support solutions, you should expect your formal training offerings to shrink. More content will be built directly into work processes in the form of help systems, decision tools, FAQs, performance support, and others, making those processes more streamlined, efficient, and easier to use. Nevertheless, overall learning opportunities may actually increase.

There will be situations when the implementation of these new learning strategies won't eliminate formal training but will change its nature. Courses that were predominantly factual may become more application oriented as employees find it easier to access the facts using the Web. Courses that once taught a subject directly may now focus more on teaching how to use new resources to learn more independently about the same content. These new approaches can shorten the time needed for some formal training. Courses that were a week long, for example, may be reduced by half, as much of the content is moved to more informal and more accessible places. Many of these scenarios will require you to redesign your training programs in much the same way as you probably did when you moved some of your training from classroom to online.

What about instructors and instructional designers? For designers, the reconfiguration of training programs in the light of the growth of KM, collaboration, and performance support initiatives should be nothing new. Courseware is always evolving, either because the content has changed or the way people learn the content has changed. Also, many professional designers schooled in the many aspects of analysis, evaluation, and message design possess an excellent set of skills that can be applied to the design and development of such "nontraining" solutions. For instructors, the changes may be more profound. Some courses may go away, and others will be radically altered. Although there will always be a need for effective teachers, instructors should also understand that what they do is evolving. Their traditional role as presenters of information ("sage on the stage") will give way to an increasing role as facilitators and coaches ("guide on the side").

True Telecom's deployment of KM, collaboration, and performance support will fundamentally change how training is perceived and managed. This can be positive. For Brian, there are now many more ways to learn and get access to information and expertise. Some of these approaches will still be classroom and online courseware. But it's likely that they will be less fact driven and less focused on known algorithmic procedures and more centered on problem solving, teamwork, and innovation. It's also likely that the artificial barrier between formal and informal learning will gradually disappear. For True Telecom and its training organization, the move to a unified and ubiquitous learning and performance architecture has started, but it is a journey more than a destination. To sustain that journey, these organizations must change just as Brian has changed.

Notes

1. Rossett, A., & Sheldon, K. (2001). *Beyond the podium: Delivering training and performance to a digital world*. San Francisco: Pfeiffer, p. 245.
2. The screen shots in this story were built with the Qexchange knowledge management application, and while there are other similar tools (some more robust and others less so), this tool effectively showcases many of the key elements on the workplace side of the learning and performance architecture. www.qinnovation.net.
3. Kaplan, R., & Norton D. (1996). *The balanced scorecard: Translating strategy into action*. Boston: Harvard Business School Press.
4. Bujold, L. M. (1999). *A civil campaign*. New York: Baen Books.
5. Schank, R. (2005). *Lessons in learning, e-learning, and training: Perspectives and guidance for the enlightened trainer*. San Francisco: Pfeiffer, p. 229.
6. Norman, D. (1993). *Things that make us smart: Defending human attributes in the age of the machine*. Reading, MA: Addison-Wesley, p. 181.

Learning Evaluation

So Much Talk, So Little Meaning

Allison Rossett

Graciela: Well, we've been gathering data forever, but there's little impact that I can see.

Riley: We always ask them if they liked the class. Maybe we ask them if they'll recommend it to others. Now we use an instrument that talks about the room temperature, food, and coffee service—got lots of responses on that. I'm not sure we can do anything about any of it, though.

Horatio: I don't think this is working anymore. We're starting to do online training, and I think there are better questions to ask. Even more of a concern is that we're experimenting with nontraining approaches in the workplace. How can we ask them if they liked the class when there is no class?

So much talk. So little meaning. Describe even a single decision made based on data gathered during evaluation. An online community in engineering launched or closed down? A marketing course revised or killed? An informational Web site enhanced with new knowledge needed by the field sales force? A customer care supervisor who added her voice to an online conversation because of increased error rate or lower customer satisfaction?

Few can name specific ways that evaluation has changed how employees learn or, more important, what they do. I know. I've asked.

Too often evaluation is activity done to justify existence or the status quo. And that's not just my opinion. A recent ASTD study asked and found that the number one reason people do evaluation is to prove their value to the organization. There is nothing wrong with that, except that the other key purposes for evaluation were variations on the same theme.

The new world of learning and performance is shouting for help from evaluation and evaluators. As we shift to distributed learning resources, available wherever and whenever, and expectations that employees will make good and habitual decisions, we need better insight into what is working and what is not. Motivation and persistence are defined differently in this new world. We need to look into the process, look hard at the assets, question the guidance systems, and worry about the results. Why? New approaches, from formal online training to a variety of workplace learning strategies, demand attention and continuous improvement based not on whim or habit, but on what's actually happening.

Here are a few questions to think about for starters:

- Are employees actively growing in their jobs? Does that growth match strategic goals?

- Are employees clear about what constitutes excellent performance? Do they self-assess in order to figure out their next steps?

- If a program involves a blend of face-to-face class and technology-based resources, do employees know what to do, where to go, why to choose one asset over another? Do they "keep on keeping on"?

- Do they enjoy and value learning alternatives that help them improve performance?

- Do they stay involved through participation in communities, reference to knowledge bases, conversations with e-coaches? Is involvement easy or a big hassle?

- How much do they use these resources at work? Which ones are favored? Why?

- Does it go two ways? Do they contribute to conversations and knowledge bases?
- When they take an online class, do they get involved? If it is a class with a defined ending—and not all of them end—do they see it through?
- Do they perceive these resources as contributing to the quality of their work? Do the numbers support their views?
- Do they talk with colleagues about the systems that are helping them get smarter and work more effectively? What are they saying?
- Are knowledge assets improved and updated on a regular basis? Are managers smarter about their employees' needs and growth?
- Are supervisors and experts involved in helping employees learn?
- What is the frequency of use of different knowledge assets? Level of satisfaction? Have they been improved to reflect use and satisfaction data? How were they improved?
- Does the system link to careers and performance management?
- Do they know what they have to do to move to new skills? The next career step?

An Accenture 2004 survey of executives found that only 18 percent received weekly or monthly reports about learning effectiveness. That number exactly matches the one U.S. Coast Guard Commander Cathy Tobias and I found when we queried workforce learning and performance professionals about their evaluation efforts.[1] Our work was done in the late 1990s. Accenture's study is much more recent. With all the chatter about Kirkpatrick's four levels of evaluation, accountability, and return on investment, there isn't much to applaud. The environment is not data rich. The data lack legs. Questions do not reflect our new technology and knowledge-rich, employee-centric world.

Evaluation is not as influential as it needs to be. Since you are dreaming new dreams about technology, learning, and performance, now is the time to commit to vivid and actionable evaluations.

Note

1. Rossett, A., & Tobias, C. (1999). An empirical study of the journey from training to performance. *Performance Improvement Quarterly*, *12*(3), 31–43.

◆ ◆ ◆

Allison Rossett is professor of educational technology at San Diego State University. Reach her at arossett@mail.sdsu.edu and at edweb.sdsu.edu/people/ARossett/Arossett.html.

Part Three

BEYOND LEARNING

When great learning comes up against an
unsupportive organizational culture, the culture
wins every time.

8

Making the Change Happen, and Making It Stick

Change is easy, except for the change part.
—*Alan Kay, personal computing guru*[1]

It would be nice to believe that applying new technologies and approaches would, by themselves, facilitate a great organizational learning revolution. It would be nice to think that just by deploying a learning and performance architecture, you would enable a smart enterprise. It would be nice, but it would be a mistake. Implementation is *not* behavior change.

Have you ever spent so much effort introducing what seems to be a great idea that you failed to notice when people either didn't care about it or didn't want it? Nothing you do will have any value if people won't use it. E-learning has often fallen into this trap. Now, as entirely new ways of looking at learning and performance begin to emerge and new technologies are available to support them, a fundamental organizational transformation is required. Careful attention must be paid to help people accept and adopt a new way of learning. Make no mistake: there will be resistance. The question is, "How can resistance be overcome?"

Change management is critical to implementing new and durable approaches to learning. This chapter presents thirteen change management success factors that must be addressed to ensure that new learning initiatives, especially those that represent approaches that are far from traditional, will endure. Ignoring even one of these factors can put innovative learning solutions in jeopardy.

The Importance of Change Management

When you're through changing . . . you're through.

—*Will Rogers*

It is important to ensure that those who will use, and are affected by, new learning approaches willingly embrace them and the changes they represent. Careful and deliberate change management is essential to the acceptance of e-learning and a broad-based learning and performance architecture.

> **Change management** is a set of strategies that focuses on ensuring that an organization and its people are committed to and capable of executing business strategies driven or enabled by innovation. Its objective is to move a business forward toward its goals by improving the readiness and motivation of the workforce to accept and take advantage of change.

Change management is about understanding and working the culture. It is neither marketing nor communications, although it makes use of both. There are critical times when you need to drive awareness of a new initiative and quicken its acceptance and adoption. Marketing and communications can help. But making people aware of something does not mean they will automatically believe in it. That is often the biggest mistake in instituting change, resulting in a failure to sustain the change in the long run. Good change management programs help users become aware of what's going to happen and then to buy into it.

What if users reject a new approach? What if they see the initiative as too disruptive or burdensome, or feel they are not adequately prepared, or that they haven't been told enough about it? If this happens, they could treat it as just another gimmick and quite possibly reject it, making the next effort even tougher.

Changing the way people acquire competence and improve performance, especially if the change is a radical departure from existing practices, has the potential for upsetting personal comfort levels or disrupting an existing organizational culture. It is tough work and not to be taken lightly. And when the change appears to add more structure or process to how people do their jobs, or when it appears to conflict with individual work styles, regardless of whether these perceptions are correct, the challenge is even greater. Research in organizational dynamics, diffusion of innovation, and change suggest that failure to pay attention to prevailing attitudes, beliefs, and practices, even when the benefits of a new way of doing things are totally obvious to all, invites disappointment and often a hardening of previously held positions.

Change Management Success Factors

The dogmas of the quiet past are inadequate to the stormy present. The occasion is piled high with difficulty, and we must rise with the occasion. As our case is new, so we must think anew and act anew.

—Abraham Lincoln

Training is often used as a change management tool. It can be an effective component of a change management strategy, but it is not a panacea. Certainly people will reject a new way of doing things if they don't have the skills to be successful at it. That's where training comes in. But it is not enough to sustain change over the long haul. A more comprehensive approach is needed to achieve a positive and lasting organizational change, including a change in how the organization learns. But what does this mean? What should be done? Here are thirteen success factors to consider when building a change management plan.

Get Leadership Onboard Early

Grassroots support is important, but nothing is more important to the success of a new learning initiative than the support of key leaders and visible role models. When leaders tout a change but refuse to use it themselves, they send two clear messages. The first is that they don't value the initiative, regardless of their rhetoric. This leads to a perception that the change reflects the "flavor of the month" and eventually will go away. The second message is that the change is for "workers," not for executives. This can be perceived as elitist and result in worsening the performance problem rather than fixing it.

> Now that e-learning is distributed to the desktop, many line managers are ill equipped to manage the learning process.
>
> —Bob Mosher, director of learning evangelism and strategy, Microsoft Corporation[2]

It is not just executive leadership that's important; frontline supervisor support is essential. Make sure managers understand the new learning initiative and their role in it. Build support for learning into their performance appraisal, and make it a criterion for advancement. If you can't get your leaders onboard, your learning initiative—be it an incremental change or fundamental transformation—may be doomed before it gets started. But when leaders at all levels—supervisors, managers, and executives—are truly involved, they encourage others to do the same. Here's a test. Look at major changes that have occurred in your organization. See where the change has taken hold and where it has faltered. Now look at the level of leadership support in and for these initiatives. There will undoubtedly be a positive correlation between leadership support, cultural change, and the adoption of the initiative.

Tout Success Stories

Nothing succeeds like success, and success is very appealing to people who are trying something new. When they hear from others like themselves that a new online training program or knowledge management system has made work easier, improved performance, or helped serve customers better, they are more likely to believe that they can benefit as well. It's simply not enough to tell people about the benefits of learning or even show them. You must find ways for potential users to envision themselves in the future state.

Whether you present these stories in live meetings, text, video, online, or any other format, the key to their effectiveness will be their authenticity. Refrain from hiring actors or trying to create overly idealistic situations. Use real people who can relate their personal experiences, perhaps including early struggles and how they overcame them. Success stories, possibly drawn from pilot projects, will give the broader population a way to truly understand that "if they can do it, so can I."

Focus on Early- and Second-Wave Adopters

Some of the best people to tell your story and motivate others to try out new formats for learning and performance are early adopters; people at all levels in the organization naturally want to embrace new things and new thinking. These early adopters tend to be more accepting of new ideas. They are first to try out new technologies and first to get on the bandwagon of new ways of doing things. But they must be more than just the first ones on the bus. They must be able to influence, explain, and show what they are doing so that they spread a positive word that helps others come onboard. The people to get involved early on are those who can and want to be great personal evangelists for your cause.

Early adopters can also be early rejecters. In fact, most change initiatives fail when early adopters reject them. So in the early stages, care must be taken to offer clear value to early adopters and to select people and groups focused on attaining that value rather than groups focused on fads or with short attention spans. Turn covert resistance to overt resistance, so it is out in the open where you can address it. Try to select people and groups with a history of trying out new things and—if the change meets their needs—sticking with them. Look at how these people reacted to other new systems introduced in the past. Look at how well their managers promote new work processes and whether these new approaches were incorporated successfully into the work culture. Use the early adopters you select in pilot programs before full-scale implementation. Monitor their use and attitudes carefully, and provide as much support as needed. These people will generate your first success stories and boost acceptance of the solution when you deploy it to the larger organization.

Early adopters are most likely to embrace change from the start, so you probably need to go further to test the change with people who are not so readily inclined to jump in right away. Second-wave adopters—those who could be persuaded to get onboard but need a little more convincing—are great candidates to test your change and your change management strategy. If they go for it, your chances for success are much improved. And there's probably a lot more of them than early adopters, so they can spread the word much faster.

Avoid Consequences, and Build Incentives

People are much more likely to adopt a new way of doing things when they believe they will benefit. But if they believe that the new system brings with it more work, lots of hassle, ambiguity, and perhaps punishment of some kind (for example, a conflict with how the boss wants work done), they'll avoid it like the plague. So when introducing a new way to learn, remove any negative consequences of participation, and provide the right incentives so that people will do more than try it out: they'll stick with it.

On the incentives side, consider how people will be encouraged to try out a new online training program, contribute to a knowledge repository, or collaborate online, for example. There are many creative approaches that can be tried to cultivate buy-in and support. Here are some examples for building adoption of knowledge management (KM). Think about including limited monetary incentives for high-value KM contributions, not just for participation (perhaps based on user feedback). Special perks for contributors or just special management and peer recognition of individuals for their expertise (removing the Rodney Dangerfield, "I get no respect" attitude) also can be useful. You might offer exclusive access to industry experts or exclusive participation in an industry event as incentives for valuable contributions. You can use opportunities for more or advanced learning in the future as an incentive to participate in learning now. And opportunities to work on innovative projects can also incentivize people to jump in. It's important to recognize that participation can be seen as new work that takes time away from other work. When potential knowledge contributors complain that they have no time, they are surfacing consequences you must deal with, either by reevaluating workloads or convincing participants that work levels will actually decrease as a result of the new KM system (maybe by using success stories or role models).

Build a Solid Value Proposition Based on a Clear Vision and Attainable Benefits

To get real and sustainable acceptance, new learning systems must offer value to users and the business as a whole. Implementing e-learning, KM, or performance support because it's "cool" technology or because everyone else is doing it is hardly a reason for serious long-term support. The value proposition must address at least two groups of people, and it may be different for each. For executives who support and fund the initiative, the initiative must bring benefits to the business. Increased productivity, that is, enabling people to learn more quickly, is one form of value. But good value propositions should be more specific. How might the new learning approaches improve sales results? Enhance the customer care component of the business? Improve the capabilities of your R&D department? The clearer and more precise you are on the value proposition—both quantitative and qualitative business results—the more likely you are to get long-term support from executives.

> Most executives would rather be in an "earning" organization than in a "learning" organization.
> —*Anders Hermre, CEO, InterKnowlege Technologies*[3]

The value proposition should address end users. Why should they accept a new way of doing things? From a change management perspective, people respond positively to a strong vision (how the organization will be better in the future) and attainable benefits (what the solution can be expected to accomplish) rather than features (how the system works and what it does). When developing a value proposition, focus on vision and benefits. Will e-learning make their work easier or save them time? Will KM improve their job performance and contribute positively to their annual review? Features, such as the tracking of online courses, the workings of a search engine, or the collaboration tools available in an online community, are inadequate by themselves to generate support and commitment. Postmortems of disappointing deployments often uncover that the failure to communicate benefits clearly is one of the major causes of nonadoption.

Involve Stakeholders and Constituents Throughout the Process

Being a part of change is much more likely to lead to success than being the object of change. Those who are involved in the creation of something new are much more likely to support it. As much as possible, those who will use new learning tools should be part of their design. One of the best ways to do this is to form a steering committee representing all stakeholders—developers, users, and managers, for example—that will have, at the least, direct input into the design of the solution and, more so, some governance or decision-making power. If necessary, because executives and users might have different interests, several groups can be formed. It is important that the input of all groups, especially end users, is incorporated into the project from the start.

These groups can serve as a ready-made pilot population, provide "eyes and ears" in the field to report back on how the system is or is not being used, and, if all goes well, serve as a strong group of advocates during deployment that can mean the difference between adoption and rejection.

In a study by England's Charted Institute for Professional Development, more than 90 percent of respondents agreed that e-learning demands a new attitude on the part of participants.[4] The bottom line is to involve stakeholders early on. This will lead them to accept the forthcoming change as being done *with* them and *for* them rather than *to* them.

Avoid a "This Won't Work" Message

"It can't be done." "It will never work." These comments are heard often when something new is introduced. Negative attitudes—seeing failure before you even get started—can be disastrous to a learning initiative. It's a mistake to think that these attitudes are entirely based on a desire to avoid something new and different. Often these feelings result from experience with previous efforts that were poorly conceived or poorly executed. Positive communications can significantly counter feelings that the project is going to fail.

Set Priorities

One person's critical issue can be someone else's trivial concern. The priorities of end users and sponsors go hand-in-hand with their view of the project's likelihood of success. People who think your initiative is critical (a high priority) but also feel that it won't succeed are bound to be the most disappointed and discouraged if the initiative does fail. And they may be more resistant the next time around. This is even worse if management attaches a high priority to the initiative but fails to instill this in those who will use the system. People will be bewildered and feel that what you are introducing is just another management fad. Again, the key is alignment: a high priority ("we need this") with a perception that the solution will actually work.

Dispel Fears of Technology

In today's Internet-savvy world, it's easy to assume that everyone is totally comfortable with technology. But there are still lots of people who are new to computers. There are also lots of people who use computers every day and still have trouble performing tasks like upgrading to new operating systems or installing software (if you're not sure about this, try playing your child's video games). Clerks who have worked for years on mainframe "green-screen" systems may have trouble moving to a Windows- or mouse-based system. Salespeople who have always gone to class for training may view online courseware with dread. Managers who have stored critical documents on their C-drive may be fearful of placing those same documents in a centralized knowledge repository. Always assume that any significant change in hard or soft technology, the way that technology is used, or in how that technology alters work or learning routines may surface some fear and trepidation.

For end users, use lots of demonstrations and testimonials. Place prototypes around work areas for people to test-drive. Provide adequate training and human support. Identify experienced technology buddies in each department to help out and serve as role models. For "techies" (who might lead the "it's impossible" charge), offer advanced technical briefings with the development team, and make sure the IT department is a full participant and that the help desk staff are well informed and prepared to offer technical support once the change is initiated.

Give People Time to Adapt

Almost all change initiatives find resistance early on. But it's far worse when people feel that they're being rushed into something they're not sure of. They want and need time to consider how the change will affect them. If something new is being launched on January 1, for example, telling people about it on December 31 is too late to expect that they'll be ready and open to the new approach. A significant period of disruption will occur as people try to figure out what it all means and whether it's "for real." This lack of preparedness can sometimes overwhelm the new initiative, and it won't catch on. Providing adequate time to help people understand, question, and ultimately accept a new technology-based approach to learning before it is launched will dramatically reduce disruption time and give the initiative a much greater likelihood of success. This calls for communication, success stories, role modeling, and demonstrations and prototypes early on, even when the system is still under development.

Don't leap too far, too fast. Some people, like early adopters, can move easily from "what was" to "what's new." Others need time. You may want to roll out your change in stages, or overlap the availability of the new solution with the old, giving people adequate time to experiment, then accept, and ultimately commit to the change. And don't forget to monitor how the change is progressing on a regular basis. It is highly likely you'll be required to make several adjustments along the way.

Don't Forget Training

Remember that training can be a vital component of your change management strategy. It begins early, before deployment. It should focus primarily on the user experience, be personalized to the user's skill and experience level, allow lots of practice, and provide realistic scenarios that depict how participants (not the designers) will use the system to get work done and how it will benefit them (value proposition). Training should not be limited to new tools, features, and functionalities, which is often the only training that is offered.

It should also address how to get the most out of those tools, features, and functionalities in the context of work, through authentic simulation and application.

Too often trainers mistakenly focus only on users and not on their managers. People in leadership and authority positions will be watched closely to see if they use new learning systems. Train them first, and make sure they understand their unique role not just in the learning initiative, but in the change process as well. Finally, the use of good online help to develop managers as "knowledge coaches," including a liberal use of examples and models, can help transfer the impact of the training back to the workplace.

Provide Ongoing Support

Change management often begins and ends with the rollout: lots of marketing, communications, training, and hoopla around the new system—and then, down the road, nothing. Initial enthusiasm can be quickly replaced with doubt and discouragement as problems arise (and they always do) without any means to resolve them. People become reluctant to change and could revert back to their old ways. It is important not to quit your change effort just because early indications are good.

This can be prevented in part through ongoing support. The best change management efforts extend well beyond initial deployment, with continued training, help lines, newsletters, support Web sites and other forms of communication (usually online), testimonials, success stories and case studies, and so forth. Even a local peer group or steering committee that meets once a week to discuss how the transformation is proceeding and offer suggestions for improvement can be invaluable.

Don't Confuse "I Can't" with "I Won't"

When implementing change management, it is important not to mistake *resistance* to change with *inability* to change. Several success factors point to approaches to get buy-in, while others focus more on building skills. For example, if you notice that people are skilled in using computers for learning but don't particularly like that approach (they may continue to prefer the classroom), skill-building efforts may not only be wasted, but may make the resistance stronger. More likely, role modeling, success stories, and incentives may be appropriate.

Many people who moved from classroom training to online training liked the fact that they could take the training any time they wanted, but did not complete online training because they didn't know how to manage their own learning. Without an instructor to keep them on task or a schedule class to carve out time for, they were lost. Here's another example: if you find employees are eager to use a new KM system but don't know how to use it effectively, continuing to sell them on the new approach may have the opposite effect, converting their enthusiasm into cynicism. Instead, focusing on a strategy that includes training, demonstrations, and support to help build their confidence and capability will more likely to reinforce and accelerate the change process.

DILBERT: © Scott Adams/Dist. by United Feature Syndicate, Inc.

From Awareness to Understanding to Preference

A good communications plan is a key element of a solid change management strategy, the goal of which is to move people through three adoption stages: from awareness ("I know I'm going to be learning differently"), to understanding ("I understand how I will learn differently and what it means for me"), to preference ("I want to move to the new way to learn"). As mentioned under "ongoing support," going beyond the rollout is also important here: too often new training programs, including online training programs, have been launched with great fanfare and celebration. This will certainly draw interest and even use—for a while. But if people don't believe in it, if they think it is something that will make their work lives more difficult, if they believe it takes away something they've become used to without giving them something better, that use spike is guaranteed to be short-lived. If you fail to go beyond awareness, as is too often the case, you will likely see a sharp rise in interest and participation in a new learning venture, followed by a severe drop-off and a return to old ways. Marketing helps build awareness. Information, supported by conversation, demonstrations, and opportunities to try it out, builds understanding. Success stories and testimonials ("I did it, so can you!"), role modeling, proper incentives, benefits ("what's in it for me?"), strong leadership, delivered over the long term, and experience with the new way of doing things build preference and staying power. (A sample change management and communications plan is illustrated in Appendix E.)

At the end of the day, no new learning initiative of any type can survive an organization that doesn't value it or won't accept it. If your investment in a solution does not include a corresponding investment in change management, you may be throwing more than your financial investment down a rat hole. You may be tossing out a big piece of your credibility too. Paying attention to change management and the thirteen change management success factors gives you a huge advantage as you introduce new ways to learn and perform. It takes time, but getting stakeholders and constituents onboard can make all the difference between a successful implementation and starting over.

Notes

1. Alan Kay, currently president of Viewpoint Research Institute and an HP fellow and founding principal of the Xerox Palo Alto Research Center, has made this comment a number of

times. Kay was also a fellow at Apple Computer and Disney Imagineering.

2. E-learning's greatest legacy. (2005, July). *CLO Magazine*, p. 14.
3. Dragoon, A. (2004, October 15). KM by any other name. *CIO Magazine, 18*(2), 65.
4. Sloman, M., & Van Buren, M. (2003, May 18). *E-learning's learning curve: Will they come, will they learn?* Presented at the ASTD Conference, San Diego, CA.

Seeing Learning Differently

Nancy Lewis

I didn't wake up one day, after many years at IBM, and suddenly think to myself, "We need to revamp our approach to learning." It took time. After all, IBM is a successful company, and we've always had a strong commitment to training. Even customers were interested in our approach to training—a winning formula, it would seem. So why mess with it? Why rethink our learning strategy?

For me, it didn't start with a new technological innovation or some stunning insight into learning theory. It started with the business. At IBM, growth is key to our future; our vision and strategy sharply focus on this goal. But you can't grow by productivity or cost savings alone. You have to create new business models to capture new opportunities—models that drill down to how people work and learn. And technology becomes a great enabler of this effort because it allows you to do things you could not have done before.

I've seen several studies where CEOs cite a lack of a skilled workforce as a major barrier to growth. Some of these skills can be outsourced, but when you get into new paradigms of innovation to make the business grow, as we are, we're likely dealing with capabilities that don't yet exist in the marketplace. We have to take it on ourselves to rethink training and learning so that as IBM changes, it will have a learning strategy aligned with its new direction.

Business leaders understand this. They know that the rate of information change is accelerating, growing faster than our ability to consume it. The result is that we will all have skill gaps all the time and that skill gaps will be a constant state of life in the future. We also know that our roles are becoming as complex as the knowledge we work with. There will never be enough time to learn everything we need to know. There is such a consistent and rapid churn of the skills and knowledge required to maintain job performance that learning can no longer be provided as a set of events. This is the new challenge for learning: enabling people to capitalize on new technologies, discoveries, and business insights, to be first to the marketplace with new solutions that exceed our clients' needs and expectations. The essence of any company's ability to adapt and grow is its ability to learn. And that involves new ways of thinking about an approach to learning.

We need to think in different ways. We looked at where learning actually takes place most of the time, and it's in the workplace, not in the classroom. We learn naturally on the job. We learn by doing, by solving problems. There will always be a need for formal training, but it will likely be much more in direct support of the capabilities that cannot be learned in the workplace.

At IBM, we think there's a pressing need for a learning model to incorporate the on-the-job aspect of how people learn. Today's training and development have undeniable strengths and have served organizations well in the past. But today's development and delivery methods are often a poor fit for tomorrow's needs and tomorrow's pace. A growing discontinuity exists between what business has become and what training has remained.

We are not working on another "program." This is a fundamental, seminal change for us. But it is also actionable and concrete. We're not just talking; we're doing. We begin by focusing on what happens on the job, what our people need to accomplish. Then we ask ourselves, "How can we support these folks in the context of their work activities rather than always removing them from work to go to training? What is it that we can do as learning professionals to amplify and ratchet up the learning that happens naturally in the workplace?" Remember that if you stop ten people in the hallway and ask them how it is that they know what they know or how they can do what they do, they *never* say, "I went to class.'"

Our On Demand Learning strategy focuses on how learning can enable people and business as a whole to change the traditional learning model. It integrates learning into the daily routines of employees, teams, functional workflows, and organizations by:

- Embedding learning in process workflows, increasing learning while doing.
- Using technology to deliver personalized, easily accessible, role-enabling, and collaborative learning.
- Driving innovation and business growth by reshaping individual, team, and organizational learning.

We want to know how we can use information transfer technologies to get best practices to our people quickly. Time matters, and anything we can do to keep people up-to-speed really matters. We want to know how we can improve work processes and tools to enable our people to focus more on performance and our clients rather than having to struggle with new and sophisticated work processes. We don't want people to have to go to class to learn how to master a complex process; we'd rather look at that process and embed the learning required to master it right into its actual workflow. We want our teams in the field to benefit from what others are doing, so we want all of IBM's best practices to be at the fingertips of all IBMers. This goes beyond codified information. Technology is increasingly allowing us to significantly enhance accessibility to people and their expertise, making it easier for employees to learn from their colleagues. And ultimately, not all work and not all business problems are created equal. Our goal is to pick the learning initiatives that will have the biggest impact on our business success.

In a few years, I would like to see that the paradigm shift has taken place, that people's mind-sets around learning in the workplace have changed, and that learning and work are indistinguishable from each other—that it's in the DNA of the company.

Learning has a lot of different responsibilities. In addition to understanding the direct correlation between learning and earning, employees understand that it helps them compete for opportunities within the company to advance their career, makes them feel that they can improve their professional expertise, and makes them want to stay with IBM. It affects the morale of the workforce. Opinion surveys tell us that our employees feel they are advantaged when the company invests in their learning and development, and it draws people to want to work for us.

For IBM, the future of learning has started. IBM Learning recognizes the importance of creating new models for learning that keep pace with the changes in our business. Just as sophisticated advances in technology enable businesses to achieve new and different goals, build new business models, and require new workforce models to achieve those goals, technology also offers—even demands—that we create new approaches to leverage learning in the workplace to advance how employees work and learn. IBM is shifting the emphasis from bringing the worker to the learning to bringing the learning to the work, an exciting new era that promises to leverage the collective expertise of employees, teams, and organizations throughout the enterprise.

◆ ◆ ◆

Nancy Lewis is vice president of On Demand Learning for IBM.

9

Championing Learning

Leadership and learning are indispensable to each other.
—*John F. Kennedy*[1]

Leadership is a funny thing. Strong leaders are highly desirable, but if the decisions that leaders make are not in keeping with your views, you might question their leadership abilities. Who doesn't think learning is good? It's like motherhood and apple pie; no one would argue that learning has no value or purpose. Whether they lead whole companies or smaller departments, almost all leaders say they support learning. The question, of course, is what constitutes support and how that support can be nurtured.

This chapter is about true learning champions: how to find them, build on their sponsorship, and use them to advance your new and expanded learning and performance strategy. It is about recognizing leadership in others and in yourself, so that you can leverage its power. Working for someone who truly buys in to what you are doing is great, but working for someone who says he or she supports you but sets up roadblocks every step of the way is just bad business. If you want to implement the new learning approaches covered in this book, you must to be able to tell the difference.

Picking the Right Sponsors

The history of training, and especially e-learning, is replete with high expectations and successes, but also big disappointments. Technology is sometimes the culprit: you spend so much time and effort getting it to work that when you do, you have little energy or resources for anything else. Other times, it is failure to focus on change management; what you think is the greatest learning program ever created is just one more distraction to someone else. But perhaps the most disarming roadblock is a lack of sponsorship, especially when you think you have it but find out too late you really don't. Picking the right sponsor is essential for any new initiative. E-learning, whether it is more traditional or part of a broader learning and performance architecture, falls into this category. When looking at potential sponsors, keep in mind that not everything is always what it seems to be.

Sponsor Styles

> The bottleneck is at the top of the bottle.
> —Gary Hamel[2]

Management consultant Nigel Barlow provides a useful way to classify sponsors. Adapted from his work, you are likely to face one or more of these four styles of sponsors (Figure 9.1): spectators, the walking dead, obstructionists, and players.[3]

Spectators. A spectator is probably the most common style of sponsor. Spectators are enthusiastic; they display a lot of positive attitude around training, learning, and e-learning. However, like spectators everywhere, they are also likely to sit on the sidelines, waiting for something to happen. If you do well, they cheer you; if not, they'll either be silent or negative and distance themselves from you and your initiative.

The danger is assuming that cheerleading equals commitment. If the going gets rough or you assume more support than is actually there, you could be left exposed down the road. For example, if you

Figure 9.1 Four Sponsor Styles

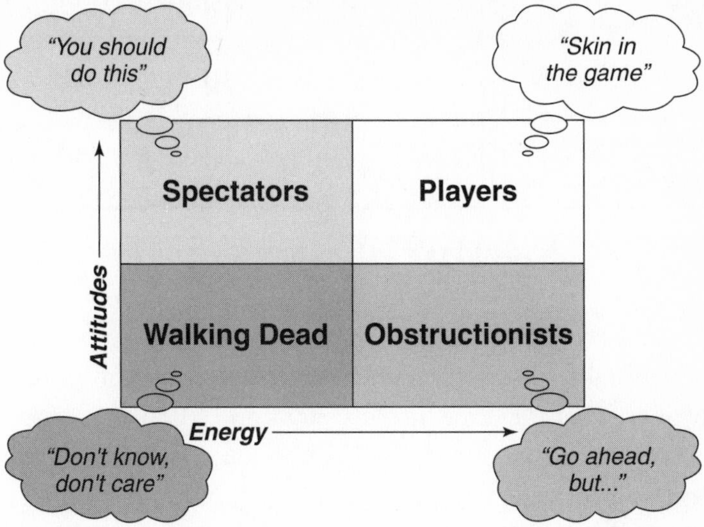

Source: Adapted from the work of Nigel Barlow.

assume support just because spectators tell you they support you and then spend a significant amount of money on learning staff, technology, or other products and services without a specific financial commitment, you may not have the backing you need when it comes time to pay the bill.

With spectators, your approach should be to show them success stories and convince them that other executives like themselves are getting involved. When they see that your ideas work and that others are already benefiting, they may get on board.

The Walking Dead. The walking dead are totally nonsupportive. Whether their views are about you and your project specifically, or the overall effort and direction of innovative learning and performance programs, trying to bring these people around is probably a waste of time; they have neither the right attitude nor the level of energy needed to be effective sponsors. They just don't care.

DILBERT: © Scott Adams/Dist. by United Feature Syndicate, Inc.

Spending too much effort trying to turn the walking dead around can be a mistake. First, you expend your resources, valuable time, and goodwill on what might be fruitless effort, and second, you are likely to miss opportunities elsewhere. Even if you could convince these leaders to support you, that support is likely to be temporary and risky, perhaps with far worse consequences than having done nothing at all.

Even if you see a great opportunity, seeking support from the walking dead is probably a showstopper. They will come around only if forced or see it in their own self-interest. Move on to other projects, even if they are smaller; your likelihood of success will be far greater. Perhaps these leaders eventually will move to another sponsorship style and you'll be able to work with them.

> When you discover that you are riding a dead horse, the best strategy is to dismount.
>
> —*Tribal wisdom of the Dakota Indians*

Obstructionists. Obstructionists have lots of energy around new initiatives. When you come to them with a new learning idea, they'll want to do it right away—if you can prove to them that it's worth it (in their eyes). They are most likely to place unrealistic barriers in your way, and once you move past them, they'll find more. Sometimes these barriers mask a hidden agenda: they may not be supporters at all but have a need to show some activity around your initiative.

You can turn obstructionists around, but you have to do it on their terms. Overcoming initial barriers in ways that make obstructionists more comfortable and secure tends to lower their resistance. Building momentum for your initiative gradually, through a series of successes, can be a good approach. Success stories and solid business case work help a great deal. Obstructionists often respond well to peers, so use allies to help you reach them.

Players.   Players are most likely to be long-term, serious sponsors. They get involved by writing checks, becoming role models, and showing how your initiative links to their business issues. Their willingness to invest their time, money, and resources in your effort will increase your likelihood of success.

Work with players even if the project is small. Here is where you can build the small success stories that will showcase what you can do in learning and e-learning. These success stories will attract the interest of some spectators and obstructionists, and eventually may even turn the walking dead to your side. But keep in mind that the commitment you get from these leaders can be shattered if your project doesn't achieve their business goals. Finding a player who believes in and supports your innovative learning project is terrific, but only if you make it work. Keep your eye on the right objectives, and don't bite off more than you can chew.

Creating Executive-Sponsor Alignment

Whether your new project represents incremental improvements, like adding new courses or upgrading your technology, or a fundamental change in your learning and e-learning strategy, be sure your sponsors are onboard as you begin. This avoids surprises and disappointments later and gets influential allies involved from the start. Understanding sponsor styles is a start. Now you can move on to executive alignment.

It is important to know whether your sponsors are on the same path with you or heading off in different directions. Ask yourself, "How do executives and other key leaders view my project? Are they truly with me, or is it just a lot of words?" You can begin with an executive alignment exercise. This tool, found in Appendix F, can help you begin to understand areas of agreement and differences with your executive sponsors. A low score on the tool strongly suggests that you work things out with your sponsors before getting started so that there are no misunderstandings along the way.

Leading Your Organization to Change the Way It Learns

Once you have solid sponsorship, you need to look at your own leadership responsibilities. Change management should guide you in developing a sound plan to get executives, managers, and users onboard. In addition to the broader organization, you must also focus directly on your own team's ability to lead the change that is represented by your new learning strategy. Carla O'Dell, of the American Productivity and Quality Center, points to five areas for consideration when leading your team to readiness: vision, value proposition, strategy, resources, and wins.[4] How do they relate to e-learning and learning and performance?

Vision. Be sure you have a vision for what you want to change and where you want to go. If your vision is weak or missing, you will be missing a foundation to guide you the rest of the way. Vision questions you should answer about the future direction of your learning and e-learning strategy include:

- Do you see yourself as in the commodity business (lots of courses and other products) or in the service business (solving problems and capitalizing on opportunities)?

- How will learning and e-learning in your organization be different a year from now? Three years from now?
- If you are successful, what will people (from executives to end users) say about your accomplishments?

Value proposition. Be sure you have a sound value proposition that goes beyond the learning benefits and speaks to business benefits. In fact, lack of alignment with business goals, and ensuing business pain, will likely result in a value proposition that is overly simplistic or unimportant. So in determining your value proposition, ask yourself not what you think is important, but what your CEO would think is important.

> If you know what's keeping your CEO up at night, you'll know what you should concentrate on during the daytime.
>
> —George Selix, senior vice president, Learning and Organizational Effectiveness, Consumer Real Estate, Bank of America[5]

Without a solid value proposition, you will not be able to justify what you are about to do, and you may put the entire initiative at risk. Value proposition questions to be answered include:

- What specific benefits will the business derive from a new approach to learning and e-learning? What will the impact be on performance and the overall value proposition?
- How will you measure the success of your efforts?
- What will motivate people in your organization to learn in new ways?

Strategy. Develop a comprehensive implementation strategy for moving forward that addresses all the components of your initiative and how they will work together to achieve the vision. Without a viable strategy, you will have less leverage across the organization around what you want to accomplish. See if you can answer these learning and e-learning strategy-related questions:

- How will you achieve your vision and deliver value to your organization?
- Are your vision and strategy aligned with senior management?
- What will change and what will remain the same around how you and the organization operate?
- How will organization structure and interdependencies change as a result of implementing your strategy? How will your department be affected?

Resources. Be sure you have the resources you need to execute your strategy. Otherwise you will likely experience considerable frustration and delay, too much of which can be disastrous in maintaining your momentum toward your goal. In planning your resource needs, think about how you might respond to these questions:

- Do you have the right people, with the right skills and motivation, to implement your learning and e-learning strategy? If not, where will you get them?
- What new skills will you and your team need? What skills will your clients and constituents need? What skills will no longer be as important?
- Do you have a long-term plan to ensure that you have the right tools and technologies in place, when you need them, without overly depending on technology as a substitute for strategy?
- Do you have committed and long-term financial resources necessary to see your plans through to full deployment and beyond?

Wins. Be able to showcase some wins. Getting support based on a promise or a future payoff can only go so far. Having some success stories, no matter how small, gives you the credibility you'll need to get long-term support for scaling your strategy. "Small" should not be confused with "insignificant." Pick something with impact and something you can handle; don't try to solve all the world's problems at once. Here are some key questions to answer regarding wins:

- Do you have success stories—even small ones—that sell your vision and strategy for learning and e-learning?
- Are you working with people who are most likely to be supportive in the early going, thus improving your chances of getting those critical early wins?
- Are you fully prepared to demonstrate your value by effectively showcasing your wins and winning over skeptics to your side?

Early in this book, you were advised not to refer to people in training as learners but rather to refer to them based on what they actually do. As you determine how best to lead your organization and how best to advocate your value, is calling yourself a trainer and referring to your function as training still appropriate? Trainers have become "performance consultants" and "learning specialists" in an effort to expand their role, and training organizations have turned to calling themselves "corporate universities," "learning centers of excellence," or "performance improvement organizations" to do the same. What an individual or an organization is called, and how successful the new label is, is very much based on the pervading culture. While changing what you are called is nothing compared to changing what you do, labels do matter, so think carefully how you really want to be seen by your constituents and stakeholders.

Governance

> If we don't hang together, we most assuredly will hang separately.
>
> —Benjamin Franklin

One critical leadership area that is often overlooked is governance: the overall decision-making process and management of your learning strategy and resources across the smart enterprise. Too often, training organizations in different departments or different business units operate too independently. Not only do they fail to partner with other organizations like IT and HR, but they often don't partner with each other. Even if you have only a single training group, you can benefit from sound governance as it will help you build better working relationships across your organization.

The history of the training business, especially in larger organizations, is full of feuding among training departments, redundant learning efforts across business units, and conflict between training and other functions, like IT and HR. As e-learning in all its forms becomes more mainstream, organizations that cannot work together and pool resources will not last very long. If you find that learning programs in different parts of the business are competing against each other, you can't agree on centralization and decentralization issues, you are indecisive or inefficient in your insourcing or outsourcing strategy, or you have difficulty allocating human, technical, and financial recourses across the business, you likely need more governance than you probably have.

Learning and e-learning governance can range from a formal decision-making body with lots of control and power to an informal collaborative body that simply keeps everyone apprised of what's going on. Either way, governance helps avoid duplication of effort and provides opportunities to leverage resources better. A governance program can give you a single voice to executive leadership, including important business unit leaders and the CIO; provide more leverage for learning among enterprise priorities; and provide everyone with a more strategic perspective. It will help you find ways to centralize scalable assets and programs, such as technical infrastructure, professional development, and vendor management, while decentralizing areas that meet diverse business or local needs, such as content development and delivery. And it will help you develop a more comprehensive staffing plan—one that best uses your precious learning and technical talent. Whatever your situation, you can build a governance effort by following ten basic principles:

- **Agreement on governance is a more important first step than the structure of governance.** The first thing you have to do is get everyone to meet and agree to form a governance body. Start with a level of governance that everyone will support, even if it is voluntary at first.
- **Live by your charter.** Governance needs rules that participants can live with. Create a charter or a set of operating principles for your governance group, and once you get agreement, stick to it. As in any form of self-government, a constitution loses its meaning if it is amended to meet every whim or resolve every disagreement.
- **There is no "land grab."** Governance is not about power and dominance. It is about collaboration and enlightened self-interest. You will never get anywhere if your governance efforts are a disguise for consolidating control.
- **Involve all constituents and stakeholders.** Not everyone can or should lead your governance effort, but everyone should be involved. People are more likely to participate if they feel that they, and the groups they represent, are valued. Consider a tip from the U.S. Declaration of Independence and strive for "consent of the governed." Governance means shared decision making. Although not everything can be put to a vote, try to have as much group direction setting as possible. This combats any possible feelings that the group is merely for show.

- **Include education.** Governance activities are ideal opportunities to educate members on a number of levels: business issues, learning strategies, technologies, and more. Use part of your governance meetings to enlighten your community about the challenges and opportunities they face.

- **Go physical and virtual.** Many of the principles for running a vibrant community of practice apply to your governance group. Live meetings can be balanced with online activities that keep members involved on an ongoing basis.

- **Make it valuable.** People stop going to meetings if they believe they are getting nothing out of them. This can kill any governance effort. Be sure you address the real business, operations, and learning needs of your members and their constituents.

- **Don't think you can do it all inside.** Today, governance in the learning and e-learning space means not just working with internal groups and resources, but also working with valued outside partners and suppliers. As the field gets more complex and technological, it is impossible to completely keep up with new skills and tools. Finding the right partners, even if they are on the other side of the globe, and forming a mutually productive relationship with them will be an increasingly important governance activity.

- **Show leadership commitment.** Governance efforts are more likely to succeed if there is support from above, outside the governance group. When you get senior executive sponsorship for your governance efforts, you increase the likelihood of having staying power and meaningful impact.

- **Get out there.** Governance should be visible. Closed-door meetings create suspicion and skepticism. Have as many open meetings as possible, and send representatives out to talk to constituents on their own turf. Communicate with them in print, over the Web, and in person as often as you can.

At a time when the pace of business and the need to constantly adapt is accelerating, learning and e-learning governance is essential. It can be the bridge between how effectively you lead your own organization and how well you build organizational sponsorship for what you do. Agreeing on governance should be one of the first things you do as you rethink your strategy.

If We Build It, Will They Come?

As illustrated in Figure 9.2, change management and communications and effective leadership are essential tools for building a culture where a smart enterprise can succeed. Together they prepare the organization for a new era in learning.

Figure 9.2 Supporting the Smart Enterprise with Change Management, Communications, and Leadership

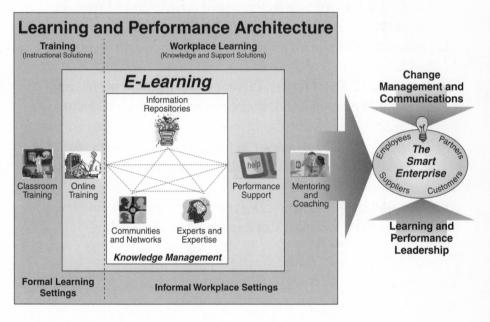

Whether you work in a training department or run it, whether you are a chief learning officer or a more traditional business executive, championing learning involves some rethinking of your role. Of course, providing and managing training is important, but learning leadership is more. It is thinking more strategically, even transformationally, about the role of learning in the organization. It is not just about training people; it is about helping them develop, grow, and deal with constant change. Building a highly trained workforce is merely a step on the way to building a smart enterprise and enhancing the organization's ability to learn and innovate. You'll never get there if you haven't moved people beyond simple awareness of new ways to learn to preferring new ways to learn. You're likely to go nowhere if you can't get sponsors onboard, or if you can't bring all your resources and allies together under one tent. But if you build it well and lead the way, they will come.

Notes

1. Kennedy, J. F. (1963). Speech prepared for delivery in Dallas on the day of his assassination, November 22, 1963.
2. Hamel, G. (1996, July 1). Strategy as revolution. *Harvard Business Review*, pp. 69–81.
3. Barlow, N. (2003, April 9). Presentation at the Chartered Institute of Personnel and Development Conference, London, England.
4. O'Dell, C. (2002, September 12). *KM in action: Looking back and looking ahead*. Human Capital Live! Webcast presented by Saba.
5. Selix, G. (2004, October 29). Presentation at Northern New Jersey ASTD E-Learning Conference, Morristown, NJ.

Is E-Learning Underhyped?

Kevin Oakes

I was thumbing through an industry magazine recently and a bold statement caught my eye: "The e-learning industry is underhyped! E-learning is a thriving industry that is still in its infancy," stated the author, a fairly well-known industry guru.

That's a cheap way to capture attention, I thought. Give me a random sampling of learning professionals who lived through the e-learning initial public offerings, the bubble burst, and the ensuing consolidation, and I'd be willing to bet that 99 percent of them would not use the term *underhyped* to describe the industry.

Yet as I thought about it, I realized that I didn't believe e-learning was overhyped. Sure, the expectations were too lofty for the e-learning industry in the late 1990s. That could be said for just about any sector during the dot-com heyday, so it's hardly a damning statement.

Still, anyone can see that the e-learning industry is far from being labeled a success. So what went wrong? Rather than being underhyped or overhyped, the longer I'm in this industry, the stronger I feel that e-learning, and learning in general, has been mishyped.

Our industry seems fascinated by the different methods of training a human being. Every consultant I meet seems to feel he or she has a better mousetrap for delivering training and stinging criticism of the status quo. We can always use new and better tools and approaches for learning, and questioning how we currently do things is healthy. But too often we lose track of the real reasons we are in this business. Why do we love to debate the means but spend so precious little time on the ends?

While learning professionals spend hours debating philosophical approaches to learning, many have failed to focus on the fact that they work in for-profit companies that primarily value only those things that ultimately increase shareholder value. The small number of real-life case studies, the deficiency of tangible metrics, and the general lack of focus on business results by the learning profession have kept the profession from being viewed as strategic; instead, they are viewed as a necessary evil in the minds of many senior executives.

One of my favorite stories in the industry was told to me by Pat Crull, whom I had the pleasure of working with during her tenure as chair of the ASTD board of directors. Pat has been the CLO at several prominent companies and one day told me about a CLO panel presentation she gave at an industry conference.

"During my presentation, I stated that as a CLO, I see myself as an officer of the corporation. I worry about improving shareowner value. If it doesn't make a difference to the bottom line, then my work has little or no value." At that point, a woman in the audience got up and left the room. "Later, during the Q&A section of our presentation," Crull continues, "someone who was sitting next to the woman who had left stood up and said, 'Do you know what she said right before she exited? That she didn't get into the training and development field to worry about the bottom line.' I was stunned. To me, that summed up the biggest problem in our profession today."

A previous ASTD board chair, John Cone, expanded on this point with me when I was researching an article for *T+D Magazine*, "A Seat at the Table," which lamented that learning professionals generally don't have a place in the strategic discussions in corporations.

"Learning professionals who have the ear of senior management come to the table to talk about business results, not learning pedagogy," said Cone. "They understand the drivers of the business, how the executives think, and the metrics that mean the most to them. They talk about business outcomes, not learning enablers. And they talk about their business using real business language and real data. They talk about revenue, expense, productivity, customer satisfaction, and other quantifiable stuff that businesspeople care about. They've learned that every conversation had better include information about money or time saved, revenue or new business generated, or customer problems solved."

Which brings me back to e-learning being mishyped. E-learning is doing more today to flesh out real business metrics than anything else that has occurred in the profession since Kirkpatrick invented the fourth level. Today robust reports and real-time dashboards are showing a direct correlation between learning programs and improvement in the core measurements that businesses care about: increasing revenue, decreasing expenses, improvement in cycle time, and rising customer satisfaction.

The companies that have applied this focus and exhibited these correlations look at learning differently. Far from a necessary evil, it has become critical to the strategy of the organization, and technology has been the enabler. The CTO at GlaxoSmithKline told my organization recently that our learning management system is the second most used application in the company, right behind Lotus Notes. He also called it one of the three hottest applications within his organization. The reason it has attained this lofty status is that they rely on it daily for many different kinds of information dissemination, collaboration, and best practice sharing. But mostly they have measured the connection between the "how's" and the business metrics, and produced attention-grabbing results. That's what you need to be strategic and mission critical.

While it certainly has been chic to criticize e-learning, the truth is that technology is now doing more to legitimize the learning business than anything else in the past several decades. What the e-learning industry needs to hype are the business success stories as opposed to the dizzying array of different applications and make sure C-level executives understand the correlation among learning, performance, and results. Once that happens, learning professionals won't need cheap ploys to capture attention; they'll be sitting at the table, front and center.

◆ ◆ ◆

Kevin Oakes is president of SumTotal Systems, the business performance and learning technology industry's largest single provider of technologies, processes, and services. He can be reached at koakes@sumtotalsystems.com.

10

From E-Learning
to Learning to Performance

We are confronted with insurmountable opportunities.
—*Pogo*

This book began with a discussion of the current state of e-learning and the reality that e-learning, and training in general, are far too limited for today's fast-paced organizations and for the accelerating rate of knowledge change. It went on to introduce the smart enterprise, where the organization forges a new relationship with learning: how it acquires, shares, and distributes knowledge and skills in support of improved performance. These new approaches work in harmony to deliver integrated skill, knowledge, and support beyond the classroom and into the workplace. Training, knowledge management, collaboration, and performance support are organized not as singular, siloed functions but as part of a broad-based learning and performance architecture. Finally, change management and leadership were introduced as ways to increase the likelihood that any learning intervention (or suite of interventions) deployed to improve both individual and organizational performance will be successful and sustainable. This final chapter puts it all together and lays out a performance-centric path to follow going forward.

Nonlearning Approaches
to Performance Improvement

Preparation is everything.

—*Motto,* Culinary Institute of America

Have you ever come up with an answer before you knew what the question was? Too often training or another learning solution is proposed before there is a clear picture of the problem to be addressed. Misdiagnosis of the problem is one of the biggest contributors to wasted efforts, training or otherwise.

Moving right to implementation, like offering a course when you don't really know if it's the right solution, is like throwing dice; you are hoping you've rolled the right numbers (that is, the right solution), but you won't know until you're totally committed and your money is on the table. You may win or you may lose. Do you want to take the risk?

When Henry Ford instituted the assembly line, he fundamentally changed the way work was done and revolutionized manufacturing. Today, much of the increase in business productivity comes not necessarily through more learning but from changes to the work environment, such as better tools and technologies (such as computers and communications devices), streamlined work processes, even changes to physical office space. When personal word processing became standard issue in most businesses, it changed the way the work got done and, to a large extent, the people who did the work. When artists use computers instead of pen and ink to create animation, the very nature of that profession was forever altered. In both cases, performance and productivity increased as the nature of the work changed.

But changing the working environment involves more than just physical enhancements. You can also improve performance by focusing on workers directly. Incentives and rewards, such as pay, recognition (for example, employee of the month), or a better work-life balance (for example, by offering telecommuting as an option), are also critical factors that play a role in improving performance. It's basic human nature to work smarter, better, and harder when the benefits of doing so, to the individual and the organization, are rewarding rather than punishing.

Hiring and firing employees, while sometimes necessary, is frightfully expensive (including the costs of constantly training and developing new workers), which is why companies pay so much attention to selection (hiring people with the right entry skills, knowledge, motivation, and potential) and retention issues.

Before you jump too quickly to a learning solution, make sure you have investigated and identified all the workplace factors that bear on performance. If people know how to do something but can't, perhaps because they have inadequate tools, other parts of the work process are broken, or the job itself is too difficult or poorly designed, learning will not help much. If people know how to do something but won't, perhaps because they are punished when they do so or are not rewarded for the effort, learning would be wasteful here as well. However, if you determine that people don't know how to do something or don't even know that they should do something, training or other learning strategies may be appropriate.

It was Thomas Gilbert, among others, who first made a strong case for looking at the whole work environment for clues to why people don't or can't perform.[1] One of the most interesting treatments comes from Ferdinand Fournies.[2] Table 10.1, adapted from his work, showcases fourteen possible barriers to performance. Only the first four would indicate some form of learning intervention as a primary solution. In the other ten issues, learning might be useful, but other nonlearning approaches are much more likely to be successful in improving performance.

Table 10.1 Performance Barriers and Possible Interventions

Performance Barrier	*Possible Interventions*
They don't know how to perform. No one showed them what to do. There are no role models or examples. There is no documentation on how to perform. There is no training, or the training didn't work.	Training Knowledge management Collaboration Mentoring and coaching Performance support
They don't know how well to perform. No one told them how well to do it. Performance expectations are unclear. There is no documentation as to what to do. There is no training, or the training didn't work.	Training Knowledge management Collaboration Mentoring and coaching Performance support Performance measurement, evaluation, and appraisal
They don't know they should perform. No one told them they should perform. Performance expectations are unclear. There is no performance documentation.	Training Change management Communications Mentoring and coaching
They don't know why they should perform. They don't see the benefits of performing. They believe they already are performing.	Training Knowledge management Collaboration Change management Communications Mentoring and coaching
They don't have the financial or technical resources to perform. There is no budget to support performance. They were told to perform without being given the tools to do so. The tools they have are outdated. The tools they have don't work. They have the wrong tools.	Funding Software applications Hardware and connectivity Technical support Mechanical tools

Table 10.1 Performance Barriers and Possible Interventions, Cont'd

Performance Barrier	*Possible Interventions*
They don't have the staff resources to perform. There are not enough people to do the work. The right people to do the work are not available. The people who will do the work are not organized appropriately.	Staffing, recruiting Teaming Resource allocation Retention Organizational design
They are not rewarded for the right performance. There is no benefit for them to perform. The reward is inadequate for the effort and risk.	Rewards and incentives Leadership and supervision
They are punished for the right performance. Following the old ways carries less risk.	Rewards and incentives Leadership and supervision
There are no consequences for doing it wrong, or for not doing it at all. There is no differentiation between those who perform and those who don't. Nonperformance carries no risk.	Rewards and incentives Leadership and supervision
The physical environment does not support performance. There is no place to perform. Workspace is not conducive to performance.	Workplace design Ergonomics Human factors
The job or task is poorly designed. The performance makes no sense. The new way of doing things is harder than the old way.	Job design Process and work flow design Performance-centered design Reengineering
They don't believe in it. They think the new way is wrong or stupid. They think the old way is better. They've tried it before, and it didn't work. They don't believe the organization truly believes in it.	Change management (may include a training component) Communications Rewards and incentives Mentoring and coaching Leadership and supervision

Table 10.1 Performance Barriers and Possible Interventions, Cont'd

Performance Barrier	Possible Interventions
They are too busy doing other things.	Prioritization
They are given too many conflicting directions.	Time management
They are overworked.	Job design
They don't know what's most important.	Process and work flow design
They are working on things that are more rewarding or easier to do.	Organization design
	Leadership and supervision
They don't have the capacity to perform.	Reassignment
They don't have the physical capacity (strength) or the intellectual capacity (aptitude) to perform.	Termination
They are prevented from performing due to physical limitation (for example, poor eyesight).	Assistance with physical disability

Analyzing Performance

If you don't know where you're going, any place will do.

—*Cheshire Cat in* Alice in Wonderland

Conducting an up-front performance analysis is crucial if you are to develop the right set of solutions to improve performance. No major training, learning, or performance improvement initiative should be initiated without doing this first. A performance analysis helps determine the exact nature of the performance problem or the performance opportunity. If the analysis shows that you need to develop skills, deliver knowledge or information, or provide support in the workplace, you will be pointed to an appropriate training, workplace learning, or support intervention for your primary set of solutions. But when your performance analysis indicates that other issues may be at play, around motivation, incentives, or resources, for example, learning may not be an appropriate solution, or it may not be the singular solution.

Jumping to the conclusion that learning is the answer before the problem or opportunity has been identified and articulated is all too common. If training or other form of learning intervention is warranted, it will be appropriate to determine what type of intervention is needed, but you are not there yet. Starting with the perception that you have a training need will lead you toward some assumed solutions and away from others before you have enough evidence. Without fully understanding the root causes of the performance problem, any solution you might come up with could be premature and perhaps little more than an educated guess.

While it is important to understand both business performance and human performance issues in the context of a performance analysis, it is also important not to confuse the two. Business performance issues, usually reflected in a business plan, are focused on organizational goals and results, such as profit, revenue, market share, customer satisfaction, and shareholder value. Human performance issues are centered on the ability of individuals and teams to execute the business plan. Your performance analysis should have the business issues and the performance issues clearly defined, and you should be able to establish that there is a linkage between the two. But your primary purpose is to address human performance issues, both individual (skill, knowledge, motivation) and organizational (process improvement, environment, resources, culture).

Having a valid and realistic picture of the state of the business in front of you from the start reduces the chances of basing your solution on assumption, chance, and guesswork. One way to approach this issue quickly is to answer the question, "What if nothing were done?" This often overlooked question is sometimes the most powerful one you can ask, because it often serves as a catalyst for people to express deeper concerns about the business.

Also remember that you can't solve all problems simultaneously, so you need to sort them by some criteria that concentrate your resources on the business's most important priorities (you may do this, or it may be done for you). If you are able to zero in on key performance and business issues quickly, you will find it easier to develop a supportable value proposition for whatever recommendations come out of your analysis.

> People problems come in many guises. They are solved by different remedies. And the one who is best at analyzing the nature of the problem will be more successful at solving it.
>
> —*Robert Mager and Peter Pipe*[3]

Your performance analysis begins with defining the current state: the way things are now and the desired state: how you would like them to be for both organizational and individual performance. You express both of these in measurable terms: the level and quality of the current state and your expectations for the level and quality of the desired state. The difference between the two is the performance gap. Identifying the gaps will enable you to link your performance analysis to the business problem or opportunity you are addressing. This will enable you to articulate the benefits of closing the gap and the risks to the organization if the gap is not closed. Once you have clearly identified the performance gap, you should also be able to identify the causes of the gap—lack of skill or knowledge, poor work environment, or lack of proper incentives, for example—which should point you to an array of possible interventions, learning and otherwise, to address the problems or opportunities you've identified here.

Way Beyond E-Learning: Revisiting the Smart Enterprise Framework

With the addition of nonlearning, performance environment interventions to the model, the smart enterprise framework is complete. Figure 10.1 depicts the complete model.

Figure 10.1   The Complete Smart Enterprise Framework

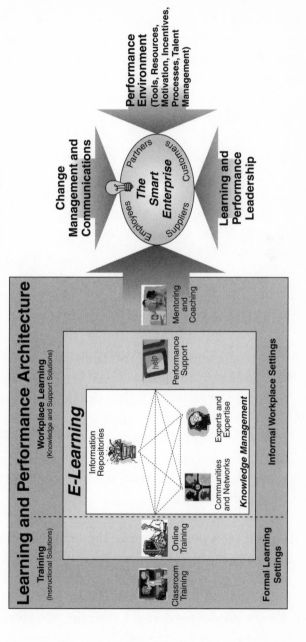

Going forward, training, learning, and e-learning, where this book started, are still important initiatives in support of workforce performance, but they are no longer the only ones. They are integrated and deployed based on a sound analysis of what is needed, not a knee-jerk reaction to do what has always been done. And they are more likely to be combined with nonlearning interventions to create a total solution. This is smart enterprise thinking in its most comprehensive and strategic sense.

> Too many people appear frozen in their view of the possibilities. Many training professionals are locked into what they do every day, with little time to consider more strategic options.
>
> —*Allison Rossett*[4]

The Road Traveled

Moving beyond e-learning is not merely doing e-learning better. It is not simply doing training better, and it is certainly not just moving to the next great technology. It is not limited to moving from training to learning or from learning to performance. It is all of these things and more. You may have already moved from a training perspective to a learning perspective, but you have further to go. As you move along this path, you will come to form three additional and important mind-sets:

• **Learning solutions are expanding to embrace the broader perspective of performance improvement.** The time has come to stop thinking about learning (and e-learning) as the same thing as training (and e-training). Learning is different; it is much more robust. The broader definition of e-learning, and the comprehensive learning and performance architecture, provides a progressive framework for rethinking what learning can be and what it can do.

- **There are many ways to improve performance that are related not to learning but rather to the environment in which the performance takes place.** As important as learning is, not all the performance improvement problems or opportunities you will face are addressable through learning, or at least not entirely through learning. There are many nonlearning approaches to performance improvement that must be considered. You should carefully analyze every situation to understand your best choices.

- **Leadership and culture play an important role in driving and sustaining a smart enterprise.** A nonsupportive culture trumps great learning. Effective leadership and change management will help counteract this. It is tough but very important. When you roll out a new initiative, you're not at the end of the solution; you are really just beginning.

Throughout your journey, you will face many challenges, including these:

- Maintaining high quality in the transition from a predominantly classroom world to much more of an online world
- Becoming a much more flexible and real-time operation
- Balancing formal and informal learning
- Reskilling your training staff
- Convincing current clients to try new approaches to learning
- Building credibility in client organizations for implementing alternatives to training
- Collaborating with other departments, especially IT, which will require lots of effort, relationship building, and trust
- Embracing nonlearning performance improvement solutions
- Finding opportunities to showcase how learning and nonlearning solutions can work together
- Measuring the impact of the performance system and each of its components

- Maintaining the impact and value of training even as you move away from a sole dependence on it
- Making learning and performance decisions, both functional and strategic, in the context of the higher-level business decisions that are being made every day
- Moving more directly into the design and support of work
- Sharing the responsibility for learning and performance with everyone in the business
- Meeting much higher expectations for learning and performance in terms of business transformation and innovation

You may have mastered some of these challenges already, but others may remain. With them come great opportunities for more impact and value. Define the role you want to play, set your course, and start turning challenges into opportunities.

Four Underlying Principles for Moving Forward

Moving beyond current thinking and perceptions of e-learning will likely require you to reinvent the way you talk about and practice it. You must reflect the need for speed and greater efficiencies, and the emergence of new thinking about learning and performance. Getting there involves adherence to four main principles:

- **Heed the warning signs.** Don't be complacent. Look around for telltale signs that your efforts are in trouble or heading that way. Embrace your strengths, but don't ignore your weaknesses. Not until you have a clear understanding of where you are will you know where you need to go.
- **Reinvent what you do.** If you have existing programs that are not accomplishing their goals, fix them. Analyze and rebuild your processes, and set the right priorities, especially in the areas of problem identification, assessing results, and supporting quality.

Reinvention is not always about trashing what exists; rather, it is about improving what you are doing and moving on from there.

• **Redefine your world.** Expand the parameters of what learning can be. Don't be held back by traditional views about what constitutes e-learning, the role of training, or the traditional function of the training organization. New technologies and new requirements are changing the landscape, so go (smartly) with the flow.

• **Put yourself in the bigger game.** Rethink and expand your role. It may be a cliché, but it's still true: fight for a seat at the table—the business leadership table. This means getting into the workplace and becoming a valuable partner in solving real business problems with the least disruption to work as possible. Figure out how to help mainstream business activities and get operational functions to embrace what you do and what you can offer.

As your journey continues, you may find that being as good as everyone else is not good enough. You may want to be, as Jerry Garcia once said about the Grateful Dead, "the only ones to do what we do." That's better than being the best; that's being invaluable.

Don't Make the Mistake the Railroads Made

> I find the great thing in the world is not so much where we stand as in what direction we are moving.
>
> —*Oliver Wendell Holmes*

In the early part of the twentieth century, the railroads carried almost 90 percent of intercity passenger traffic in the United States, especially on trips of over three hundred or so miles. They were reasonably priced, safe, and comfortable, and they were constantly improving, albeit incrementally. In the 1920s and 1930s, airplanes began flying people between cities. Travel by air was expensive, risky, and uncomfortable, but it was faster. Air travel was, by any measure, a radical change in how people got from point A to point B.

The railroad goliaths looked at these fledgling airlines with amusement. If they wanted to, they could have bought up all the airlines for pocket change. Today, passengers might be flying the Burlington Northern Airline, the Santa Fe Airline, or even the Amtrak Airline. But the railroads made a fundamental mistake in their thinking: they saw themselves in the railroad business, not the transportation business. They defined themselves narrowly, around businesses and concepts they knew and understood very well. They didn't see change coming and stuck to their safe, comfortable ways. Today, 90 percent of intercity passengers travel by air.

You have a similar choice to make when it comes to moving beyond e-learning. Like the railroads, you can stick to what you know and do well. You can continue to focus on training and continue to see yourself in the training business. A highly trained workforce is essential for a successful business, and there will always be a need for quality classroom and online training. So, of course, do training well, but don't stop there.

The railroads didn't see themselves in the broader transportation business, but you can position yourself and your organization in the broader learning business and, more important, in the performance business. You can embrace both the classroom and the workplace by embracing different and expanding roles, with new responsibilities, increased challenges, and greater impact. Moving beyond e-learning is not simply moving to new technologies or new approaches for training or learning. It is a transformation of the first order; the relationship that people have with what they know, how they know it, and what they do with it is profoundly changing. The learning and performance field is being redefined in the emerging smart enterprise, and the train is leaving the station. Are you onboard?

> Go out on a limb—that is where the fruit is.
>
> *—Anonymous*

Notes

1. Gilbert, T. (1996). *Human competence: Engineering worthy per-formance*. Amherst, MA: HRD Press. (Originally published in 1978).
2. Fournies, F. (1988). *Why employees don't do what they're supposed to do*. New York: McGraw-Hill/Liberty Hall Press.
3. Mager, R., & Pipe, P. (1997). *Analyzing performance problems*. Atlanta, GA: CEP Press.
4. Rossett, A., & Sheldon K. (2001). *Beyond the podium: Delivering training and performance to a digital world*. San Francisco: Pfeiffer, p. xiii.

Afterword

E-Learning: Advancing Toward What Will Be

John Larson

Progress lies not in enhancing what is, but in
advancing toward what will be.
—*Kahlil Gibran*, A Handful of Sand on the Shore

When Alexander Graham Bell began his early experiments with vocal communication, he wasn't thinking about the telephone—far from it. His initial goal was to help hearing-impaired people communicate—*to make speech visible to the deaf*—so they could fully participate in a speaking world. And while there is some speculation surrounding Bell's "accidental" invention of the telephone, it seems fairly clear that as he was moving along one path pursuing a singular objective, the potential for seizing on a new and largely unanticipated objective revealed itself. Such is often the course of discovery and innovation. And e-learning, as an emerging technology and practice, appears to be unfolding along a similar path of surprising twists and turns, where expressed intended ends are replaced by (or at least expanded to embrace) new goals and possibilities.

In the beginning, its original intent, even before it was dubbed *e-learning,* was to expedite learning—to streamline the delivery of instruction in support of learning outcomes. Education professionals and training practitioners alike, armed with the oft-invoked promise of increased learning gains and reduced training time (not to mention the wholesale displacement of some nasty incidental expenses like travel, hotels, and lost opportunity costs), set about developing and promoting e-learning venues to advance, hasten, and support the acquisition of learning outcomes.

As learning professionals continued to pursue advances in e-learning technologies, however, they began to uncover and exploit new ambitions, objectives, and ends that are redefining the development of the technology and the practice. Whereas e-learning systems initially focused on supporting learning, more recently their development seems headed in quite a different direction—an unexpected direction driven by the necessity for faster and broader communications and knowledge sharing and made practicable by creeping possibilities of technological innovation. In an attempt to perfect the technology as a means to supporting one outcome, learning, it has exposed new and often more valued goals and objectives that are, and should be, vigorously pursued. Emerging e-learning systems (as demonstrated in their features and the way they are being designed, applied, and used) seem to be evolving along a path that is less about learning and the internalization of knowledge and more about access, knowledge exchange, and collaboration—access to a variety of reference, data, and performance support assets and exchange and collaboration among and between users, experts, and content providers.

While e-learning systems continue to offer entrée to an array of learning programs (including courseware), the advancement of these systems and the expansion of their associated feature sets and capabilities (for example, collaborative tools, knowledge sharing, performance support, user content evaluation and content contributions, data mining agents, usage analysis algorithms, affinity features) appear to be serendipitously prompting some new ways of thinking about how these systems can best be used, and to what new ends *beyond learning* they may be applied.

> Emerging e-learning systems are no longer preoccupied with building a better mousetrap—now they are going after different prey.

It seems that the real power of "e," as it is evolving and being applied in a variety of so-called learning contexts, is that it can circumvent (or reduce demand for) learning in the first place, while providing for the broad distribution of essential knowledge for immediate use. Applying "e" to what heretofore were considered learning situations seems to present an opportunity to redefine the desired objective or end. Innovations in e-learning are not just about streamlining the means (learning delivery mechanisms) to an end; rather, they are putting forth new desired ends. When one has easy instantaneous access to required up-to-date information that addresses whatever the task at hand is, at a level that is meaningful to the users and meets them at their starting point, why would it be necessary for users to take the time to internalize this information before they exploit it or use it?

Following this line of thinking, e-learning design has been plotting a slightly divergent path of development—a path more appropriately suited to supporting and enhancing performance and productivity directly. Emerging e-learning systems are including a number of fanciful features that have the capability (and the purpose) of elevating individual competence, performance, and productivity more immediately rather than just refining their capacity to mediate and support instruction. The feature sets of emerging e-learning systems are focusing more on expanding and promoting instant access to current information, resources, and expert knowledge, as well as promoting the just-in-time exchange of intellectual assets and the enhancement of user collaboration capabilities.

Traveling along that path of invention, Bell discovered new and unexpected opportunities and set additional far-reaching goals for his emerging technology that expanded well beyond his original intent. With the willingness to accept change, follow divergent paths, and construct new goals and objectives that may be served by our emerging "e" technologies, who knows what remarkable wonders lay beyond e-learning?

◆ ◆ ◆

John Larson has more than twenty years of experience in performance and learning systems analysis, design, and development. He has held management and thought leadership positions at four major corporations and served as adjunct faculty at Teachers College, Columbia University, and the University of Central Florida. His Ph.D. in instructional systems is from Florida State University.

Appendix A:
Nine E-Learning Warning Signs

Warning Sign 1:
Technology Without Strategy

Are your goals defined more by technology than by learning and performance requirements?

You May Have a Problem If . . .	You're on the Right Track If . . .
• Your investments in technology and infrastructure have so overwhelmed your actions, decisions, and budgets that you have little left for other critical areas like content development, staff skills development, or assessment. • Your technology sits idle while you struggle to deliver enough content to justify the investment. • Your sponsors and executives believe that investment in technology is, in fact, a complete e-learning strategy. • You have no defined plan or strategy for your e-learning initiatives. • You have a poor or nonexistent working relationship with your IT department.	• You balance your technology and infrastructure investments with other investments (for example, high-quality content, professional development), making sure that you do not get ahead of your capabilities with too much technology that can't be justified. • You recognize, and have educated your sponsors, that while technology is a critical *enabler* to achieving e-learning success, it is not, by itself, an e-learning strategy. • You add technology iteratively and carefully, using prototypes, pilots, and interim tools to build a level of comfort and confidence before significant, long-term investments are made. • You have a defined strategy for e-learning that focuses on business and organizational needs and how those needs will be addressed before you invest in technology.

Risks	Benefits
Significant investment that can't deliver, disillusioned sponsors, no business impact. In addition, there may be a danger of incompatible technologies that could have a negative impact on business operations.	More prudent technology investments, at the right time, yield higher e-learning productivity and better utilization of network and infrastructure resources with less risk to business operations.

Warning Sign 2: Weak Focus on Business and Performance Requirements

How well are you tied into the business?

You May Have a Problem If . . .	You're on the Right Track If . . .
• Your deployment strategy is to offer up as many courses as you can, allowing people to select whatever they want. If you don't have what they want, you'll get it. • You fail to distinguish between critical and noncritical learning and performance requirements, resulting in too much investment in marginally beneficial courseware. • Your constituents can't discern what e-learning programs are appropriate and important for them (your guidance is weak or nonexistent). • Establishing an e-learning program becomes its own goal. You feel compelled to get into e-learning (or expand an existing effort) without truly understanding why you are doing so. • Your sponsors and other constituents, including users, hold the view that e-learning is "nice to have" but not a business necessity.	• While continuing to offer variety, you emphasize critical learning and performance needs of the business and you help employees (or customers, partners, and suppliers) identify what learning programs are important to them. • You take care to use e-learning only when it is appropriate rather than touting it as a miracle cure. You avoid the overhype that e-learning works for everything, all the time. • You show specific linkages between e-learning efforts and important business requirements. You have built a solid value proposition for e-learning. • You demonstrate e-learning's ability to solve business problems more efficiently than traditional training models. This has won you praise from your constituencies.

Risks	Benefits
Unfocused activity, solving the wrong problem, significant waste, and no business impact	More focused use and greater linkage to business problems, resulting in more credibility for e-learning

Warning Sign 3: Minimal E-Learning Expertise

Are you and your organization ready to do e-learning well?

You May Have a Problem If . . .	You're on the Right Track If . . .
• You launch an e-learning initiative before you (or your staff) are ready *and* you fail to recognize this lack of readiness. • You assign e-learning responsibilities to those who have the time to do it rather than the necessary expertise. • You do not invest significant time or money in developing e-learning expertise in your people (or yourself), and you do not have permission or resources to recruit needed e-learning talent.	• You take an iterative, developmental approach to building and deploying e-learning that tracks with the development of expertise within your team. • You have an e-learning skills development program in place for you and your staff (and, to some extent, for your constituents and clients). The professional development program is balanced among technical, instructional design; project management; evaluation; and other skills. • You avoid assigning e-learning development projects to unqualified staff members just because they have some free time. • You have a better sense of what skills you have and what types of expertise you need to bring in (for example, consultants, vendor partners).
Risks	**Benefits**
Getting in over your head, poor-quality outputs, missed opportunities for innovation	Better decision making, more efficient operations, higher-value and better-performing products, more e-learning innovation

Warning Sign 4:
No Attention to the Unique
Attributes of E-Learning Design

Do you know what it takes to create great e-learning?

You May Have a Problem If . . .	You're on the Right Track If . . .
• You believe that classroom training can be put online with minimal modifications. • Your e-learning programs follow the same design strategies as your classroom programs. • Your programs do not take true advantage of the capabilities of e-learning for interactivity, reference, reuse, and assessment (for example, putting slide presentations online without doing much to make the experience interactive or reusable on the job).	• You recognize that quality classroom and quality e-learning development require different approaches, tools, and skill sets. • You use instructional design effectively to restructure classroom training for online use, and you take full advantage of design technology to build in interactivity, good use of media, frequent assessments, and other capabilities. • When you do put slide presentations online, you label them as information, *not* instruction.
Risks	Benefits
Inefficient and boring training, failure to achieve desired learning and performance results	Greater use of the natural advantages of technology to facilitate more efficient learning and performance

Warning Sign 5:
Weak Assessment

Do you really know how good your e-learning is?

You May Have a Problem If . . .	You're on the Right Track If . . .
• Your failure to link your e-learning efforts with critical business needs (see Warning Sign 2) leaves you with an unclear view of what results you should be looking for (or what results you are actually getting).	• In addition to participant satisfaction and learning gain, you are tracking the impact of learning on job performance and business results.

You May Have a Problem If . . .	You're on the Right Track If . . .
• You have no significant review process to determine if the e-learning you are about to deploy is accurate, authentic, instructionally valid, and easy to use. • You are primarily using traditional training measures (enrollments, user satisfaction and pre- and post-tests) to determine e-learning success. • You have no process to get quality feedback from users and other constituencies.	• You are documenting productivity gains by using more efficient e-learning approaches rather than exclusive use of classroom delivery. • You use a series of prototypes (testing of working components or models) and pilots (testing of near-final products) to continuously improve your product during its development. • Your e-learning project management approach includes processes for quality review (for example, rechecking content accuracy and appropriateness, navigation, screen design, assessment) prior to deployment.
Risks	**Benefits**
Inability to report results in performance or business terms, resulting in weaker documentation of e-learning efficacy; false sense of security about e-learning's value	Significantly stronger justification for e-learning; greater evidence of e-learning's contribution; ability to catch problems and implement improvements before deployment, when the cost of modifications is still relatively low

Warning Sign 6:
No Focus on Workplace Learning

Are you abdicating responsibility for learning that takes place outside the classroom (or outside the online course)?

You May Have a Problem If . . .	You're on the Right Track If . . .
• You view your role as focusing almost exclusively on formal classroom and online training; therefore, you limit e-learning's role to augmenting or replacing formal classroom training.	• You work more closely with line organizations to build learning directly into work processes.

You May Have a Problem If . . .	You're on the Right Track If . . .
• You view informal learning in the workplace as someone else's job, perhaps the manager's responsibility.	• You seek to improve work documentation and processes (for example, providing information in the context of work, making the process simpler) so that workers can access knowledge at the moment of need. This will reduce the need for training but increase performance efficiency.
Risks	**Benefits**
Minimal involvement where most learning takes place—on the job and in the context of actual work, resulting in reduced influence in the workplace	Costly, unnecessary training is avoided; fewer work disruptions; work processes are improved

Warning Sign 7: No Governance

Do you have a process for making enterprise decisions about e-learning?

You May Have a Problem If . . .	You're on the Right Track If . . .
• Your e-learning efforts are characterized by competing programs and organizations. • You are unable to reach agreement as to what e-learning functions should be centralized and what should be decentralized. • You cannot arrive at an agreed and beneficial outsourcing and vendor management strategy. • You are having difficulty allocating e-learning resources to various groups across the enterprise.	• A cross-organizational governing body sets priorities, allocates resources, and resolves disputes. • An enterprise e-learning technology strategy coordinates technology investments and efficient use of e-learning platforms. • Where appropriate, common processes and services are centralized (for example, vendor management, technology tools and support), while resources and capabilities unique to a department, business unit, or region (for example, content development) are decentralized.

Risks	Benefits
Significant waste, redundancy, and infighting, resulting in lost credibility	Faster implementation of organizational e-learning strategy with reduced costs; greater efficiency and increased collaboration; easier to make enterprisewide adjustments as the market dictates

Warning Sign 8: Weak Sponsorship

Do you have real support from senior executives?

You May Have a Problem If . . .	You're on the Right Track If . . .

• You do not have solid backing from senior leaders (although you may have great lip-service). Examples:
  • Verbal support without financial and staff resources to get the job done
  • Verbal support accompanied by unattainable requirements (such as guaranteed or proven return on investment) to gain the resources you need
  • Verbal support in private, but no willingness to go public
	• You have identified sponsors who are willing to invest in and publicly promote e-learning.
	• You have identified executive sponsors willing to share the risk (and reward) with you, even if they represent smaller parts of the business.
	• You have identified sponsors who will be great advocates for your e-learning successes.
	• You have successfully negotiated reasonable and realistic expectations about results (return on investment), which may be different for early efforts (pilots) than for ongoing implementation.

Risks	**Benefits**
False sense of security around the approval you have to proceed; constant proving yourself consumes all your time, resulting in extra cost and lots of wasted efforts	Greater likelihood of success; builds allies in the executive wing; satisfied sponsors make future investments easier to come by

Warning Sign 9:
Failure to Manage Change

Is your organization ready to accept e-learning?

You May Have a Problem If . . .	You're on the Right Track If . . .
• You fail to prepare people for the change long before the change actually happens (you focus on the rollout exclusively rather than on preparation for the rollout). • Your e-learning rollout is characterized by lots of short-lived fanfare rather than a long-term, comprehensive communications and change management plan. • You cannot distinguish an inability to change ("I don't know how") from resistance to change ("I don't want to").	• Your change management strategy begins long before the change itself and continues long after deployment. • You employ the right incentives, role models, informational communications, and leadership activities in addition to more traditional marketing. • You effectively balance teaching people about the change and helping them to embrace the change.
Risks	Benefits
Initial interest and enthusiasm in e-learning, followed by a rapid decline in use as people revert to their previous positions. Resistance increases, and it becomes harder to win over people the next time.	Long-term buy-in to the e-learning initiative and a sustainable change to the culture that reflects acceptance and preference for the new way of learning. Easier to roll out subsequent change initiatives.

Appendix B:
Knowledge Management Features, Functionalities, and Challenges

Knowledge management systems can have many different features, and some systems have more features than others. Following are the key features that many knowledge managements systems will employ, organized into three major categories: services and tools, collaboration, and content.

Services and Tools		
Knowledge Management Feature	Functionality	Challenges
Portal	• Allows users to select from a variety of functional modules, depending on need. • Allows companies to position certain modules as required and others as optional. • Provides a common design environment for future module building, resulting in a high degree of interoperability and reusability. Once created, the module can be used anywhere within the portal framework. Multiple departments and users can reuse the functionality. • Allows different business units opportunities for differentiation, while	• A common portal technology is essential to create enterprise or organizational impact; multiple portal technologies can create confusion and waste. • Decisions will be needed as to who can build new modules and what standards to adhere to. This is a governance issue. • Portals can become too

Services and Tools, Cont'd		
Knowledge Management Feature	Functionality	Challenges
Portal (*continued*)	preserving a common platform and look-and-feel and other enterprise-required elements. • Emerging suppliers provide increasingly robust tools so that creating a portal from scratch may not be necessary.	crowded with too many choices. Continuous usability testing is critical.
Document Management	• Provides a common repository for critical documents. • Provides a common and easy way for people to access documents. • Ensures a higher level of reliability through version control, access to authors, document ownership, and expiration strategies. • Has flexible entitlements to allow permissions at the user, organization, and document level. • Has metatags that accurately define the document and its uses and makes searching easier.	• Quality control of incoming documents will be an issue. • Balancing "open publishing" with quality assurance and other screening requirements will be important in preserving quality without discouraging participation.
Content Management	• Archives, tracks, and manages a wide array of content objects, including graphics, text, animations, video and audio, and code so that it can be accessed, updated, and reused efficiently. • Can be a general content management system, which has broad application across	• Successful implementation requires a great deal of discipline and process management, across the organization, to use the tool uniformly and appropriately.

Services and Tools, Cont'd		
Knowledge Management Feature	Functionality	Challenges
Content Management *(continued)*	the business, or a learning content management system, which is more tuned to the needs of the training function.	Otherwise the benefits will not be realized.
Search	• Can search across all knowledge repositories and file types. • Does an analysis of the search request and finds or orders results based on user requirements or needs (personalized search). • Can save searches for future and regular use. • Adjusts results based on value, past searches (dynamic searching). • Can use metatags and filters to refine searches.	• Personalized search is difficult but very valuable. • Getting search engines to work across different databases is challenging. • Reducing the number of irrelevant hits will help make the search more valuable. • Inaccurate tagging of content may result in inaccurate search results (for example, missing items, wrong items).
Work Flow	• Ensures that knowledge flows to the right people in the right sequence. • Allows individuals in the work flow to perform one or more operations or tasks (such as editing or approval) on the knowledge asset before passing it along. • Very useful in managing processes, especially where sign-offs are required.	• Can get very complex. • Cannot substitute for effective project or program management, although some people may see it that way.

Services and Tools, Cont'd		
Knowledge Management Feature	**Functionality**	**Challenges**
Work Flow *(continued)*	• Leaves an electronic "paper trail" for compliance and other requirements. • Useful for quality assurance purposes.	
Publishing	• Creates a process and a tool set to ensure that knowledge assets (such as documents and Web sites) are added to the knowledge base (repository) in a similar manner. • Can disperse document publication to multiple authors. • Can be combined with templates and other support tools to ensure consistency and ease of publication, as well as improving quality over time. • Strongly linked to document management.	• Publication tools are essential whether the publishers are a special central group or dispersed to end users. • Governance of the process will be critical so that publishers can effectively balance freedom to contribute within style, quality, confidentiality, approval, and other necessary guidelines.

Alerts	• There are two basic types of alerts:
	
	  • "Notify Me": end user sets some parameters within the system to monitor activity. When a change (addition, modification) occurs that matches those parameters, an alert is created.
	  • "Notify You": publisher (content owner or author) makes a change (addition,
		• Too many alerts can overwhelm the end user.
		• Publishers may need to use discretion in determining who really needs to be alerted, lest they alert virtually everybody about everything.
		• The same alert approach should

Services and Tools, Cont'd		
Knowledge Management Feature	Functionality	Challenges
Alerts *(continued)*	modification) and generates an alert to a predetermined set of end users who were previously identified as interested in the information. • Alerts can appear directly in the portal or in e-mail with a link to the knowledge asset. • In sophisticated systems, alerts can be generated through the matching of user profiles and metatags.	be used across all the applications of the knowledge management system. • Alerts, by their very nature, imply a priority or a sense of urgency. Too many dilute their value.

Personalization	• There are multiple levels of personalization (in increasing level of sophistication):
	  • Portal: using portal technology allows the end user to select which functional or content modules are on his or her screen.
	  • Filters/metatags: allows the user to personalize a search based on filters and metatags that are meaningful to him or her.
	  • Profiles: the end user's profile (role, expertise, interests, and so forth) is used by the system to present content that matches the profile.
	  • Previous work: the system monitors the end user's work and searches on the portal and attempts to find new material based on past use.
		• The more complex the personalization, the more complex the system (but also the more effective).
		• Personalization improves efficiency and user satisfaction, but can be hard to do and maintain.

Services and Tools, Cont'd		
Knowledge Management Feature	Functionality	Challenges
Filters and Metatags	• A coding scheme that categorizes knowledge assets by domain (sales, technology, HR), type (budget, technical manual, user guide), or other taxonomy. • Publishers establish the metatags when publishing a knowledge asset; end users use metatags as filters when searching; administrators use the metatags as knowledge asset inventory control points.	• Metatags are normally used to categorize and filter knowledge assets. Using them to organize expertise or people is often ignored but should be explored (see personalization).
Security (Entitlements)	• Restricts access by unauthorized users and allows differing access for authorized users according to a predetermined scheme. • Enables knowledge owners to manage access to information by any number of criteria (level, location, role).	• Creating the right security around the right content without overly restricting access. • Ensuring that security and entitlements requirements are followed (governance).
Mobility	• Enables information to be received by workers who have mobile or virtual jobs or who travel extensively. • Promotes more 24/7 access and availability to key personnel. • Promotes just-in-time and "just enough" information access at the moment of need (performance support).	• Filtering information so that only essential content is transmitted. • Security. • Multiple platforms and devices may require multiple instances of the solution.

Collaboration		
Knowledge Management Feature	Functionality	Challenges

Communications	• Communication tools are essential for community building and collaboration.
	• There are several communication approaches:
	  • Real-time: one-to-one or group tools enable "conversations" on the Web (chat, instant messaging).
	  • Asynchronous: one-to-one or one-to-many tools that enable the capturing of ideas and content (e-mail, discussion groups).
	  • Conferencing: one-to-one or group tools enable interaction with content through collaborative tools and document sharing.
	• These tools can be provided independently from a portal but, ideally, there are links to them within a portal.
		• There is an equal danger of overuse of these tools, leading to a glut of conversations or content that loses its value, or an abandonment of these tools, diminishing the collaborative benefit of the system.
		• The key is to make the tools easy to use and establish specific purposes for their use; incentivize and reward contributions made through these tools.
		• Capturing and codifying collaboration content is often difficult.

Application Sharing	• Enables people to work in a collaborative way on documents, presentations, spreadsheets, business software, and other material in real time. • Promotes efficiency by reducing time for feedback and development of ideas and reports. • Creates a sense of team by allowing more inclusive participation in knowledge development.	• Need protocols for managing the development. • Does not replace good document management and approval work flows.

Collaboration, Cont'd		
Knowledge Management Feature	Functionality	Challenges

Community Building	• Can associate people and the content they own and create collaboration opportunities.
	• There are two types of communities:
	  • Vertical: resembles an organizational hierarchy, consisting of different roles and levels organized around a specific function (for example, everyone in a technology organization).
	  • Horizontal: cuts across organizations to bring together people with common roles, skills, interests (for example, all Java developers).
	• Allows new communities to be established and dissolved as needed.
	• Membership in multiple communities is allowed.
		• Need to control proliferation of communities; some should be controlled centrally.
		• Communities will not succeed without leadership within a community; identify specific people to lead or facilitate communities.
		• Communities can conflict with organizational charts and existing lines of authority.
		• Communities may represent significant cultural change.

Expert Locator	• Provides an opportunity for experts to surface (either appointed or through self-nomination). • Enables the organization to identify expertise that otherwise would be hidden. • Enables experts to be recognized for their expertise. • Expertise can be shared online or off-line (or in combination).	• Experts often resist being identified, as it represents additional work that is often unrewarded. • Danger of creating a schism between experts and novices.

Content		
Knowledge Management Feature	Functionality	Challenges
Directories	• Provides direct, one-click access to employee information (external contacts also possible). • Allows individuals to update their own information, ensuring greater accuracy. • Can evolve into personal pages that can contain more than contact information (expertise, projects, interests). • Can be linked to an on-line organizational chart (dynamically generated).	• Ease of access to e-mail addresses could result in a significant amount of e-mail traffic (not necessarily bad). • Important to instill responsibility for individual maintenance of personal information.
Learning and Development	• Direct links to course registration, competency assessment, learning plans, university education and other forms of training, often managed by learning management systems. • Can use other features of a portal to add value to the learning program (for example, communities, access to knowledge assets).	• Effective learning plans and programs require manager involvement; it's important to integrate this component, or the process could create conflicts between employee and manager.
Bookmarks	• Placing bookmarks on the portal instead of on the browser allows access from any networked computer. • Adds additional personalized value to the portal for the end user.	• Too many bookmarks may overwhelm the portal space.

Content, Cont'd		
Knowledge Management Feature	Functionality	Challenges
Internal Content	• Serves as a uniform internal news source. Key organizational information is pushed to all employees or to selected employees based on their profile. • Replaces e-mail as key news source, although alerts can be sent through e-mail with links to the portal. • Ensures message consistency. • Examples: corporate press releases, stock price, product information, IT policy, organizational chart. • Can consist of enterprisewide news and/or content and news tailored for specific business units, roles, departments, regions, or other divisions.	• While internal news is critical to keeping employee attention focused on the knowledge management system, it will be important not to let the content of the page be controlled too much by any one source. • It will be important to balance internal company news with external news about the company (adds relevance, authenticity).

Syndicated Content	• Content acquired from outside, specialized content vendors.
	• There are two types of fee-based syndicated content:
	  • General: news, weather, sports, entertainment (CNN, ABC, *New York Times*, Reuters).
	  • Specific: news related to a specific industry (telecommunications, travel, financial services).
	• These services are either provided to users in a set pattern, or users can select the
		• Content services can be free or subscription based, sometimes part of the portal service. Special services may carry license, copyright, or usage restrictions that can be costly.
		• For industry-specific content sources, it will be important to determine content accuracy and relevance to the

Content, Cont'd		
Knowledge Management Feature	**Functionality**	**Challenges**
Syndicated Content (*continued*)	syndicated content modules they are interested in.	business (avoiding wrong or contradictory information).
Dashboards	• Collects information from a specific set of sources (internal or external) and presents the information in a unique way to give the user a customized view of an organizational process, business results, progress toward a goal, status of resources, or sales figures, for example. • Pulls data from different databases and presents a dynamic representation of the information. • Some dashboards can be set up and managed centrally; more sophisticated versions can be customized by the end user.	• Important to select the right data and not overwhelm the user. • Accuracy of the data will be critical; if the data are inaccurate, the business can be severely affected if decisions are based on dashboard information.

Appendix C:
Collaboration Technologies

Technology: E-Mail		
What It Does	**How It Supports Collaboration and Learning**	**Challenges in Use**
As ubiquitous as the telephone (or more so), e-mail has become the primary messaging technology of the modern organization, as well as for individuals.	People use e-mail to ask questions, distribute information, and update each other. It is an excellent vehicle to notify people (provide alerts) of the availability of new information or distribute knowledge to entire communities or organizations. In addition, it can be used by members to "subscribe" to information resources so that they receive the content as soon as it becomes available.	As instantaneous as e-mail seems, it is primarily a one-way medium. When people use it to hold synchronous conversations, the technology becomes cumbersome, as delays in sending and receiving each piece of the dialogue tend to interfere with collaborative nature of the conversation. Furthermore, e-mail is often used by individuals to archive content (in personal e-mail folders). This makes it difficult for other members of the community to access the information when they need it, adding more delay and noise into the conversation.

Recommendation: Use e-mail primarily to inform or alert community members of new content, community activities, work assignments, or other information appropriate for the membership. URLs of new content or features can easily be transmitted to members (and subgroups of members). Do not use e-mail to transmit the actual content, as it is usually unsearchable by the community and is subject to loss or deletion by individual members.

Examples: News organizations such as CNN and MSNBC use e-mail to alert subscribers when critical events important to them are posted on their Web site.

Technology: E-Mail, Cont'd
Medical sites like WebMD use e-mail to alert users when new advances in specific areas of medicine are announced. This makes users aware of the existence of new information by making it common knowledge. This is critical because if you don't know knowledge exists, you can't learn from it.

Technology: Instant Messaging		
What It Does	**How It Supports Collaboration and Learning**	**Challenges of Use**
IM has taken the desired immediacy of e-mail and removed the delay in sending and receiving each individual piece of the dialogue. The format of IM more accurately represents conversational behavior. In addition, multiple and group conversations can be held just as easily (much more so than conference calling on the telephone).	The instantaneous nature of IM allows single or multiple conversations to begin at the moment of need, making it much more convenient than telephone or e-mail communications. More important, community members who share IM "buddy lists" can instantaneously see who is online at any particular time. This "presence awareness" enhances collaboration by facilitating easy connections among community members.	Community members might remove themselves from "availability" (going "invisible") or withdraw completely from the community if they perceive that the IM traffic they are receiving is more than they can handle or if it is not valuable enough for them to pay attention. If this happens a lot, IM conversations are either ignored or become more background noise. Like any other communication or collaboration technology, it can be overused and abused. Also, IM may hog bandwidth and is perceived to be less secure than e-mail. Some corporate networks block IM traffic.

Recommendation: Use instant messaging as a primary real-time communication vehicle inside communities. The IM functionality can be incorporated directly into your community work space, or it can be one of the many external commercial tools that are available. Try to limit IM conversations to community- or business-related activities so that users will not get overwhelmed and turned off by all the chatter.

Examples: Accenture uses IM to enable experts within the firm and those seeking expertise to use IM to build and manage their own personalized knowledge

Technology: Instant Messaging, Cont'd

networks (see the case study in Chapter Five). Because these IM lists are personalized to each user, they have more value and are more likely to be used and trusted. This makes the information shared more trusted as well, and when trust within a collaborative environment is high, more learning is likely to take place.

Of course, why IM another person when you can query an automated agent? Often called a *bot* (short for *robot*), this type of software can find information for you; all you have to do is ask. The sophistication of bots is always increasing; they can be "trained" by users to find particular types of information or cover specific domains of knowledge.

Technology: Discussion Threads and Chatrooms		
What It Does	**How It Supports Collaboration and Learning**	**Challenges of Use**
These tools allow structured Web sites to be developed where individuals can ask and respond to questions in a way that allows users to follow the logic of the conversation.	These tools overcome the limitations of e-mail by allowing all members of a community to have access to all discussion threads. This enables everyone to see the contributions of everyone else so that responses can more easily reflect group thinking. All conversations can be archived for future reference. This can be very effective for problem solving, for example, because everyone in the community can see how people previously talked about and resolved an issue. Many technical support Web sites use this technique so that customers can learn from prior discussions rather than ask the same questions over and over again.	Logging on and using these tools requires significant motivation—a need to solve a specific problem or ask a specific question, for example. Once the issue is solved, users don't often return to the site until it's needed again. Characteristically, then, users often get very involved in a discussion thread for a short time, until their need is met, and then don't come back. So there is a great deal of work to keep interest and involvement in discussion forums high over time. This is where facilitators, alerts, and a careful attention to ease of use become important. Without these extra efforts, most discussion threads and chatrooms are either used by just a very small group of enthusiasts or quickly wither and die.

Technology: Discussion Threads and Chatrooms, Cont'd
Recommendation: Use discussion threads and chatrooms for specific topics, issues, and problem-solving activities, not for general dialogue or interaction among community members. Be sure that important threads are monitored or facilitated and that access to these services is as easy as possible. When new ideas emerge or problems are solved, do not expect that all community members will check the thread to learn about them; be proactive in publishing the findings using other collaborative and alert tools.
Example: IBM wanted to query its thirty-two thousand managers about the role of the manager in the twenty-first century. More than eight thousand of those managers submitted ideas, stories, questions, and suggestions over a forty-eight-hour Web discussion event called "Manager Jam." The company created the high level of participation, and collaborative learning, by tying the event to a critical business issue, providing extensive technical facilitation and leadership support, and limiting the time frame to create a sense that this was special.

Technology: Web Conferencing		
What It Does	**How It Supports Collaboration and Learning**	**Challenges of Use**
Allows individuals and groups to collaborate over distance. Combines audio conversations with codified knowledge assets, such as presentations, documents, Web sites, and applications, and can allow groups to talk and work with these resources collectively. Many of these tools employ a form of	Training organizations have embraced this technology for virtual course presentations. When used well, these programs allow participants to use the technology to share ideas and ask questions in ways that can approach the interactivity advantage of the traditional classroom. More interesting, however, this technology allows work teams and communities to collaborate on projects by working on knowledge assets and applications in real time.	Often this technology is used primarily for one-way knowledge dissemination (for example, one-way delivery of training content). This is an acceptable and efficient use of Web conferencing because it facilitates the distribution of knowledge and expertise to large numbers of people in a short amount of time. But it is not collaboration, because participants have little opportunity to share what they know and discuss what they are doing or learning. The danger is in confusing the two purposes: if communities tout one-way presentations as a

Technology: Web Conferencing, Cont'd		
What It Does	**How It Supports Collaboration and Learning**	**Challenges of Use**
instant messaging for communication between presenters and participants or between participants themselves.		form of collaboration, members may get frustrated and tune out of future collaborative opportunities or wait for the recording of the event to become available and watch it, asynchronously, at a later time.

Recommendation: Use Web conferencing to create opportunities for members to work interactively on an application, document, presentation, or something else. Use the application sharing features of the tool to enable real-time participation, and be sure to post the work so that it can be accessed asynchronously later. It is also appropriate to use these tools for one-way information and training presentations, but be sure not to promote them as pure collaborative activities.

Example: A retail company used Web conferencing to enable buyers to collaborate on retail trends, competitive positioning, vendor status, and other issues important to buying decisions. Buyers in different parts of the company were able to learn about and comment on new products as a team in a much shorter time frame. This allowed the company to address the buying decisions, vendor management, and supply chain issues faster and more uniformly, and it also provided a forum for each buyer to offer guidance and ideas to the group. Over time, this collaboration created a great deal of trust in the buyer community, resulting in a stronger and more innovative team.

Technology: Knowledge Network Building Tools		
What It Does	**How It Supports Collaboration and Learning**	**Challenges of Use**
Although almost everyone builds some sort of personal knowledge network, specialized software can aid this effort by identifying people who are likely	These tools address one of the great promises of collaborative learning: if people could easily find others with experience and expertise in the same area they are working in, the knowledge that could be shared would be significantly greater. Just	While these tools have tremendous potential for linking people, projects, and expertise, the fact is that in order to do this, they have to "snoop" around your work activities, e-mails, and other aspects of your virtual life. While most ask for permission first, some

Technology: Knowledge Network Building Tools, Cont'd		
What It Does	**How It Supports Collaboration and Learning**	**Challenges of Use**
to be working on similar projects or who have similar expertise. Some tools analyze the resources people use to find affinities, while others might look at e-mail or discussion threads to help people answer common questions like, "Who can help me answer my question, or show me what to do?" or "Is there anyone else out there working on the same things I am working on?"	being aware of others working on similar projects or in the same knowledge domain as you are opens up learning opportunities that would be impossible if the knowledge continued to go undiscovered.	people may feel this violates privacy rights, although privacy rights inside corporations can be debated. More challenging is the tendency of some people to hide or protect what they are doing, thus running counter to the knowledge-sharing goal. Establishing the right balance between the advantage of work and knowledge affinities across an organization, and creating a sense of being spied on or being overly intrusive, will always be difficult.

Recommendation: Use knowledge network building tools carefully. Where people all agree to use this approach, the results can be very beneficial, especially in bringing expertise together, fostering innovation, and reducing redundant work. However, caution is advised when launching these tools to be sure that they are being used for the right purposes and have some limitations on where they can look.

Example: Two groups of managers in two different countries are working on very similar projects. Using a knowledge management system that has an affinity component, one group queries the system to identify anyone else who has accessed documents similar to the ones they are using. They discover the other group by seeing documented usage patterns almost identical to their own. After contacting the second group, they all decide to pool resources and complete the project more quickly and at lower cost. As each group contributes its knowledge, the expertise of both groups increases, and the confidence everyone has in the final results is much stronger.

Technology: Weblogs (Blogs)		
What It Does	**How It Supports Collaboration and Learning**	**Challenges of Use**
Enables almost anyone to be an instant publisher of content on the Web. Weblog software creates a templated environment where "authors" publish news, commentary, and other items, usually in reverse chronological order (most recent at the top). No programming skills are needed. Most blogs can handle a rich variety of media.	Extensive use of hyperlinks allows "bloggers" to link to related content, creating a vast interconnected web of related knowledge. Weblogs tend to focus on specific knowledge domains and therefore attract a community of people interested in the same topics. Some weblogs allow readers to post commentary back to the blog. Because of their ease and immediacy, weblogs can be an ideal way to generate new ideas for comment by a larger audience.	The reliability and accuracy of information on weblogs vary greatly, depending on the author. Multiple blogs can have competing, sometimes contradictory information. This may be fine in the arena of public debate, but in a business, this could have the undesirable effect of communicating inappropriate or wrong content, providing conflicting direction, or even putting the organization at risk from a legal standpoint. Proper management and publishing permissions can reduce this problem. Blogs can also get very long, and some early information can become dated. Keeping up with content accuracy will be a constant challenge. Finally, while the use of a great many links to other resources contributes to a richer blog experience, users can get lost in the process. Good and consistent navigation protocols can help here.

Recommendation: Weblogs can be useful tools to communicate important and immediate information to communities of practice or an entire organization. They can generate interest and participation in knowledge creation. But they can get out of hand. Start slowly and carefully, and be sure to restrict blog authoring, at least initially, to those who know the content well, are highly responsible, can write well, and have some journalistic sensibilities.

Example: A company is about to launch a major product update. Many groups (sales, marketing, manufacturing, distribution, and others) must be updated on a regular basis. Resellers, advertising agencies, and other partners need time-critical information as well. The product manager starts a weblog containing all relevant

Technology: Weblogs (Blogs), Cont'd

information about the launch. Other project leaders can submit information and links. Everyone who is authorized to have access to the blog has a secure log-in and password, so the weblog is protected. Not only does the blog keep everyone informed, but it provides a history of the project. The information it contains can be transferred to more structured knowledge repositories and training courses, so others can learn from the experience in the future.

Appendix D:
Primary Knowledge Management
Development Activities

Twenty key knowledge management (KM) development activities are described, organized first by process steps (diagnosis, solution definition, design and development, and implementation) and then by framework component (strategy, management and governance, procedures, applications and tools, and technical infrastructure and architecture).

KM Development Process Step: Diagnosis		
KM Development Activity	**KM Framework Component**	**Description**
Plan for needs assessment and current state analysis	Strategy	Establish your approach for determining what the key needs and requirements the business has for KM and what the current state of KM is in the business. Determine the data collection techniques that will best give you a reliable picture of what is currently going on.
Assess current management of intellectual capital, issue resolution	Management and governance	Determine how knowledge is currently managed in the organization. Is information sharing chaotic? Is information hard to find? How does the organization deal with redundant knowledge? How are disputes around knowledge processes and resources resolved? What is the level of senior executive support for KM?

KM Development Process Step: Diagnosis, Cont'd		
KM Development Activity	**KM Framework Component**	**Description**
Define how knowledge is currently created, archived, and distributed	Procedures	Determine how information is currently captured, archived, and disseminated. Describe processes currently in place. Identify process deficiencies and breakdowns, if any. Highlight positive practices that should be preserved.
Assess capabilities of current tools; define gaps	Applications and tools	Inventory tools and applications currently used to manage knowledge. Determine redundancies and gaps. Does the organization have competing tool sets? Are the tools adequate for moving the KM initiative forward? Will the tools scale?
Assess capability of current platform, infrastructure	Technical infrastructure and architecture	Assess how well KM will integrate into the organization's overall IT infrastructure. What changes and upgrades will be needed to the overall architecture, end user platforms, and other areas? Determine if any other applications, such as enterprise resource planning or customer relationship management will be affected.

KM Development Process Step: Solution Definition		
KM Development Activity	**KM Framework Component**	**Description**
Build a rationale and business case for KM	Strategy	Document the current and future state for KM, and identify the gaps between the two. Develop and justify the value proposition for KM and get buy-in and long-term support from senior management.

KM Development Process Step: Solution Definition, Cont'd		
KM Development Activity	KM Framework Component	Description
Define KM operating model, jobs, and roles	Management and governance	Specify the specific roles, responsibilities, competencies, and interdependencies for personnel involved in KM. Determine how KM should be managed (what is centralized and what is decentralized). Establish parameters for KM governance and overall management, making sure to involve key stakeholders.
Define KM operating procedures	Procedures	Establish preliminary procedures for content creation, content reviews, work flow, publishing, archiving, distribution, community memberships, entitlements, and other aspects of system operation.
Define KM technical model	Applications and tools	Specify how the KM system will work from a technical perspective. Develop a technical framework, including system specifications, use cases, and standards. Identify preliminary tool classes (search, document management, portal, and others). Develop tool selection criteria.
Define KM infrastructure and platform	Technical infrastructure and architecture	Specify modifications and enhancements that are required in the organizational IT infrastructure for the KM system to be introduced and operated. Specify any end user platform changes that may be required.

KM Development Process Step: Design and Development		
KM Development Activity	**KM Framework Component**	**Description**
Establish a road map for KM system development and deployment	Strategy	Develop and publish a specific project management plan for KM system development and deployment. Ensure that all plan elements (for example, software development, management and governance, change management, training, and support) are considered and approved.
Build and test job descriptions, governance model	Management and governance	Create and assess pilot KM roles and organizations. Develop a KM charter. Begin KM governance meetings while the system is being built.
Specify a knowledge architecture	Procedures	Define knowledge domains for the KM system, and identify interdependencies among them. Establish, test, and refine metatagging and filtering scheme for the knowledge base. Test rules and procedures for creating, archiving, publishing, and distributing content. Test entitlements and content approval work flow.
Evaluate best-of-breed tools, build interfaces, run pilots	Applications and tools	Identify and acquire KM components and tools. Design system interface and navigation strategies. Develop style guides. Construct and test system prototypes (controlled environments) and pilots (business environments).
Upgrade infrastructure and test platform	Technical infrastructure and architecture	Integrate KM system into organizational IT infrastructure. Validate end user platform.

KM Development Process Step: Implementation		
KM Development Activity	KM Framework Component	Description
Roll out system, implement change management	Strategy	Implement the system incrementally according to a scalable deployment plan, making sure that the rollout does not proceed too quickly or too slowly. Make sure a change management plan is in place and operating. Control use initially, and observe buy-in and use. Correct as necessary.
Implement ongoing KM management and governance	Management and governance	Deploy the KM operating organizations, including, but not limited to, central management team, local management teams, content owners and developers, community members, technical support, and content review and approval designees.
Deploy appropriate training and support	Procedures	Provide classroom and online training as needed. Implement online help and Web-based support. Establish a help line for user issues (especially important at deployment). Specify an ongoing training and support strategy.
Integrate tools into common system	Applications and tools	Roll out the KM system into the mainstream business.
Integrate KM system into business operations	Technical infrastructure and architecture	Link KM system to existing business processes. Make the KM system as seamless as possible within the organization's overall technology services.

Appendix E:
Sample Change Management
and Communications Plan

The Situation

A major retail company determined that its IT knowledge (technical assets, documentation, system specifications, human resource information, and inventories) was a mess. Most of the information was outdated, in peoples' heads (although the company didn't always know *whose* head), or just plain missing. The business embarked on a knowledge management strategy (other learning and performance solutions would work the same way) to get its IT information, operational and strategic, in order. Congruent with its KM strategy, the firm developed a twenty-five-point change management and communications strategy:

Change Management and Communications Specifications and Tactics	Adoption Stage(s)
1. Identify selected employees as resources and influencers to their peer groups and communities. Employees can become surrogate trainers and serve as role models and opinion leaders.	Awareness, Preference
2. Establish a steering committee of key leaders and stakeholders who will serve as advocates for the change. Make sure the steering committee members are representative of and respected by potential users.	Understanding
3. Post articles of interest to employees, as well as links to prototypes, on the project Web site.	Awareness, Understanding

Change Management and Communications Specifications and Tactics	Adoption Stage(s)
4. E-mail project updates from the project team, the steering committee, and upper management. Use to encourage use of the new system, detail employee responsibilities, and provide a vehicle for employee feedback.	Awareness, Understanding
5. Attend senior leadership meetings to update team personally on project status. Respond to questions from the team, and present briefings on project status, technology, change management efforts, and other issues.	Understanding
6. Provide regular e-mail updates to all constituents. There should be two parts to the update: one from the executive leadership and the other from the project team or steering committee.	Awareness, Understanding
7. Create a special section on the project Web site that articulates the business case, and provide similar collateral material for managers to use with their teams. Collateral material can include presentations to be given to team members, project fact sheets, sample screens, and testimonials.	Understanding
8. Attend department meetings to help provide support for managers as they introduce the solution to their teams. This helps position the solution in the right light with employees.	Awareness, Understanding
9. Identify managers to serve as role models. Provide special training, and introduce the role models early in the change management process.	Awareness, Understanding, Preference
10. Create prototypes of the solution, and position them in kiosks at strategic locations. At times, provide a coach to assist people in using the prototype. To give people enough time to get comfortable, make sure the prototypes are available long before the system is launched.	Understanding, Preference
11. Allow the steering committee, senior leaders, and employees to experiment with prototype tools and products.	Understanding, Preference

Change Management and Communications Specifications and Tactics	Adoption Stage(s)
12. Establish communities of practice for interested groups—for example, early adopters, role models, techies, the steering committee, and the development team.	Preference
13. Establish and announce a governance structure for the new solution. Communicate the governance structure to all employees. Incorporate governance issues into workshops, training, and other communications. Create feedback mechanisms that allow all employees to have input into the governance structure. Appoint broad representation across the organization (the governance body could be the steering committee). Establish scope of authority.	Understanding, Preference
14. Restructure the organization as necessary to reflect changes brought on by the introduction of the new system. Determine how work will change, and move aggressively to document new changes and ensure that they are supported within the organization. Communicate changes, and integrate changes into other vehicles, including training and senior management messages. Ensure that restructuring is not tied to job security issues. Be sure that all managers are on board with any changes.	Awareness
15. Make frequently asked questions (FAQs) easily available, and update frequently. FAQs can be derived from feedback from various meetings, e-mails, and the insights of the steering committee members and the project team.	Preference
16. Host informal brown bag lunches on topics related to the new system. People voluntarily attend if the topic is of interest. Sample topics: benefits, technology, how work will change, new roles and responsibilities.	Preference
17. Build expert recognition into the culture to encourage contributions. Content owners and contributors should be recognized, especially if they offer themselves as experts.	Preference

Change Management and Communications Specifications and Tactics	Adoption Stage(s)
18. Adjust performance appraisals to recognize participation and contributions to the effective use of the new system. Create criteria for performance assessment, vehicles for people to measure the value of their participation, and coaching guides to help managers improve the quality of their local leadership of change. Provide clear information on inappropriate behavior.	Preference
19. Create special communications focused on the value of the system to users and the benefits and rewards of using it. This can be linked in with some testimonials. Reflect on current state of work and the frustrations uncovered in the needs assessment. If appropriate, have more senior managers also comment.	Preference
20. Deliver a special workshop for managers on the new system and their role in facilitating adoption and change.	Understanding, Preference
21. Provide an in-depth technology briefing for steering committee members, managers, and others, and post it to the project Web site. Enable constituents and stakeholders to explore some of the recommended technology in more detail and provide feedback.	Understanding
22. Create specific leadership messages about the new system. Each manager reviews these messages with his or her team at team meetings.	Awareness
23. Provide training in the use of the new solution. Everyone in the organization will have an opportunity to take the training; however, the bulk of the support for learning the system will be in the form of a help system and a guided tour. Create special manager training, and deliver it early.	Understanding, Preference
24. Create appropriate help systems, user guides, guided tours, and other online help.	Understanding

Change Management and Communications Specifications and Tactics	Adoption Stage(s)
25. Provide testimonials and success stories on the use of the new system (ease of use, value, benefits). Consider developing a video or capturing some of the testimonials for replay on the Web.	Preference

A full-blown change management and communications plan would also include time frames, milestones, resources, and roles and responsibilities.

Appendix F:
E-Learning Readiness Assessment: Executive Team Alignment

A critical piece of evaluating readiness for e-learning in any form is understanding the extent to which the senior executive team is aligned around the strategy and critical factors for success. The following ten questions begin to shape the scope and extent of alignment work, as well as highlight specific areas of weakness in the team's alignment. The focus of the questions is on the overall, broad-based strategy, not on individual initiatives and actions that are part of the strategy.

Directions

1. Determine your operational definition of e-learning, ranging from instruction only to one that might include knowledge management (information repositories, communities and networks, experts and expertise) and performance support. Do this before you use this instrument, and be sure that all who respond understand and are in agreement with your definition.

2. Answer each of the following questions from two perspectives:
   - How you would answer the question individually
   - The rating you would give to the senior leadership team as a single group

3. Answer each question on a scale of 0 to 5 as follows:

> 0 = I don't know the answer
>
> 1 = Definitely no
>
> 2 = Leaning to no
>
> 3 = I think so
>
> 4 = Pretty likely
>
> 5 = Definitely yes

The Questionnaire

1. There is a *clearly defined* and *compelling* opportunity for e-learning within the company's core business operations.

   My Response   _____

   My Score for the Executive Team as a Group   _____

2. There is clarity around executive team *commitments and accountabilities* for the success of the e-learning strategy.

   My Response   _____

   My Score for the Executive Team as a Group   _____

3. There is a common and shared understanding of the *strategic intent (that is, the business objectives)* behind the e-learning strategy.

   My Response   _____

   My Score for the Executive Team as a Group   _____

4. There is a shared and intricate understanding of the *financial and operating performance objectives* for the e-learning strategy.

   My Response   _____

   My Score for the Executive Team as a Group   _____

5. There is a shared and intricate understanding of the *priorities and actions* to realize the full value of the e-learning strategy.

   My Response _____

   My Score for the Executive Team as a Group _____

6. Realizing the *objectives* for the e-learning strategy is a significant factor in positioning the company for success.

   My Response _____

   My Score for the Executive Team as a Group _____

7. The executive team has a strong *performance culture and track record of results* from cross-organizational and technology-enabled initiatives like e-learning.

   My Response _____

   My Score for the Executive Team as a Group _____

8. There is a high degree of *energy and enthusiasm* for what the e-learning strategy makes possible for the company.

   My Response _____

   My Score for the Executive Team as a Group _____

9. The organization views the e-learning *leadership team as highly credible and effective* in driving change throughout the organization (assumes there is a person or set of people chartered specifically with the e-learning agenda).

   My Response _____

   My Score for the Executive Team as a Group _____

10. We are satisfied with the *pace, progress, and results* coming out of the e-learning initiative.

    My Response _____

    My Score for the Executive Team as a Group _____

Scoring and Actions

Step 1: Sum up the total score for your individual response:

_____

Step 2: Sum up the total score for your rating of the senior executive team: _____

Step 3: Assess as follows for either individual or senior team rating:

- For any question that was answered with a 0, collect information to answer the question, and then rescore.
- If the total score is lower than 20, the data suggest a need for broad executive alignment work that should take priority over activities that are under way.
- If the total score is between 21 and 35, the data suggest a need for broad executive alignment work that should occur in parallel with activities that are under way.
- If the total score is between 36 and 45, the data suggest a need for focused alignment work (in areas of weakness) in parallel with activities that are under way.
- A total score over 45 suggests there is little need or value in alignment activities. *There is strong alignment for moving forward.*

Step 4: Compare your total individual score to total group rating. Discrepancies over 15 points indicate a significant difference between key initiative stakeholders and senior executives that suggests a need for a session to get aligned on the critical success factors and more frequent interactions and updates.

Appendix G:
Additional Resources

Books

There many good books on learning, e-learning, and performance improvement that will help you implement the ideas presented in this book. The following list, covering strategy and fundamentals, design and development, knowledge management, collaboration and communities, implementation, leadership and change management, performance improvement, and the human-technology interface, will get you started.

Learning, Learning Technology, and E-Learning: Strategy and Fundamentals

Brinkerhoff, R., & Gill, S. (1994). *The learning alliance: Systems thinking in human resource development*. San Francisco: Jossey-Bass.

Kelly, T., & Nanjiani, N. (2005). *The business case for e-learning*. Indianapolis: Cisco Press.

Rosenberg, M. (2001). *E-learning: Strategies for delivering knowledge in the digital age*. New York: McGraw-Hill.

Rossett, A. (2001). *Beyond the podium: Delivering training and performance to a digital world*. San Francisco: Pfeiffer.

Rossett, A. (Ed.). (2002). *The ASTD e-learning handbook: Best practices, strategies, and case studies for an emerging field*. New York: McGraw-Hill.

Schank, R. (2005). *Lessons in learning, e-learning and training: Perspectives and guidance for the enlightened trainer*. San Francisco: Pfeiffer.

Shank, P., & Carliner, S. (2006). *E-learning: Lessons learned, challenges ahead (voices from academe and industry)*. San Francisco: Pfeiffer.

Online Training Design and Development

Aldrich, C. (2005). *Learning by doing: A comprehensive guide to simulations, computer games, and pedagogy in e-learning and other educational experiences.* San Francisco: Pfeiffer.

Carliner, S. (2002). *Designing e-learning.* Alexandria, VA: ASTD.

Clark, R. (2002). *E-learning and the science of instruction: Proven guidelines for consumers and designers of multimedia learning.* San Francisco: Pfeiffer.

Driscoll, M., & Carliner, S. (2006). *Advanced web-based training: Adapting real world strategies in your online learning.* San Francisco: Pfeiffer.

Garrett, J. (2002). *The elements of user experience: User-centered design for the web.* Indianapolis: New Riders Press.

Horton, W. (2002). *Designing web-based training.* New York: Wiley.

Knowledge Management

Collidon, C., & Parcell, G. (2001). *Learning to fly: Practical lessons from one of the world's leading knowledge companies.* Milford, CT: Capstone Publishing.

Davenport, T., & Prusak, L. (1998). *Working knowledge: How organizations manage what they know.* Boston: Harvard Business School Press.

DeLong, D. (2004). *Lost knowledge: Confronting the threat of an aging workforce.* New York: Oxford University Press.

Goldsmith, M., Morgan, H., & Ogg, M. (Eds.). (2004). *Leading organizational learning: Harnessing the power of knowledge.* San Francisco: Jossey-Bass.

Stewart, T. (1998). *Intellectual capital: The new wealth of organizations.* New York: Doubleday.

Stewart, T. (2001). *The wealth of knowledge: Intellectual capital and the twenty-first century organization.* New York: Doubleday.

Collaboration and Communities

Cross, J. (2004). *The hidden power of social networks: Understanding how work really gets done in organizations.* Boston: Harvard Business School Press.

Saint-Onge, H., & Wallace, D. (2003). *Leveraging communities of practice for strategic advantage.* Burlington, MA: Butterworth-Heinemann.

Surowiecki, J. (2004). *The wisdom of crowds: Why the many are smarter than the few and how collective wisdom shapes business, economies, societies and nations.* New York: Doubleday.

Wenger, E. (2002). *Cultivating communities of practice.* Boston: Harvard Business School Press.

Implementing and Leading Learning and E-Learning, Including Change Management

Conner, M., & Clawson, J. (2004). *Creating a learning culture: Strategy, technology and practice*. Cambridge: Cambridge University Press.

Cross, J., & Dublin, L. (2002). *Implementing e-learning*. Alexandria, VA: ASTD.

Drucker, P. (1999). *Management challenges for the twenty-first century*. New York: HarperBusiness.

Horton, W. (2001). *Leading e-learning*. Alexandria, VA: ASTD.

Kotter, J. (1996). *Leading change*. Boston: Harvard Business School.

Performance Improvement

Fournies, F. (1988). *Why employees don't do what they're supposed to do*. New York: McGraw-Hill/Liberty Hall Press.

Rossett, A. (1999). *First things fast: A handbook for performance analysis*. San Francisco: Pfeiffer.

Stolovitch, H., & Keeps, E. (Eds.). (1999). *Handbook of human performance technology*. San Francisco: Pfeiffer, and Washington, DC: International Society for Performance Improvement.

Stolovitch H., & Keeps, E. (2004). *Training ain't performance*. Alexandria, VA: ASTD.

The Human-Technology Interface

Dawson, R. (2002). *Living networks: Leading your company, customers, and partners in the hyper-connected economy*. Upper Saddle River, NJ: Pearson.

Norman, D. (1993). *Things that make us smart: Defending human attributes in the age of the machine*. Reading, MA: Addison-Wesley.

Web Sites

A number of Web sites provide up-to-date information, perspectives, and ideas on the topics presented in this book. Some of the sites represent professional associations that offer educational programs and conferences.

Ageless Learner. An eclectic and independent site focusing on learning in general and e-learning in particular. Lots of valuable information, commentary, and links not easily found anywhere else. www.agelesslearner.com. See also www.learnativity.com.

American Productivity and Quality Center. Knowledge management focus area has a wealth of valuable resources. Conference. www.aqpc.org.

American Society for Training and Development. The largest professional training organization in the world. International and TechKnowledge Conference. www.astd.org.

Brint.com. An extensive portal on knowledge management issues. www.brint.com.

CIO's E-Learning Research Center. From *CIO Magazine*, a focus on e-learning issues with extensive links to other related sites. www.cio.com/research/elearning.

CIO's Knowledge Management Research Center. From *CIO Magazine*, a focus on knowledge management issues with extensive links to other related sites. www.cio.com/forums/knowledge.

CLO Magazine. Magazine focused primarily on e-learning strategy and enterprise applications. Resource-rich Web site. Conference. www.clomedia.com.

destinationKM. An online newsletter with interesting articles about knowledge management. www.destinationkm.com.

The eLearning Guild. A growing, resource-rich community of e-learning practitioners. Multiple conferences. www.elearningguild.com.

E-Learning Post. An excellent collection of articles and other features related to e-learning and knowledge management. www.elearningpost.com.

EPSS Central. One of the leading sites devoted to electronic performance support systems. www.epsscentral.net.

International Society for Performance Improvement. Focused on the broad field of human performance technology, ISPI is the professional home of many of the leading thinkers in the areas of learning and performance improvement. Conference. www.ispi.org.

Internet Time Group. A great deal of information, insight, and perspective on e-learning. Long time e-learning commentator Jay Cross's e-learning blog is well established and worth reading. www.internettime.com.

KM World. A rich resource on knowledge management concepts, vendors, publications, and conferences. Conference. www.kmworld.com.

Learning Circuits. On the ASTD site, this webzine covers broad issues in e-learning. www.learningcircuits.org.

Web-Based Training Information Center. An extensive portal devoted to online training resources. www.webbasedtraining.com.

About the Author

Marc J. Rosenberg is a management consultant, educator, and leading figure in the world of training, organizational learning, e-learning, knowledge management, and performance improvement.

He is a veteran of almost three decades in the field of organizational learning and was a pioneer in the development of electronic performance support systems. His career includes eighteen years in management positions at AT&T, where he developed the company's education and training strategy and directed major corporate initiatives in learning technology, performance management, and education and training reengineering. He also served as the e-learning and knowledge management field leader for the consulting firm DiamondCluster International. His first book, *E-Learning: Strategies for Delivering Knowledge in the Digital Age* (2001), continues to be a best-seller in the field.

A highly regarded and much-sought-after presenter, Rosenberg has spoken at the White House and at well over 150 professional and business conferences. He has authored more than forty articles and book chapters and is a frequently quoted expert in major business and trade publications. He is a past president of the International Society for Performance Improvement (ISPI); a founding editorial board member of *Performance Improvement Quarterly*; coeditor of ISPI's *Performance Technology: Success Stories*; and a contributing author to the *Handbook of Human Performance Technology*, as well as the American Society for Training and Development's (ASTD) *Training and Development Handbook* (fourth edition), *Models for Human Performance Improvement,* and the *2002 ASTD E-Learning Handbook.* He is a member of the ASTD E-Learning Brain Trust Advisory Board and also serves on the advisory board for The eLearning Guild. Rosenberg holds a Ph.D. in instructional design, plus degrees in communications and marketing. He also holds the Certified Performance Technologist designation from ISPI.

Index

What will you find on pfeiffer.com?

- The best in workplace performance solutions for training and HR professionals

- Downloadable training tools, exercises, and content

- Web-exclusive offers

- Training tips, articles, and news

- Seamless online ordering

- Author guidelines, information on becoming a Pfeiffer Affiliate, and much more

Discover more at www.pfeiffer.com